The Future of Regionalism in Africa

Ralph I. Onwuka
Amadu Sesay

ST. MARTIN'S PRESS　　　　　　　　　　New York

© R.I. Onwuka and A. Sesay, 1985

All rights reserved. For information, write:
St. Martin's Press, Inc., 175 Fifth Avenue, New York, NY 10010

Printed in Hong Kong

Published in the United Kingdom by Macmillan Publishers Ltd.
First published in the United States of America in 1985

ISBN 0-312-31482-5

Library of Congress Cataloging in Publication Data
Main entry under title:
The Future of regionalism in Africa.
    Includes index.
    1. Africa – Economic integration – Addresses, essays, lectures. 2. African cooperation – Addresses, essays, lectures.
I. Onwuka, Ralph I.   II. Sesay, Amadu
HC800.F87 1985   337.1'6   84-40335
ISBN 0-312-31482-5

Acknowledgement
The authors and publishers are grateful to McGraw Hill Book Company for permission to use extracts from *Africa in the 1980s, A Continent in Crisis* by Legum et al.

We wish to dedicate this book to all those who believe in a brighter future for Africa. It is also dedicated to all those who have, and continue to sacrifice, suffer and die in the name of Africa's liberation, for theirs is the future kingdom of Africa.

Contents

Editors' Preface ix

Abbreviations xi

Introduction
Ralph I. Onwuka and Amadu Sesay 1

**Part One Continentalism in Africa:
Past, Present and Future** 7
1 Towards a Political Economy of Regionalism in Africa
  Timothy M. Shaw 8
2 The ECA/OAU: Conflict and Collaboration
  Isebill V. Gruhn 22
3 African Development Bank/African Development Fund:
  Problems and Prospects
  I. Diaku 36
4 An African Common Market or African Free
  Trade Area: Which Way Africa?
  Ralph I. Onwuka 58

**Part Two Regionalism in West Africa:
Problems and Prospects** 73
5 ECOWAS/CEAO: Conflict and Cooperation in
  West Africa
  S.K.B. Asante 74
6 The Future of the Central African Customs
  and Economic Union – UDEAC
  Wilfred A. Ndongko 96
7 ECOWAS Defence Pact and Regionalism in Africa
  Tom Imobighe 110

8 The Mano River Union: Politics of Survival
  or Dependence?
  Amadu Sesay 125
9 Transnational Corporations and Regional Integration
  Ralph I. Onwuka 149

**Part Three Regionalism in Eastern and Southern Africa:
              Trials and Failures** 171
10 The End of the East African Community: What are the
   Lessons for Regional Integration Schemes?
   Arthur Hazlewood 172
11 The Southern African Development Coordination
   Conference: Politics of Dependence
   Layi Abegunrin 190
12 The Future of Regionalism in Africa
   John Ravenhill 205
13 The Southern African Customs Union:
   Politics of Dependence
   Robert D.A. Henderson 225

Conclusion
Ralph I. Onwuka and Amadu Sesay 254

Notes about Contributors 258
Select Bibliography 259
Appendix: African Regional and Sub-regional Economic
              Institutions 265
Index 267

Editors' Preface

The idea of providing a text that would comprehensively examine the various sub-regional and continental integration schemes in Africa struck our attention while we were attending an International Seminar on the Future of Africa collectively organised by the Department of International Relations at the University of Ife, and the Department of Political Science at Dalhousie University, Canada, in May 1981. The discussions at the seminar coupled with the various gloomy predictions about Africa's future only reinforced our determination to go ahead with the project. We believed then, as we still do, that Africa's future would be determined by a variety of factors – one of them being the success or failure of the many integration programmes that have been proposed or set up in Africa since the dawn of independence. We believe that the success of integration arrangements in different sub-regions of the continent would go a long way in tackling some of the perennial development problems in Africa.

The actual work on the book started in Ife in June 1981 and, for one reason or another, we sought the help of many people. It is thus with a sense of pleasure as well as from a sense of duty that we would like to express our indebtedness to the contributors who responded promptly to our call for chapters. We are grateful also to the following copyright owners: Basil Blackwell, for permission to reproduce Hazlewood's 'The end of the East African Community: What are the lessons for regional integration schemes?', from *Journal of Common Market Studies* Vol. XVIII, No. 1, September 1979, pp. 40–58, and Timothy M. Shaw and 'Sola Ojo (eds), for Ralph I. Onwuka's 'Transnational Corporations and Regional Integration in West Africa', from *Africa and the International Political System* Washington DC UPA, 1982, pp. 269–99.

Our gratitude must also go to the typists who prepared the first and final drafts of the manuscripts, especially our departmental typists Mr Mathew Adekunle, Mr Waheed Olaniyi and of course Mr Segun Oyedepo who took valuable time off from his academic pursuit to type the final draft. Lastly but by no means the least, we wish to express our love and gratitude to our families who lovingly accepted our odd working hours in the course of the book's preparation.

Ralph I. Onwuka
Amadu Sesay

Abbreviations

AAFC	Allied Armed Forces of the Community
ACP	African, Caribbean and Pacific Countries/States
ACM	African Common Market
ADB	African Development Bank
ADF	African Development Fund
AEF	Afrique Equatorial Française
AFTA	African Free Trade Area
AGC	African Groundnut Council
ANC	African National Congress
BCDI	Community Bureau for Industrial Development
BCEAO	Banque Centrale des Etats de l'Afrique de l'Ouest
BLS	Botswana, Lesotho and Swaziland
CAR	Central African Republic
CARICOM	Caribbean Community
CCCE	Caisse Centrale de la Coopération Economique
CDG	Carl Duisberg-Gesellschaft
CEAO	Communauté Economique de l'Afrique de l'Ouest
CET	Common External Tariff
CFA	Coopération Financière Africaine
CFTC	Commonwealth Fund for Technical Cooperation
CIB	Union Curriculum Planning Instructional Materials Production and Book Development Project
CIEC	International Council of Commerce Employees
CIMAO	Cimens de l'Afrique de l'Ouest
COMECON	Council for Mutual Economic Aid/Assistance
CPA	Cocoa Producers Alliance
DELCO	Sierra Leone Development Corporation
EAC	East African Community
EADB	East African Development Bank
ECA	Economic Commission for Africa
ECE	Economic Commission for Europe
EEC	European Economic Community

ECLA	Economic Commission for Latin America
ECOSOC	Economic and Social Council
ECOWAS	Economic Community of West African States
EFTA	European Free Trade Association
ESAPTA	Eastern and Southern African Preferential Trade Area
ESCOM	South African Electricity Supply Commission
FAC	Fonds d'Aide et de Coopération
FAO	Food and Agriculture Organisation
FCD	Community Development Fund
FTA	Free Trade Area
GATT	General Agreement on Tariffs and Trade
GDP	Gross Domestic Product
GNP	Gross National Product
IACO	Inter-African Coffee Organisation
IBRD	International Bank for Reconstruction and Development
IDU	Industrial Development Unit
ILO	International Labour Organisation
IMF	International Monetary Fund
INGO	International Government Organisations
ITU	International Telecommunications Union
LAFTA	Latin America Free Trade Association
LAMCO	Liberian, American and Swedish Mineral Company
LDCs	Less Developed Countries
MFN	Most Favoured Nations
MNCs	Multinational Corporations
MRU	Mano River Union
NATO	North Atlantic Treaty Organisation
NIEO	New International Economic Order
OAS	Organisation of American States
OAU	Organisation of African Unity
OCAM	Organisation Commune Africaine Malagache et Mauriçienne
OCPE	Community Trade Promotion Office
OECD	Organisation for Economic Cooperation and Development
OMVS	Organisation pour la Mise en Valeur de la Fleuve Sénégal
OPEC	Organisation of Petroleum Exporting Countries
PAC	Pan-African Congress
PPM	Mauritania People's Party
PTA	Preferential Trade Area
R and D	Research and Development

SACU	Southern African Customs Union
SADCC	Southern African Development Coordination Conference
SATCC	Southern African Transport and Communications Commission
SEATO	South East Asia Treaty Organisation
SELA	Latin American Economic System
SWAPO	South West Africa Peoples' Organisation
TAZARA	Tanzania-Zambia Railway
TCR	Taxe de Coopération Régionale
TNCs	Transnational Corporations
UAR	United Arab Republic
UDE	Union Douanière Equatoriale
UDEAC	Union Douanière et Economique de l'Afrique Centrale
UDI	Unilateral Declaration of Independence
UMOA	Union Monétaire Ouest Africaine
UN	United Nations
UNCTAD	United Nations Conference on Tariffs and Trade
UNDP	United Nations Development Programme
UNESCO	United Nations Educational, Scientific and Cultural Organisation
UNIDO	United Nations Industrial Development Organisation
UNITAR	United Nations Institute for Training and Research
US/USA	United States of America
USAID	United States Agency for International Development
TBV	Transkei, Bophuthatswana and Venda
VALCO	Volta Aluminium Company
WARDA	West African Rice Development Association

Introduction

This collection of essays is concerned with investigating the present state and the future prospects of regionalism in Africa. Regionalism, in this context, refers to the various forms and contents of economic integration arrangements (common markets, free trade areas, and harmonisation of policies) prevailing, or proposed, at both regional (as in the cases of the African Common Market and the African Development Bank) and subregional (where there exists a cluster of economic institutions, e.g. ECOWAS, SACU and SADCC) levels. Attempts have been made to include in *The Future of Regionalism in Africa*, as many of the economic institutions in Africa as are allowed by space and time.

The rationale and motivations behind the editing of this comprehensive list of essays in a single volume are twofold. First, since 1967, when Arthur Hazlewood assembled a team of able intellectuals to investigate integration and disintegration in Africa, nothing of similar focus and scale has emerged on that issue on a regional scale. A lot has happened since then as new interests and forces have been projected successfully or otherwise. SADCC, ECOWAS and the Mano River Union are among the emergent institutions that deserve the consideration given them in the book. The East African Community has collapsed and new challenges have faced old economic organisations in Central and Southern Africa as well as the African Development Bank.

Secondly, since 1967, there have been increased conflicts and contradictions in perceptions and projections about the future of regionalism, and indeed about development in Africa. This becomes obvious when one composes the hopeful schemes of the OAU's *Plan of Action* with the World Bank's gloomy predictions found in *An Agenda for Action*. These reports and other similar resolutions helped to shape the authors' prognostic assessment of African economic integration schemes. In assessing the present and in foretelling the future of African regionalism, the book is blessed with the support of

1

many masters of advanced thought on African integration from Africa, Europe, Canada and the USA. Such experts have the merit of looking at regionalism in Africa from different perspectives and persuasions – normative, descriptive, radical and conservative.

Nearly all the contributors agree that, judging from the past, the future of African regionalism is at a crossroads. A look at the integration conditions will help in predicting the future in Africa. We have a great diversity of cultures, languages and even races on the continent. Besides, we have a proliferation of states (some of them are actually micro-states) – over fifty of them, tenaciously clinging to a fragile political sovereignty and independence. These states differ not only in physical size, but in their populations and their endowment with natural resources, as well as in their levels of economic development and external commitments. Furthermore, there is serious ideological and personality incompatibility among African states and their leaders, resulting in continual conflicts. The list can go on almost indefinitely. All these factors have in one way or another, placed serious obstacles in the way of regional integration in Africa. Thus, the 'obstacles to regionalism' as identified above, must be taken into account in any discussion of the prospects for regionalism in Africa either at present or in the future.

What lessons, then, can we learn from previous experiments in regionalism? Perhaps the most general is that there is no such thing as an 'ideal' community, or criteria or size. We have in mind here such factors as the number of cooperating states, their populations and market sizes, and so on. For instance, the defunct East African Community brought together three contiguous former colonies with almost identical colonial experiences: Kenya, Tanzania and Uganda. Nonetheless, as Hazlewood correctly pointed out, the community was saddled with many problems, such as the personality differences between Nyerere and Amin, on the one hand, and between the radical and the conservative leadership in Kenya and Tanzania, on the other. Besides, the cooperating partners adopted different development strategies. Tanzania was socialist, while Uganda under Amin, and Kenya, both pursued capitalist strategies. Finally, the three states were at differing levels of development, with Kenya the most developed. The combination of these factors drowned all other advantages, resulting in constant frictions and misunderstanding among the members, and the eventual demise of the Community in 1977. Thus, what seemed an ideal community was more complex than one might have thought.

We can also learn from the Mano River Union arrangement between Sierra Leone, Liberia and Guinea. Again, under normal circumstances, one would be tempted to say that the Union is ideal. The three members are contiguous. They have ethnic groups which straddle their common borders, and all are poor developing states. But underneath these apparent similarities there are deep-rooted differences. First, there is a serious language barrier between Anglophone Liberia and Sierra Leone, and Francophone Guinea. The three states operate different national currencies: the Leone in Sierra Leone and the Guinean Franc in Guinea. Both currencies are inconvertible. On the other hand, we have the almost universally acceptable American dollar as legal tender in Liberia. This situation automatically gives undue advantage to Liberia in terms of investment opportunities. Apart from the convertibility of the dollar, Liberia, unlike Sierra Leone and Guinea, does not have foreign exchange control regulations. Thus, investors can bring in their dollars and take them out without any fuss from the government in Monrovia. The result is that investors, both local and foreign, tend to prefer Liberia to the other two states. This creates friction within the community because Liberia does not like its nationals doing business with their Guinean and Sierra Leonean counterparts only to accumulate inconvertible local currencies. This problem explains the slow take-off of intra-union trade, and is a serious obstacle to the eventual integration of the economies of the members.

But, if small groupings have problems, are bigger schemes like ECOWAS or SADCC more fortunate than their smaller counterparts? The problems seem to be multiplied several times over in the case of much bigger arrangements such as ECOWAS. For instance, the language barrier is much more pronounced in ECOWAS since it encompasses three, instead of two, linguistic divisions: Portuguese, French and English. Again, the states are at different levels of development as well as greatly varying sizes both in terms of their population and their territory. There are therefore diplomatic problems over the relative political weight and influence of member states. The differing past colonial experiences and degrees of dependence of member states also raise the questions of the place and impact of external influences, both of the former colonial powers – a theme in several of the chapters on West African integration – and of regional powers such as South Africa, discussed in part three.

The collection opens with a general introductory chapter by Timothy Shaw on the political economy of regionalism in Africa. The orthodox analysis of the political economy of the continent still prevails, but there is a slowly emerging radical school. In the words of Professor Shaw, 'attempts to compare these two rather divergent modes of analysis is further complicated by the dominance of the literature in the orthodox tradition in contrast to the paucity of work in the radical genre.' This is naturally reflected in the book.

Some chapters in the anthology analyse the tenuousness of economic integration in Africa. For example, Arthur Hazlewood details, in his case study of the East African Community, the lessons to be learned by future African integrationists from the covergence of crises that led to the demise of the East African attempt. These crises were both internal and external. In the 1970s the most intense integration activities have been found in West and Southern Africa, with the formation in particular of the Economic Community of West African States (ECOWAS) and the Southern African Development Coordination Conference (SADCC). Though dissimilar in institutional and functional scope, their recent integration successes are being threatened by diverse forces of disintegration, treated in a comparative study in this volume by John Ravenhill. ECOWAS has opted for a gradualist approach to a common market yet it has remained ambitious and multidimensional in scope. S. K. B. Asante has treated, however, the overlapping membership and duplicating objectives of ECOWAS with the Mano River Union and the CEAO, as a source of strain to ECOWAS in particular, for its future depends on the collaborative (or conflictual) role of the other unions. Apart from this, the French role in African economic institutions is very great. In both West and Central Africa especially, France has demonstrated its interest in determining the state and direction of economic integration movements. The SADCC on the other hand, has its existence threatened by its closeness to South Africa. The multiple programmes found in the Preferential Trade Area and SADCC need to be reconciled with the Southern African Customs Union, made up of some members of SADCC – Botswana, Lesotho, Swaziland and South Africa. A major problem confronting economic arrangements in Southern Africa remains the compelling influence of South Africa in the sub-region.

The issue of inequality and assymetrical exchange is taken up in Layi Abegunrin's chapter on SADCC. He argues that one of the main reasons for its creation in 1980 was to enable its members to free themselves from the economic, political and military stranglehold of the racist regime in Pretoria. SADCC, then, should be seen as a continuation of the 'ever-evolving African strategy of achieving the total liberation of Southern Africa.' In doing this, however, there are numerous problems involved. First, there are the countermeasures taken by the apartheid regime in South Africa to frustrate the efforts of the black African states, which are striving to end their dependence on the Republic. Botha's constellation of states should be seen in that light, as being used by him to exert subtle pressure on the independent African states, especially SADCC members, to ensure that they 'cohere with the white minority regime in South Africa'.

In his chapter on the ECOWAS Defence Pact, Tom Imobighe also sees a threat (though remote at present) from racist South Africa. Like the activities of the Southern Nine, those of ECOWAS are seen in Pretoria as a major threat to its apartheid policies. Thus, the Republic could decide on a 'pre-emptive action on selected ECOWAS targets'. Imobighe points out that the threat to ECOWAS is not posed by Pretoria alone. The threat is also posed by the great powers 'with imperialistic interests in the region. Neo-colonial powers lurking around in the region will find the situation (future success of ECOWAS) rather uncomfortable and may decide on hostile action against selected targets' in the Community. This is because the success of the Community, *inter alia*, would make its members less dependent on the developed western countries which had been exploiting the resources of these states cheaply.

A central issue extensively treated by most of the contributors to this book, including Amadu Sesay, W.A. Ndongko, Ralph I. Onwuka, and John Ravenhill is the sometimes pervasive role of international finance and technology in integration movements. This sharpens the question of the relative costs and benefits of integration; there is no clear answer. Traditional provisions are nevertheless made for Fund/Development Banks for cooperation and compensation, and for rectifying and balancing the anomaly of uneven development in the integrating Union, but there is scarcely enough internal capital for these programmes. International financial institutions (e.g. the IMF and World Banks) and International Multinational Corporations are always around to close up the gap, sometimes under difficult conditions for the integrating states. The experience of the African Development Bank demonstrates a case of an undue external dependence on the West for survival. As I. Diaku explains, the capital subscription was originally by only a handful of African countries (see chapter 3) and Nigeria was adamant in keeping it that way until the dire need for external finance forced the African leaders to change their original nationalistic stand. The snowballing political and economic effects of maintaining Development Banks that depend on the developed countries for capital transfusion cannot be overemphasised.

The future of regionalism in Africa requires moderation and self-sacrifice if self-reliant development is to be achieved. The *Lagos Plan of Action* which intends to erect an African Common Market by the year 2000 does not fully appreciate the disruptive influence of the 'multiple ailments' in Africa extensively analysed in this volume. A continuous gradualist approach towards a continental common market would augur well for the future of regionalism and economic development in Africa.

Part One

Continentalism in Africa:
Past, Present and Future

1 Towards a Political Economy of Regionalism in Africa

Timothy M. Shaw

Introduction

Africa is not only the largest regional sub-system in terms of territorial size and number of states;[1] it is also the least industrialised and one characterised by the most inequality. Its colonial inheritance – of 'dualistic' economies, authoritarian regimes and high levels of ethnic and racial consciousness – is not an advantageous one and if current projections materialise with regard to both its continued inability to meet basic human needs and the incidence and impact of growing inequalities, its future prospects are rather gloomy.[2] Nevertheless, despite its unfortunate inheritance and mixed performance, Africa has emerged as an important actor in the contemporary arena of world politics.

Ambiguities and contradictions in the past and present characterise the political economy of Africa; in addition it is a Southern continent in a global system still dominated essentially by the interests and actions of the North. The discontinuities and dilemmas of 'economic' dependence and 'political' interdependence are revealed most poignantly in the very tenuous and vulnerable form of 'independence' presently achieved by African countries. The uneven rates and results of development – with its interrelated political, economic, social and strategic components – have served to exacerbate inequalities and tensions both within and between the states of Africa as well as between continental and global actors.[3]

The position and prospects of Africa in an unequal world order pose problems for both analysis and action, perception and prediction. This chapter is concerned, therefore, not only with the comparative study of Africa as a regional sub-system, but also with alternative approaches to analysis as well as alternative development strategies. In particular, it will consider and contrast both the more 'orthodox' and 'radical' modes of analysis and modes of production, taking into account the interrelationship between theory and policy. The paradoxes and dilemmas of Africa's role in the world system are relevant to the comparative analysis of regionalism, to comparative explanations of integration and to comparative policy choices.

Authority and Influence Patterns in Africa

The revival of ideology in Africa is one aspect of a broader trend towards divergent political economies caused by the highly uneven impact of incorporation into the world system. The myth of equality dies hard amongst scholars as well as statesmen, and the emergence of a few leading powers on the continent is forcing a reassessment in both perception and policy. Nevertheless, the orthodox school sticks doggedly to the assumption that the continental system consists of essentially equal and similar actors, while the radical approach attempts to relate novel concepts – such as that of 'sub-imperialism'[4] – to changes in Africa's position in the world order. Both modes of analyses retain their currency in a global system characterised by a return to Realpolitik and power politics. Nevertheless, Zartman continues to assert that 'it is simply not possible to understand the relations of the continental system through a study of the few states which, through a combination of such elements of national strength as location, area, population, GNP and foreign policy interest, might be counted as the powerful of the continent.'[5]

Nonetheless, the orthodox approach has moved some way towards recognition of the growing inequalities on the continent, conceiving of them, however, as changeable and unstable phenomena rather than as reflections of a gradual evolution in Africa's substructure. Instead of treating Africa's new group of 'middle powers' as indicative of changes in the international division of labour, Zartman views them merely as centres of momentary conflicts and coalitions. According to him, the three major features of the leading African states are:

> temporary initiatives on the regional level, delicate positions of predominance within a subregion, and limited arrays of resources available as a power base even for the strongest ... in short, African states have little with which to threaten and little to share, and they are not in a position to win or enforce long-term commitments. At best, they can command temporary advantages, since most African states' resources are meagre.[6]

By contrast, the radical mode sees regional powers as being less transitional, not restricted to strategic issues alone and more structurally defined. From this viewpoint, the emergence of sub-imperialism on the continent is related to the evolving international division of labour in which some limited forms of industrialism can take place albeit under the auspices of the multinational corporation, in the 'semi-periphery'.[7] As production is restructured within corporations and centre states so certain countries may advance from the periphery into the semi-periphery, but technological, financial and administrative controls are largely retained in the centre.

Internationalisation of production does not mean internationalisation of control. Rather, the centre is able to secure favourable terms and attitudes by offering some limited degree of semi-industrialisation to cooperative regimes or countries with particularly valuable natural or organisational resources. According to Wallerstein's world system framework, a few African states, either by invitation or by accident, will come to enjoy upward mobility in the international hierarchy, while the majority will continue to stagnate and remain underdeveloped in the periphery.[8] The possibility or prospect of advancing into the semi-periphery serves to reinforce confidence in orthodox development theory as well as to encourage quiescence in established spheres of influence. In turn, a few semi-industrial states dominate their own regions of the continent partially on behalf of centre interests.

In the mid-term future, semi-industrialism in the semi-periphery may reinforce confidence in orthodox development strategies and in the continent's ability to maintain order. However, in the longer term, as Langdon and Mytelka suggest, the sub-imperial 'solution' may generate its own contradictions and demise because of its association with the established capitalist international division of labour.

Export manufacturing in Africa, then, will undoubtedly increase – as the signs of change in such countries as the Ivory Coast, Senegal, Ghana and Kenya suggest. But this manufacturing is likely to be largely under the direction of foreign enterprises and integrated into the structure of internationalized production. In consequence, the linkage, employment, and income effects of such manufacturing will be fairly limited within Africa – and probably will be enjoyed mainly by those local elites who will extend their import substitution symbiosis to the export sector. Significant restructuring of African economies, with wide dynamic advantages for African majorities, cannot be expected to emerge from this export-manufacturing growth.[9]

Interdependences in Relationships

The emergence of inequalities and regional powers on the continent may, paradoxically, serve to increase the level of interaction in Africa, at least in the short run and amongst the group of emergent middle powers. To date, the proportion of intra- versus extra-continental exchange has been very limited, because of Africa's dependent status within the world system. Economic interaction and military relations have been concentrated at the subregional level, increasingly under the dominance of a few regional centres and cities – such as Dakar, Abidjan, Lagos, Nairobi and Cairo – that serve as intermediaries between metropolises and peripheries.

Interdependences based on integration in Africa remain largely an aspiration rather than a reality. Despite resolutions, declarations, constitutions and diplomacy, integration as measured in terms of economic, communications and social transactions remains at a stubbornly low level. The orthodox view of this situation is that integration takes time and that, given Africa's colonial inheritance, its post-independence performance is quite promising. By contrast, the radical perspective sees extra-continental economic dependence as an essential characteristic of the capitalist world system; it does not expect high levels of continental integration while Africa remains incorporated within global networks.

So, whereas the orthodox approach sees no necessary incompatibility between global, continental and regional integration, the radical school considers continental and regional self-reliance to be incompatible with global and transnational integration. Regional exchange has a rather mixed record, with inter-African trade rising less slowly than extra-African trade; i.e. inter-African exchange continues to fall as a percentage of total African trade. Moreover, most of this trade is either transit of non-African goods to landlocked states, or the export of manufactures by multinational branches located in regional centres such as Abidjan, Lagos and Nairobi.

Intra-African trade is unlikely to increase much until the continent escapes from its colonial heritage of North-South links and produces goods with markets on the continent as well as outside. A regional industrialisation policy is necessary to maximise compatibility and exchange; yet this cannot be designed or realised until decisions made by foreign countries and corporations are transcended. This, in turn, requires a degree of autonomy that can only be achieved through collective action. Hence, the vicious circle of exogenous rather than endogenous growth, of a highly open rather than relatively closed continental system. Jonathan Chileshe points to this paradox:

Cooperation in the promotion of intra-African trade is a challenge which promises better lasting results in as far as the region's rate of economic growth is concerned than continuous dependency on foreign aid and trade with outside economic blocs.[10]

The exclusiveness of intra-African exchange is reflected in the underdeveloped state of the continental infrastructure. Communications by land, sea, air and telegraph are improving but still by no means balance extra-African connections. Moreover, this is so despite the major efforts of external agencies to enhance Africa's infrastructure, even if only to improve extra-continental links. The prevalence of nationalism in a balkanised continent does not improve the prospects for infrastructural development. Nevertheless, successive OAU and ECA meetings along with a variety of functional organisations have provided plans for a network of road, rail, sea and air routes, such as the Trans-Saharan, Trans-African, Trans-Sahelian and Cairo-Gaborones highways.[11] But the use to which such routes might be put is problematical until Africa's development strategies are clarified. Moreover, like other aspects of regionalism, these routes tend to reinforce rather than reduce inequalities, with Lagos, for instance, being the terminal of three continental routes – Trans-African, Trans-Sahara and Trans-Coastal. And as has already been indicated, semi-industrial growth in the semi-periphery may not produce a change in Africa's global position but merely reflect a modification in the essentially unequal international division of labour.

Regional Foreign Policy Behaviour

The established African response to colonialism and underdevelopment has been advocacy of nationalism at the state level, Pan-Africanism at the continental level and nonalignment at the Third World level; all these reactions call for a redistribution of authority and resources without involving a real transformation in Africa's world position. These three clusters of values have constituted the core of Africa's collective foreign policy and have led to current demands for NIEO. However, with the emergence of inequalities on the continent and the reappearance of ideological cleavages, common international positions have tended to fragment. The espousal of 'alternative' development strategies, such as the 'non-capitalist path' and various forms of socialism, inspired by Marxist-Leninist rather than traditional thought, have undermined the continent's ideological consensus and have led to a variety of foreign policy orientations and emphases.[12]

The orthodox approach, recognising Africa's common heritage and transition, still emphasises commonalities in the continent's foreign policies; the radical approach, reflecting changes in the political economy of parts of the continent, accepts and examines contradictions in the foreign relations of participating state and onstate institutions. The orthodox perspective, based on certain sociological, cultural and psychological affinities already identified, conceives of Africa's foreign policy as being singular and consensual. It appreciates the imperative of unity if Africa's voice is to be heard, and recognises the importance of 'externalisation' for continental integration as well as extracontinental effectiveness. Under the impact of various associations, however, it has begun to accept that there may be different foreign policy emphases or nuances, particularly based on membership of, say, the Commonwealth, the Francophone States, the Arab League or Islamic States:

> The recognition of overlapping systems in interpreting foreign policy alternatives and possibilities for states with dual membership is both a more helpful and more realistic way of looking at foreign policies than is the attempt to force such states exclusively into one area or the other.[13]

While African states may belong to a variety of international institutions, their foreign policy choices may be quite limited, particularly by their selection of a development strategy. The comparative study of foreign policy in Africa remains rather embryonic although a few frameworks for analysis now exist.[14] One major factor in foreign policy-making is, of course, choice of development strategy which, given Africa's dependence and openness, means essentially how to respond to external pressures and opportunities. Donald Rothchild and Robert Curry have proposed a trilateral typology of such responses that may also serve as a framework for comparative foreign policy analysis. They identify three policy options – accommodation, reorganisation and transformation,[15] which span the spectrum from acquiescence to resistance, respectively. But, in agreement with the general tenor of the orthodox school, they treat these as mere policy responses rather than as political strategies that reflect underlying structural contradictions.

By contrast, the radical perspective concentrates on development alternatives rather than on foreign policy, and attempts to relate these to modes of production and incorporation rather than to international associations and ideologies. More radical African scholars such as

Micah Tsomondo and Teti Kofi argued in this genre that Pan-Africanism is representative of 'bourgeois' interests and needs to be transcended both in analysis and practice by a more 'scientific' variety of socialism. Moreover, they see the adoption of socialism at the continental level as a prerequisite for effective unity based on an appreciation of class politics and the adoption of a continental industrial strategy. In other words, they conceive of socialism as a response to fragmentation and functionalism on the one hand, and to dependence and underdevelopment on the other hand.[16]

The orthodox approach, however, still sees Pan-Africanism as a reaction to colonialism and does not go much beyond the re-Africanisation of the continent as an objective. It still has faith in orthodox theories of convergence and 'trickledown' development, and extroverted strategies of growth. By contrast, the radical approach has largely abandoned the assumptions and remedies of the orthodox perspective in favour of an approach that is more introverted and self-reliant, based on an appreciation of the international division of labour as it affects Africa.[17]

This debate or dichotomy over foreign and development policies has begun, in turn, to affect regional politics.

Regional Institutions

The orthodox approach has analysed attempts at regional integration in Africa as part of a diplomatic strategy to improve the balance of forces between the continent and the rest of the global system. This approach conceives of regionalism, not so much as a development strategy or an attempt to restructure the international division of labour, so much as a diplomatic tactic designed to enhance Africa's visibility and autonomy – a collective form of decolonisation. Its focus has been on regional constitutions and institutions – the form rather than the relationship – and on mediation and liberation rather than structural transformation. From this perspective, the process is as important as, if not more than the results. And although one motive of the Pan-African movement has been to reduce balkanisation and to transcend nationalism, in fact the record of the OAU to date has served to reinforce fragmentation and to reify the state:

> From the start the existence of the OAU has been far more important to African statesmen and politicians than any functional role it may perform in promoting economic cooperation or even the

alignment of foreign policies ... By merely being there, the OAU does indeed perform one vital role in African diplomacy – it bestows legitimacy on its members and on the movements and causes which they chose to recognize ... It has always been the OAU's main task to set the seal of legitimacy on both the distribution of power within African states and on those liberation movements, mainly in Southern Africa, which were contesting power with colonial or minority regimes.[18]

By contrast with the orthodox school's focus on diplomacy and legitimacy, the radical approach considers the developmental and economic impact of nationalism. And whereas the orthodox school tends to produce relatively positive evaluations, the radical approach leads to essentially negative conclusions. The OAU network may have served to stabilise the continental system in terms of decolonisation, mediation and consultation, but the ECA and its 'subregional' associates have not yet begun to escape from a position of economic dependence on the world system.

The OAU has shown a remarkable resilience in its ability to weather the storms of 'dialogue' and 'détente' with South Africa, of conflict in Katanga/Shaba, Southern Sudan, Nigeria, Eritrea, Chad and Western Sahara, and of OPEC and Afro-Arab divisions. But these rather ephemeral, 'diplomatic crises' are seen by the radical school as merely reflections of fundamental contradictions that the OAU-ECA system has yet to seriously confront. Despite a growing range of proposals, meetings and institutions – such as the OAU Declaration on Cooperation, Development and Economic Independence, the African Development Bank and Fund, Ministerial Conferences on Trade, Development and Monetary Problems, and participation in EEC-ACP negotiations, United Nations Conference on Trade and Development (UNCTAD) preparations and International Council of Commerce Employers (CIEC) debates – regional interactions have not yet led to significant advances.[19] As Zdenek Cervenka laments:

> Compared with the progress made by the OAU on decolonization, and the success of its international campaign against apartheid, its performance in the economic field has been disappointing. After fourteen years of the OAU, the real struggle for the liberation of the continent of Africa from economic domination by outside powers has hardly begun.[20]

The radical school suggests that the reason for this condition is the continued integration of Africa into the world system. Whereas at the level of diplomacy and ideology, the OAU can score pyrrhic victories, at the level of exchange and capital and the continental political economy, it cannot, with profound implications for both metropolitan and African elite interests. Given the close transnational links between the new class and foreign countries, corporations and classes, such a prospect is unlikely to continue, either for statesmen or scholars.

In an attempt to make Africa's powerlessness and assertiveness compatible with each other, Zartman has recognised the discontinuity between continental dependence and demand while ignoring the structural contradictions that generated such ambiguity:

> in a world where Africa does not have the power to protect itself and promote its own goals, it proposes a new system of international relations that emphasizes its rights and deemphasizes the classical means to attain them. The inherent contradiction, sharpened by the fact that the faster developing states in Africa do in fact seek to increase their power and use it in classical ways, is typical of an idealistic view of international relations.[21]

If the orthodox approach, with its emphasis on the new diplomacy, is 'idealistic' in tone then the radical perspective, with its emphasis on the old dependence, is 'realistic' in orientation. This analytic and existential dichotomy is also reflected in patterns of contemporary regional cooperation and conflict.

Regional Cooperation and Conflict

The OAU system, established to reflect and advance the interests of national leaderships on the continent, seeks to achieve cooperation without further reducing sovereignty and to minimise conflict without resolving fundamental issues. It has to avoid both progress towards supranationalism and escalation towards warfare. This would be a fine line even if the region as a whole has a higher level of autonomy, but given its dependent status, the achievement of satisfactory levels of cooperation and conflict control is quite problematic. The continent continues to be the target of two distinct types of external pressures, one of which is recognised by the orthodox school, the other of which is emphasised by the radical school.[22]

The orthodox approach conceives of extracontinental intervention in essentially strategic and diplomatic terms, focusing on the role of foreign bases, troops, diplomats and intelligence networks.[23] Like the nonalignment movement, it overlooks any constraints imposed by

Africa's position in the international division of labour and conceives of cooperation as a collective diplomatic response to external threats. And it emphasises intervention from the socialist states, particularly Russia and Cuba but also China as endemic, whereas the role of capitalist powers is assumed to be more benign.

Because of the pervasiveness of external involvement in Africa, however, some students within the orthodox tradition have attempted to treat at least some, albeit the more superficial, aspects of dependence and underdevelopment. Nevertheless, they continue to see the processes of intervention and conflict as sporadic and crisis-related rather than structural and normal. Raymond Copson, for instance, has recently argued that

> The persistence of conflict on the African continent is deeply rooted in the underdevelopment of African states ... political and economic underdevelopment (is) a cause of international conflict in Africa ...[24]

Copson attempts to explain the absence of regional order, the regularity of boundary disputes, the existence of regional power centres and diplomatic disagreements, in terms of national underdevelopment, the results of which are seen as insecure regimes, limited capabilities, economic stagnation, colonial borders, regional underdevelopment (as evidenced in, for instance, the absence of strong organisation), regional imbalances and local arms races. Some of these issues are, as we shall see in chapter 4, responsible for the delay in the possible emergence of an African common market. Copson avoids notions of political economy, such as dependence and class, and opts instead for a more critical form of systemic and realist analysis, concluding that conflict is the unavoidable consequence of the underdevelopment of African states and of the African states system.[25] Chime also conceives of foreign intrusions in these terms, taking into account the history of bloc politics and 'feudal' networks in the international system. He characterises external intervention as 'the Godfather syndrome' in which foreign actors capriciously determine events and outcomes on the continent through activating their spheres of influence.[26]

The radical perspective on intervention and blocs is that they are the result of Africa's incorporation into the world system and of current transnational linkages between rulers on the continent and those in the centre. External involvement from this viewpoint is neither capricious nor sporadic but structural and routine; an aspect of Africa's part in the international division of labour. On this view cooperation against such a status is either idealistic or merely part of a continual quest for a better bargain by African leaders caught between cautious foreign associates and impatient national constituencies. The emphasis from this perspective is not on strategic and diplomatic disputes but rather on structural constraints imposed not by socialist armies and advisers but by corporate branches, foreign technology and external exchange. Such extracontinental involvement cannot readily be resisted, particularly given ubiquitous transnational class linkages that maintain global interdependence rather than continental integration.[27] Any response involves not only African cooperation (a somewhat unlikely prospect given different transnational orientations and expectations), but also disengagement and restructuring (also unlikely prospects unless intranational pressures come to demand it).

To date, much regional cooperation in both strategy and economic issues has advanced rather than reduced external involvement. The arms trade with Africa and the continuing associations with Western and Eastern armies, particularly those of France[28] and Cuba, reflect not only foreign interests but also the insecurity of regimes and states.[29] And much regional economic cooperation – from the Entente and ECOWAS to ECA and Asian Development Bank (ADB) – serves the interests of foreign aid agencies, consultants, and corporations from both socialist and capitalist states.[30] Many of the benefits of such regional integration have flowed back to centres of foreign investment, aid and technology; most dependent industrialisation is by corporate branches rather than by indigenous institutions and has served to advance the symbiotic interests of semiperipheral and centre states rather than those of the region as a whole.[31] Reflecting the radical approach, Langdon and Mytelka note:

> The contemporary crisis of regional integration in Africa is not, however, a purely nationalistic affair in which states are pitted against each other in conflicts over the interstate distribution of the gains from integration. Rather, this interstate conflict is a reflection of more fundamental problems that are associated with the distribution of gains between national and international capital, as the Multinational Corporation (MNC) seeks to structure not only national but also regional markets around its own needs and interests.[32]

The difficulties and dilemmas of regional cooperation in Africa have led to the decay as well as the creation of institutions, e.g. the now defunct East African Community; it has also led to a new awareness of different forms and strategies for regionalism on the continent.

Notes

1 See Leon Gordenker 'The OAU and the UN: Can They Live Together?' in Ali A. Mazrui and Hasu H. Patel (eds), *Africa in World Affairs: The Next Thirty Years* (New York: Third Press, 1973), pp. 105-19.

2 For a description of the debate about Africa's future see Timothy M. Shaw and Malcolm J. Grieve, 'The Political Economy of Resources: Africa's Future in the Global Environment', *Journal of Modern African Studies* 16:1 (March 1978), pp. 1-32.

3 For an introduction to these see: Timothy M. Shaw 'Discontinuities and Inequalities in African International Policies', *International Journal* 30:3 (Summer 1975).

4 See Timothy M. Shaw, 'Inequalities and Interdependence in Africa and Latin America: Sub-Imperialism and Semi-Industrialism in the Semi-Periphery' *Cultures et Developpement* 10:2, 1978, pp. 231-63.

5 I. William Zartman, 'Africa as a Subordinate State in International Relations', *International Organisation* 2:3 (Summer 1967), p. 571.

6 *Ibid.*, p. 574.

7 See, for instance, Timothy M. Shaw, 'Kenya and South Africa: Sub-Imperialist States' *Orbis* 21:2 (Summer 1977), pp. 375-94; and 'International Stratification in Africa: Sub-Imperialism in Eastern and Southern Africa', *Journal of Southern African Affairs* 2:2 (April 1977), p. 145-65.

8 See Immanuel Wallerstein, 'Dependence in an Interdependent World: The Limited Possibilities of Transformation within the Capitalist World Economy', *African Studies Review* 17:1 (April 1974), pp. 1-26.

9 Steven Langdon and Lynn K. Mytelka, 'Africa in the Changing World Economy' in Colin Legum *et al*, *Africa in the 1980's: A Continent in Crisis* (New York: McGraw-Hill, 1979), Council on Foreign Relations, 1980's Project, 204.

10 Jonathan H. Chileshe, *The Challenge of Developing Intra-African Trade* (Nairobi: East African Literature Bureau, 1977), p. 151.

11 See Guy Arnold and Ruth Weiss, *Strategic Highways of Africa* (London: Friedmann, 1977); and 'Land Transportation', *Africa 80* (April 1978), pp. 69-70.

12 For overviews of foreign policy in Africa, see Christopher Clapham, 'Sub-Saharan Africa', in his collection on *Foreign Policy-Making in Developing States: A Comparative Approach* (Farnborough: Saxon House, 1977), pp. 75-109; W.A.E. Skurnik, *Sub-Saharan Africa: Information Sources on International Relations*, (Detroit: Gale, 1977); and Mark DeLancey, 'Current Studies in African International Relations', *Africana Journal* 7:3, 1976, pp. 195-239.

13 Zartman, *op. cit.*, p. 581 (see note 5 above).

14 For a review of these, see 'Conclusion', in Douglas G. Anglin and Timothy M. Shaw, *Zambia's Foreign Policy: Studies in Diplomacy and Dependence*, (Boulder: Westview, 1979).

15 See Donald Rothchild and Robert L. Curry, *Scarcity, Choice and*

Public Policy in Middle Africa (Berkeley: University of California Press, 1978), pp. 48–91 and 301–335.

16 See Micah S. Tsomondo, 'From Pan-Africanism to Socialism: The Modernization of an African Liberation Ideology', *Issues* 5:4 (Winter 1975), pp. 39–46; and Teti Al Kofi, 'Principles of a Pan-Africa Economic Ideology', *Review of Black Political Economy* 6:3 (Spring 1976), pp. 306–30.

17 See Folker Frobel, Jurgen Heinrichs and Otto Kreye, *The New International Division of Labour* (Cambridge University Press, 1980), part 3.

18 James Mayall, 'The OAU and the African Crisis', *Optima* 27:2, 1977, p. 86.

19 See Zdenek Cervenka, 'The Organisation of African Unity in 1976', in Colin Legum (ed.) *Africa, Contemporary Record, Annual Survey and Documents*, Volume 9, 1976–1977, (London: Rex Collings, 1977) A68–A75; and *The Unfinished Quest for Unity* (New York: Africana, 1977).

20 See Timothy M. Shaw, 'Inequalities and Conflict in Contemporary Africa', *International Perspectives*, (May/June 1978), pp. 44–9; and 'The Organisation of African Unity: Prospects for the Second Decade, *International Perspectives* (September/October 1973), pp. 31–4.

21 Cervenka, *The Unfinished Quest for Unity* (New York: Africana 1977), pp. 176 and 190.

22 Zartman, *op. cit.*, p. 390 (see note 5 above).

23 For a powerful comparison and critique of both, see *Tanzania Rejects Western Domination of Africa: Statement by President Mwalimu Julius K. Nyerere*, (Dar es Salaam: Government Printer, June 1978).

24 See, for instance, Robert M. Price, *US Foreign Policy in Sub-Saharan Africa: National Interest and Global Strategy* (Berkeley: Institute of International Studies, 1978). Cf. Tom J. Farer, 'Soviet Strategy and Western Fears', *Africa Report* 23:6 (November–December 1978), pp. 4–88.

25 Raymond W. Copson, 'African International Politics: Underdevelopment and Conflict in the Seventies', *Orbis* 22:1 (Spring 1978), p. 228.

26 *Ibid.*, p. 245.

27 See Chimelu Chime, *Integration and Politics among African States*, (Upssala: Scandinavian Institute of African Studies, 1977), pp. 391–97.

28 See Timothy M. Shaw *Towards International Political Economy for the 1980s: from dependence to interdependence* (Dalhousie University Centre for Foreign Policy Studies, 1980)

29 See James O. Goldsborough, 'Dateline Paris: Africa's Policeman' *Foreign Policy* 33 (Winter 1978–9), 1974–90.

30 Cf. the rather unfortunate and premature prediction of Zartman, made in the mid-1970s, perhaps the period of greatest continental cohesion and autonomy: 'Nor are there outside agents – peripheral or intrusive members of the system – that appear willing and able to exert decisive influence for change. Even before the detente of the early 1970s, Africa had lost its position of the early 1960s as a cold war battlefield, and outside of some noisy skirmishes in various nonaligned conferences the Sino-Soviet Schism has not had much effect on regional relations. These characteristics too seem unlikely to change in the short run.' (Zartman, *ibid*, p. 593).

31 See Timothy M. Shaw, 'Regional Cooperation and Conflict in Africa', *International Journal* 30:4 (Autumn 1975), pp. 671–88.
32 Langdon and Mytelka, *op. cit.* (note 9 above), pp. 178–9.

2 The ECA/OAU: Conflict and Collaboration

Isebill V. Gruhn

Any Addis Ababa taxi driver can take you to the headquarters building of the Economic Commission for Africa (ECA). You are, however, fortunate to locate an experienced driver who knows the location of the headquarters building of the Organisation of African Unity (OAU). In 1958, when Ethiopia's Emperor Haile Selassie wanted Ethiopia's capital, Addis Ababa, to be the centre of African affairs, Africa Hall was inaugurated as part of the headquarters building of the United Nations Economic Commission for Africa. Today, Africa Hall is surrounded by several administration buildings housing a staff of hundreds. The complex sits on a slight hill overlooking post-revolutionary Ethiopia's Red Square, conveniently close to major hotels, in a city scented with the odour of eucalyptus and surrounded by scenic mountains. One can suppose most citizens of Addis Ababa have noticed daily fleets of often expensive cars with their blue and white unlicensed plates converging on the Africa Hall complex and disappearing behind its barriers. Important conferences are held at Africa Hall, including large meetings of the Organisation of African Unity (OAU). The citizens of other African nations and people around the world can tell from the wire services of the press that Africa Hall in Addis Ababa is a place where leaders of the African continent meet and seek to forge unity and direction out of frequent family quarrels.

In rather sharp contrast, there stands at the outskirts of Addis Ababa an office building or two designated as Unity House. This is the location of the general secretariat of the OAU, with facilities for small meetings, but not large conferences. When the OAU was founded in 1963 Haile Selassie offered it free use of a new office building originally meant to house a police academy. In 1973, as part of the OAU's tenth anniversary celebrations, Emperor Haile Selassie held a special ceremony to hand over the title deeds to the lands and buildings. Ethiopia was anxious to keep the OAU on its soil, and this was an occasion which allowed the country to confirm its commitment to host the OAU. Many of the local citizens who walk or drive past it on their way to work or to shops in the centre of town are scarcely conscious of passing anything other than a modern office building which stands some distance away from the dusty main road.

Even the superficial differences do not end here. In the early 1970s, a time when the total OAU budget came to 2.5 million US dollars, the budget of the ECA was close to double that. A similar comparison pertains to the staff. By the mid-1970s, ECA's professional staff was three to four times as large as that of the OAU. The OAU has been and continues to be a shoestring operation. In 1964 it had eighteen full-time paid professionals with which to address the African continent's problems. Today there are about one hundred. In addition, the budgetary situation is consistently uncertain since member governments cannot be counted on either to pay their annual assessments in a timely fashion, or, in the case of two dozen governments, to pay them at all.

I can recall an occasion in the mid-1970s when a delegation of West Africans came to Addis Ababa to attend a technical conference at the ECA. During a pause in their meetings, three or four of the West African delegates felt drawn to visit Unity House, not so much to confer but to pay their respects, to see somehow what the OAU 'felt like', and in some fashion to make their presence known. Upon arriving at the OAU the West African technocrats were dismayed to learn that only some office staff were in residence, all the professional staff having gone to the local airport to welcome a visiting delegation. No one at the OAU quite knew whether anyone on the professional staff could be expected back that day. The West Africans returned to their respective countries with something less than a glowing image of the OAU as a well-functioning, vibrant, and productive mechanism upon which they might count to improve the future of their people. On the other hand, the lengthy, boring, and often wearing meetings at ECA which they had attended had concluded the first phase of institution-building to establish a mechanism for setting up standards for the inter-state trade of locally manufactured products. Of course, the heart of the matter regarding the work of the OAU and ECA and their relationship to each other lies in something beyond the symbols of buildings, their location, and work ethics and mores of their staffs. But, in politics symbolism plays its role, and in a consideration of the organisations' capacity for economic and social development it is useful to bear in mind, staff, budgets, and even work ethic, to help illuminate what has been, what is, and what can be expected.

The Origins and Structure of the ECA and the OAU

The United Nations Economic and Social Council (ECOSOC), through its resolution of 29 April 1958, established the Economic Commission for Africa. Like other UN Regional Commissions, such as the Economic Commission for Latin America (ECLA), the Economic Commission for Europe (ECE), etc., the ECA operates under the general supervision of the Economic and Social Council and the General Assembly. The terms of reference of the ECA require that the Commission initiates and participates in measures to relieve the economic and technological problems of Africa; that it makes or sponsors investigations into economic and technological problems of development; that it undertakes to sponsor the collection, evaluation and dissemination of economic, technological, and statistical information; that it performs such advisory services as countries of the region may desire, provided that these do not overlap with those provided by other bodies of the UN or its specialised agencies; that it assists the Economic and Social Council, at its request, in discharging its functions within the region in connection with any economic problems including those in the field of technical assistance; that it assists in the development of coordinated policies for promoting economic and technological development in the region; and that it deals, where appropriate, with the social aspects of economic development and with the relationship between economic and social factors.[1]

As can be seen, the terms of reference of the ECA are broadly gauged, though clearly focused around economic and social policy. Because the terms of reference of each of the UN's regional commissions were so broad, each could, and did, develop its own special character. ECA operates within the framework of the policies of the UN and is subject to overall supervision of ECOSOC. ECA's administrative machinery forms part of the UN Secretariat under the control of the UN General Assembly. The core of ECA's operations and institution maintenance is funded from the regular UN budget, though this is augmented through bilateral and other multilateral funding. ECA's programmes and priorities too are subject to review by ECOSOC. Nevertheless, apart from budgetary links and the complex and cumbersome UN personnel structure to which it is tied, most of ECA's day-to-day operations, its policies, and priorities, are largely governed by ECA itself and with the approval of its membership through the Council of Ministers and more informal consultation with African governments and institutions. The membership of ECA is virtually identical to that of the OAU – in both cases all independent black-majority-ruled African states, but the organisations differ in their sources of authority and control.[2]

By 1963, when the OAU came into existence, ECA had already been in operation for five years. The OAU founded in 1963 was a far cry from Nkrumah's vision of 'union government for Africa'. At best it was perceived as a compromise between different blocs and factions among African states of the time. Leaders were eager to reach some agreement, and substantial compromise took place under the aegis of Ethiopia.[3] The OAU charter established a two-chamber political government for the organisation: a Council of Ministers and an Assembly. The secretary-general was to be elected by the Assembly, and the daily work was to be carried out by the general secretariat. The OAU followed the UN's scale in assessing contributions from members. Indeed, the operational budget is wholly dependent on the membership meeting their assessments. The purposes of the OAU appear in Article II of the OAU Charter; they are much broader than those of the ECA:

1 The Organisation shall have the following purposes:
A To promote the unity and solidarity of the African states;
B To coordinate and intensify their cooperation and efforts to achieve a better life for peoples of Africa;
C To defend their sovereignty, their territorial integrity and independence;
D To eradicate all forms of colonialism from Africa; and to promote international cooperation, having due regard to the Charter of the United Nations and the Universal Declaration of Human Rights.
2 To these ends, the member states shall coordinate and harmonise their general policies, especially in the following fields:
A Political and diplomatic cooperation;
B Economic Cooperation, including transport and communications;
C Educational and cultural cooperation;
D Health, sanitation and nutritional cooperation;
E Scientific and technical cooperation; and
F Cooperation for defence and security

It can be seen, then, that the OAU was charged with a much more broadly gauged and multi-functional set of tasks than that of ECA, and that only purposes B, C, D and E under number 2 fall squarely in the area of potential or actual overlap of purposes and tasks. Indeed, under Article XX of the OAU Charter, Specialised Commissions were envisaged which included, among others, an Economic and Social Commission, an Educational and Cultural Commission, a Health, Sanitation and Nutrition Commission, and a Scientific, Technical and Research Commission. Although some of these Commissions have never become fully operational, it is important to note that the Charter's intent was conscious duplication and overlap in functional areas and purposes with those of the ECA.[4]

Why would the OAU seek to duplicate some of the functions of ECA? I think it is fair to say that by 1963, at the founding of the OAU, a certain amount of disillusionment had set in with respect to the ECA. The early sixties were years of euphoria regarding independence and very high expectations that Africa's economic and social ills could be turned around in visible ways within a few years. In this context, a fledgeling UN regional commission focusing its attention on doing background and feasibility studies and collecting and disseminating statistics, easily generated criticism that it engaged in too many studies and too little action. The ECA was also perceived as something other than a 'genuine African institution.' Though Africanising rapidly, it was still staffed largely with non-Africans at the professional level, and it was often said in the early 1960s that a UN agency could not serve strictly African needs. Under the circumstances, especially the more radical African governments such as those belonging to the so-called Casablanca Group,[5] wanted to make sure that economic and social affairs would be structured into the purposes of the OAU, whose authority and control were firmly in African hands. From its very inception, though ECA was not entirely to blame, it had been seen as an English-speaking organisation. Most of the Africans on the ECA staff, and the first long-term executive secretary, Robert Gardiner, a Ghanaian, came from English-speaking Africa. There were a number of reasons for the predominance of English-speaking staff, including French post-colonial policy, inter-African organisation among French-speaking states, and the low level of availability of trained Africans in some of the smaller and less developed former French colonies. This English-speaking character of ECA was to some degree self-perpetuating. French-speaking African governments placed low priority on ECA, which in turn gave ECA an even more English-speaking flavour, which in turn produced even further alienation from ECA amongst French-speaking countries. By 1963, this process had gone far enough to add French-speaking African voices from moderate governments to those of the more radical states, calling for the OAU to take responsibility for what had been ECA's province: fostering African economic and social activities. The political disposition of a governing number of states at the foundation of the OAU was to establish it as the continental body charged, along with its other purposes, to act on behalf of African interests in economic and social matters.

Now that there were areas for potential overlap, duplication and conflict, it was up to the two organisations to discover how to avoid conflict and to structure cooperation. A history of the leadership, programmes, activities, and institutional economic and political circumstances in the years following 1963 will serve as background for assessing the current relationship of the two organisations and the future prospects for that relationship.

Uneasy Coexistence 1963–81

Superficially, 1963 commenced on a gracious note. At its fifth meeting in Kinshasa in February the ECA extended good wishes to the forthcoming founding conference of the OAU, and even prepared a background document for the conference on economic integration and cooperation. But by 1965 there was sufficient unease between the two organisations to make it necessary or desirable to have a formal agreement between them.[6] The OAU Administrative Secretary and the UN Secretary signed an agreement on 16 December 1965 pledging cooperation between the two institutions within their respective spheres of responsibility.[7] At ECA this agreement was taken to mean that ECA's proper sphere of responsibility was in the economic realm and the OAU's was in the political realm. Even if the OAU gave this agreement a different reading it did not much matter: owing to lack of staff and funds, it could not do anything in the economic realm even if it wanted to. In addition, the increasing verbal rivalry during the second half of the decade was much affected by the personalities of the heads of the respective organisations.

Robert Gardiner from Ghana assumed the post of Executive Secretary of the ECA in 1962, after extensive experience in both Ghanaian and international service. His style, and much of his background, set a certain tone within ECA, and for ECA, both in Africa and internationally. He had what in those days was described as a moderate political outlook. He operated with a low-keyed and diplomatic style and placed long-term infrastructure building ahead of more flashy enterprises.[8] Gardiner believed that ECA's future as an important mechanism for African development, its viability among its membership, and respect for it internationally, lay in keeping ECA out of controversy. He sought to avoid conflict and great care was taken to treat member governments with kid gloves. ECA documents and reports were written in ponderous UN bureaucratic language, taking care never to criticise directly any government or its policy in an identifiable fashion. Similarly, Gardiner's low-key and moderate posture won him friends within the UN system and bilaterally among donor countries. For example, the US government seemed pleased to be dealing with Gardiner and welcomed his style and manner as well as the good sense with which he was seeking to build infrastructure and institutions. Gardiner's penchant for doing background and feasibility studies came as welcome news to the US Agency for International Development, which operated in a similar fashion. However, Gardiner's good notices as a reasonable, caring and trustworthy international official should not be seen merely as a reflection of his personality and style; it must also be seen in juxtaposition to his rival at the OAU, Diallo Telli.[9]

Telli was formally elected to head the OAU in July 1964. He had his mandate renewed in 1968, but failed to get re-elected at the OAU's ninth session in 1972. The eight years during which Telli was in office constituted the OAU's formative years, just as Gardiner's 1962–75 reign at the ECA constitued that organisation's formative years. Telli, a Guinean, could fairly be described in 1960s terminology as a radical socialist. His background provided the best sort of French colonial education from Ecole Normale William Ponty right through Ecole Nationale de la France d'Outre-Mer. He also studied law and history at the Sorbonne. By the time Telli took charge of the OAU he had developed an international reputation, including high visibility in the US where he was a prominent member of the African Group at the UN. Telli sought to fight colonialism and neo-colonialism on all fronts. He associated himself with the views of Sekou Toure whose political stand was perceived with some alarm both within the UN and amongst western powers.[10]

It can now be seen that Gardiner and Telli were unlikely, on a personal level, to have much in common or to find it easy to achieve smooth, mutually supportive relationships. Telli worked tirelessly and rhetorically to give the OAU visibility as the African organisation charged with eradicating colonialism, neo-colonialism, and white racism in Southern Africa and improving the conditions of African governments. Telli was political, radical, and often petulant. He urged members to bring the ECA under the OAU's political control.

Throughout the 1960s the ECA took comfort in the fact that it was relatively better staffed and financed. This made OAU claims that it could act in the area of economic development merely rhetoric. However, Telli's claims and his actual or potential level of support among African states regarding the OAU's political activity made the

ECA very nervous. Below the surface, and more openly at OAU and ECA meetings and conferences, the battle escalated. Disillusionment with national progress and with the ability of ECA to improve things visibly gave leverage to Telli's charges against the ECA. In turn, the absence of any effective work in the economic realm on the part of the OAU gave substance to Gardiner's assertion that Telli's speeches were mere talk. Internationally, Telli's pronouncements and the resolutions of the OAU frequently alarmed Western governments, but note was also taken of them.

The characters and style of the two leaders also clearly affected the working styles of the respective organisations. Gardiner's low-key style not only kept the ECA out of the political fray, but also undercut its attempts to become a high-powered think-tank. Even by 1975 ECA could not claim to have made its mark as an imaginative institution with a distinctive organisational ideology. Gardiner's style and personality led to genuine institutional failings, and exposed ECA to OAU charges of ineffectiveness. By the same token, Telli's style, his shortcomings as an administrative leader, his failures to find and keep competent staff and to achieve an institutional work ethic, also constantly cast doubt on any claims that the OAU had anything but rhetorical capacity in the economic and social realms.

Throughout the 1960s, periodic calls for cooperation took place, as well as charges and counter-charges. The ECA felt ill at ease about the OAU and the OAU was handicapped by its own financial and other weaknesses. In 1969, however, the matter was taken up by the Africa Group at the UN in New York. The Africa Group, composed of heads of UN missions, became influential in the UN General Assembly. African countries were asking for a greater say in the formulation of UN economic policy for Africa in general. In 1969 they demanded that ECA, as a UN agency, be compelled to take the OAU view on matters seriously. The language used was still 'cooperation' but it was clear that the OAU was meant to be the political voice certifying policies and strategies to be carried out by the ECA. Since the ECA membership was the same as the group asking for this policy, the ECA basically had no choice but to accept the OAU's primary responsibility for all cooperation among African states, including economic cooperation. The terms under Article 11 of the UN Charter were recognised by the ECA at its ninth session held in Addis Ababa in February 1969.[11] In a resolution on the Relationships with the Organisation of African Unity, the following was agreed to:[12]

> African ministers and senior officials working within the framework of the ECA and the OAU Economic and Social Com-

mission should be 'constantly guided by decisions of the Assembly of Heads of State and the Government of the OAU in economic and social matters'
and
Reports on activities of the ECA should be presented regularly for consideration of the Assembly of Heads of State and Government of OAU, 'in order that the Commission might enjoy the necessary political support.'

Superficially, the redefinition of the relationship between the OAU and the ECA seemed to take root. The programme of priorities adopted by the OAU summit of 1970 served as the blueprint for the 'African strategy for development in the 1970s' as approved first by the meeting of the Conference of Ministers of the Economic Commission for Africa at their February 1971 Tunis meeting.[13] By 1973, and already in the post-Diallo Telli period of the OAU, the OAU and ECA cooperated in the 'Declaration on Cooperation, Development and Economic Independence, adopted by the African ministerial conference on trade, development and monetary problems, organised jointly by the OAU and ECA. This Declaration set out Africa's demands for the New International Economic Order (NIEO). The global call for NIEO came at the sixth Special Session of the UN General Assembly, which adopted the resolution calling for NIEO in May 1974.[14]

This process of OAU-ECA cooperation in setting out African strategies continues into the 1980s with the so-called *Lagos Plan of Action* for the Implementation of the Monrovia Strategy for the Economic Development of Africa. The Lagos Plan of Action was recommended by the ECA Conference of Ministers responsible for Economic Development at its sixth meeting, held in Addis Ababa on 9–12 April 1980. It was then presented to the first Economic Summit of the Assembly of Heads of State and Governments of the Organisation of African Unity in Lagos on 28 and 29 April 1980. Amendments were made at the OAU summit, and the final text, henceforth known as the *Lagos Plan*, contains a blueprint and an inventory of needs, and calls for sectorial and inter-sectorial development strategies. In most ways it echoes an annual report of the ECA. But it is also the latest illustration of the OAU politically-certified working agenda to meet Africa's needs. In this sense, the process begun in 1969 has become by 1980 more fully a matter of practice.

However, the more potent public OAU role in defining African development strategy masks the continued reality: the ECA is a reasonably well staffed and internationally funded mechanism able to produce studies and reports, while the OAU continues as before, as a shoestring operation, especially as it pertains to economic and social expertise and capacity.

To a casual observer the 1970s and 80s have been a period of ongoing cooperative ventures between the OAU and the ECA. Meetings, including fairly technical ones in the economic and social realm, are co-sponsored with frequency. There have also been reciprocal representation and participation at meetings, and some joint use of information, and many documents and working papers carry an ECA/OAU designation. Since 1969 there has been some intersecretariat machinery in place to help coordinate meetings and conferences, and ECA has given the OAU some administrative and technical assistance, especially in meetings and conferences held on ECA premises. In short, some cooperation, some give and take, has taken place. However, it is also the case that most of the actual work, the writing of reports, the undertaking of feasibility studies, has been done by the staff of ECA. So, what often appears to be joint work of the ECA and the OAU frequently is no more than a co-sponsorship of the final ECA product or activity. But while the OAU has profited by seeming to have some role and expertise in the vital economic realm, ECA has profited from the legitimising cover provided by the OAU. It has been a marriage of convenience. At times both organisations have publicly profited from the relationship; at other times they have had to bear to burdens of each other's shortcomings and failures, as perceived both by clients and by the international community.

It is important to recall that the founding heads of each organisation had a good deal to do, not merely with the nature of the respective organisations, but with the relationship between them. Since Diallo Telli stepped down, the leadership of the OAU has been in the successive hands of continentally and internationally less visible individuals, such as Nzo Ekangaki and William Eteki Mboumoua. In contrast, Robert Gardiner's successor, Adebayo Adedeji, has been more visible, vocal, and political than his predecessor. In fact, Adedeji has travelled far and wide, especially on the African continent, dealing with the politics of economic development. While the current leadership of each of the organisations has inherited an institutional structure and a set of perceptions inside and outside the organisation, the reversal in leadership styles poses interesting new questions regarding the future of both the OAU and the ECA.

Adebayo Adedeji, who took over the reins of the ECA in 1975, hails from Nigeria, has degrees from both Harvard and London University, and served, among other things, as Minister of Economic Development and Reconstruction in Nigeria. He has a Ph.D. in Economics, and his experience in various federal posts in Nigeria has given him the background and experience to be a salesman and lobbyist. His general demeanour, unlike that of Gardiner, has not been that of international servant, but rather that of an activist for certain strategies. The State of economic crisis in which much of the continent finds itself today, the population explosion (estimates are that the continent's population will double from its current 400 million to 800 million by the turn of the century), and the sluggishness with which the international system is responding to Africa's needs, are all themes to which Adedeji addresses himself in his tireless travels around the continent. In fact, in recent years, Adedeji has been the most audible voice dealing with Africa's economic and social development needs and defining regional strategies. Indeed, he has been far more visible than a succession of OAU secretary-generals during that organisation's post-Diallo Telli period. In this sense Adedeji has called attention to himself, to some extent to the ECA, and to a great extent to Africa's development problems.

On the other hand, the OAU, even without a visible head of its secretariat, still has a reasonable claim to speak for Africa on political issues. OAU support is now regularly sought for outlining strategies and aims for the allocation of development resources on the African continent, and for exerting leverage to achieve an NIEO.

What remains unclear is the degree to which the OAU actually can or should duplicate the capacity of the ECA to generate and formulate, and/or execute economic and social development at the technocratic level. It is clear that in 1983 the ECA continues, in spite of its own internal weakness, to be far more viable in the economic field than the OAU. The really intriguing questions arise in regard to the future.

Questions for the Future

First, with the much more activist and political leadership of Adedeji, for instance, will most African states see that the past criticism of the ECA is no longer as valid as it once was? If this is the case, then the fears and concerns of 1963, that the ECA was not really an 'African organisation,' might lessen somewhat and thus make it less urgent and less desirable to seek to duplicate the efforts of ECA by fleshing out the Economic and Social Specialised Commissions of the OAU. As the ECA takes a more agressive and activist role in speaking for Africa, as opposed to mainly serving the UN in Africa, it might be more cost- and manpower-effective and more politically feasible to mothball these duplicating Commissions. The almost totally Africanised ECA professional staff should help. Central to this issue is whether the quality of ECA's work in the years to come will merit such confidence and political support.

Second, it is also worth considering whether such sub-regional efforts as ECOWAS and functionally specific mechanisms like regional development banks and technical organisations might not gain increasingly active membership support and also financial and manpower resources from member governments. Under such circumstances, many among the OAU membership might prefer mothballing some of the OAU provisions for special Commissions in favour of supporting sub-regional efforts.

Finally, if the ECA can, in the years to come, achieve respect and recognition as speaking for Africa on economic and social issues, it could then become customary for the OAU to adopt with some comfort the strategies and blueprints worked out by ECA and sub-regional internally-run organisations. This would still leave open the question of the extent to which ECA operates as a think-tank to hammer out strategies, options, and goals, and thus leaves implementation to other African and/or appropriate international mechanisms, and the extent to which ECA should also be an executing agency. In any event, the OAU itself could turn from the economic and social realm, and instead give political support and direction.

The reader will see that by default rather than by design, the OAU has in fact done this. The question for the future, therefore, is whether the rhetoric should more closely coincide with the reality, or whether African states seriously wish to divert manpower and financial resources from the national, subregional, and continental levels, to give the OAU new resources and capacities, even though they will, for the near future, duplicate the activities of both the ECA and an assortment of sub-regional and other continental institutions and mechanisms.

For the time being, these questions are undecided. OAU conferences typically revolve around issues of political leadership, strategies vis-a-vis southern Africa, coping with inter-state conflicts, etc. The OAU, via the *Lagos Plan of Action*, is, however, again on record as wishing to link political and economic issues quite properly in their political context.

The division of labour between the OAU and ECA in regard to economic issues depends very much on how each organisation shapes and reshapes itself in the decade to come. The theme set out in the *Lagos Plan of Action* for the eighties calls for a good deal of African collective self-reliance. Such strategy calls upon African governments to replace rhetoric about economic cooperation with genuine action including providing inter-state mechanisms with adequate and well-trained staff and reliable financial bases for carrying out their task. In many ways, history has shown that African governments have a high level of commitment to the concept of the OAU without necessarily making good on this commitment. All the good intentions of the OAU to contribute meaningfully to African developments are undermined by the fact that member governments cannot be counted upon to pay their annual assessments. Under the circumstances, it may well be realistic to assume that the ECA can and should command the manpower and financial resources from the UN system. However, if Executive Secretary Adedeji's calls for recognising the crisis proportions of the continent's economic dilemmas are taken seriously, business as usual for both the OAU and the ECA will not be adequate to face the future.

This chapter has suggested that there are a number of alternative ways in which each organisation can play a role minimising overlap, duplication, and the waste of resources in short supply. In the end, whether the main task for certain economic and social activities at the continental level are left to the ECA or shared by the OAU, each organisation has a very large task ahead. Improving an organisation's effectiveness, the quality of its work output, and generating a sensible work agenda, are most easily accomplished if clients (member governments) follow a carrot-and-stick policy. That is, to allocate the necessary resources to give adequate support and cooperation, but also to demand that the quality of the work output live up to the resource investment which the membership has undertaken. In the final analysis, the OAU and ECA will live up to African government expectations individually and cooperatively only when member governments make serious demands on the respective institutions, and – more important – when member governments make serious demands on themselves to support economically and politically inter-state cooperation on the African continent. Until that happens, the rhetoric of good intentions will drown out, and even undermine the modest achievements that the ECA, in particular, has managed to contribute to African economic development. Some encouragement can be taken from renewed cooperative efforts such as the *Lagos Plan of Action*, but the urgency of the tasks ahead and the history of the past twenty years precludes undue optimism.

Notes

1   See especially introduction in Isebill V. Gruhn, *Regionalism Reconsidered: The Economic Commission for Africa* (Boulder, Colorado: Westview Press, 1979)

2   For a careful comparison of the ECA and the OAU structures, see Berhanykun Andemicael, *The OAU and the UN* (New York: Africana, 1976), chapter vii.

3   Gruhn, *op. cit.*, chapter 2 (see note 1 above).

4   Andemicael, *op. cit.*, chapters vii and viii (see note 2 above).

5   The Casablanca group consisted of those states who participated at a conference held in Casablanca in January 1961. Representatives from Egypt, Libya, Ghana, Guinea, Mali, Morocco, and Algeria attended. The Casablanca group came to stand for states dubbed as radical, in juxtaposition to the so-called Brazzaville group or Monrovia groups, each named after respective meetings in those locations, but attended by what were then perceived as less radical states.

6   Zdenek Cervenka, *The Unfinished Quest for Unity: Africa and the OAU*, (New York: Africana, 1977), see especially chapter X.

7   UN Document A/6174 of 16 December, 1965.

8   Extensive interviews with ECA officials at headquarters in the spring of 1966.

9   Gruhn, *op. cit.*, chapter 11 (see note 1 above).

10   Michael Wolfers, *Politics in the Organisation of African Unity*, (London: Methuen, 1976), chapter 11

11   See Cervenka, *op. cit.*, chapter X (see note 6 above).

12   E/CN.14/Res/190(LX) of 11 February, 1969.

13   See Cervenka, *op. cit.*, chapter X

14   General Assembly Resolution 3201 (S-1 VI) and 3202 (S-VI), 1974.

3 African Development Bank/African Development Fund: Problems and Prospects

I. Diaku

The Origin and Rationale

In Africa, the period between 1950 and 1960 was dominated by the demand for and the achievement of political independence by many countries. The attainment of independence meant the immediate takeover of responsibilities formerly assumed by colonial administrators. The promotion of economic growth and development, the raising of the living standards of the native population and the maintenance of political stability became the dominant concern of the young African states. It soon became apparent that African development cannot be successfully and rapidly achieved without a suitable institutional framework for regional cooperation. In particular, the need was felt for a suitable financing institution for channelling resources to desirable developmental activities. This feeling was most clearly reflected in the view of the Economic Commission for Africa:

> A suitable financing institution for Africa, if efficiently organized, could play an important supplementary role in mobilizing additional outside investment. This conclusion was confirmed by the existence of other regional financial institutions. An African Development Bank could also provide services not performed by existing financial agencies especially in co-ordinating regional and sub-regional development projects and in facilitating the region-wide study of national development programmes. By acting as an investment promotion and information centre, the institution could assist in formulating sound projects and reveal new investment opportunities to potential foreign investors.[1]

The scope of the Bank's operations was to include 'hard' commercial lending operations, 'soft' non-commercial lending support for pre-investment expenditure and assisting in providing guarantees for loans from other sources.

The idea of establishing the Bank was positively expressed in a resolution adopted at the close of the Second All-African Peoples' Conference held in Tunis in January 1960. This arose from the widespread belief in the developing countries in the need to establish their own regional development banks. A number of regional development banks had been established in Asia (the Asian Development Bank) and Latin America (the Inter-American Development Bank).[2]

The desire for an African Bank arose from a number of considerations:[3]

(a) African countries, mindful of their colonial antecedents, thought rightly that they needed a lending institution that would pursue an African mission by concentrating on African development problems.
(b) A proposal to establish a special United Nations Fund for Economic Development had failed to materialise. African countries thought that establishing their own lending agency would give them an opportunity to participate effectively in the management of aid resources.
(c) An African Development Bank would represent, like other regional banks, a political resistance to the dominance of developed countries in international lending arrangements.
(d) The operational style of the World Bank took no account of African circumstances and the Bank was not particularly active in Africa until the early 1960s.

In view of the strong need for an African Development Bank, Resolution 27 (III) was adopted on 16 February 1961 by participants at the fiftieth plenary meeting of the United Nations Economic Commission for Africa (ECA) urging 'the Executive Secretary to undertake a thorough study of the possibilities of establishing an African Development Bank.'

A Panel of Experts therefore met twice between October and December 1961 in Addis Ababa, Ethiopia, and after carefully examining the financial resources at both the bilateral African and multilateral levels, advised that the Bank be established.[4] It rationalised the establishment of the Bank as we have already indicated above.

The Panel of Experts gave primary consideration to the problem of providing adequate funds for the proposed Bank. It estimated that the sum of 40 million American dollars a year or 200 million dollars in five years represented the amount African members might reasonably be expected to contribute. However, considering the African development needs, a contribution of 800 million dollars would be required from non-African sources.[5]

The consideration of sizeable non-African contributions naturally raised the question of non-African participation in the equity capital of the Bank. Anticipating problems that might arise from the existence of two categories of share capital, category A shares were to be primarily for African members and category B shares for non-African participants with limited voting rights. The Panel also suggested an arrangement for the management of the Bank's resources if the share capital of the Bank were to be primarily confined to Africans. Where this turned out to be the case, 'the share capital and the contributions for general purpose loans might be managed separately from the special purpose contributions grants and *ad hoc* fund. The latter group, the Panel felt, might be subject to special agreement between donors and the Bank'.

In 1962 the UN Economic Commission for Africa met in its fourth session and after considering the reports of the Panel of Experts decided by resolution 52 (IV) to accept the principle of establishing the Bank but subject to further detailed investigation. The Commission immediately constituted a Committee composed of nine member countries, namely Nigeria, Sudan, Mali, Tanzania, Cameroon, Ethiopia, Guinea, Tunisia and Liberia, and entrusted it with the responsibility of making this investigation. Among other things the Nine-country Committee agreed was that the purpose of the Bank was to promote and accelerate the economic and social development of African nations individually and collectively.[6]

It further insisted that the contribution of non-African countries to the resources of the Bank could be made in the form of loans, grants, trust funds and purchase of debentures. But non-African participation in the resources of the Bank should not endanger or impair the essentially 'African character' of the institution. In the absence of a carefully spelled-out developmental philosophy with an African bias in content, it was not clear what 'the African character' of the Bank really was. One would expect that an African character (short of the dominance of African personnel) would imply the application of developmental criteria specific to African conditions and circumstances. One searches in vain in the official documents establishing the bank for what constitutes an 'African character' from an operational point of view.

It soon became apparent from the limitations of its resources, that the Bank could not experiment on or even prescribe alternative strategies for Africa's development. This is because during the first decade of its operations, the Bank sought for revenue-generating projects with quick financial returns demonstrable within the framework of conventional investment appraisal.[7]

With regard to the management and control of the Bank, the

Committee recommended, and the national governments generally agreed, that the Board of Governors and Board of Directors should be composed exclusively of Africans and that the Chief Executive, staff and deputy, should also be Africans. It was also generally agreed that the Bank should be managed on 'sound banking principles' by highly qualified management staff and its policy should be determined by purely technical considerations.[8]

Major Functionaries of the Bank

The powers of the Bank are vested in the Board of Governors, composed of one Governor appointed by each member country, although, with some exceptions the powers of the Board of Governors are delegated to the Board of Directors. The Board of Governors meets once a year and additional meetings may be fixed by the Board itself or by the Board of Directors on request either by five members or by members having one-quarter of the total voting power of the member states. A quorum is formed at the meeting of the Board of Governors when a majority of the total number of Governors or their representatives are present. They should, however, represent not less than two-thirds of the total voting power of members present.

The Bank's other principal organ is its management which comprises the President and the Vice-Presidents supported by an administrative staff. The Agreement establishing the Bank clearly stipulates that the President shall be a national of a member country and shall be a person of the highest competence in matters relating to the Bank's activities, management and administration. He is normally elected for a period of five years by the Board of Directors, by a majority of the total voting powers of members of the Bank. He is the chief executive and the Bank's legal representative. He presides over the meetings of the Board of Directors at which he has no votes except a deciding vote to resolve a tie.

The appointment of Vice-Presidents was more problematic. The Bank was to have one or more Vice-Presidents elected by the Board of Directors, based on the President's recommendation. Essentially the Vice-Presidents were expected to share the administrative and managerial functions with the President but the statute establishing the Bank made no specifications about their responsibility. Similarly, it was silent on the delegation of powers of the President and on the number of Vice-Presidents. This last error of omission was particularly serious because of the diversity of the Bank's membership, the regional groupings of members, and their economic, political, linguistic and cultural affiliations. These factors led to the demand that the choice of Vice-Presidents should be based on the principle of 'equitable geographical representation'. It became inevitable that member states politicised the choice of Vice-Presidents. Thus the choice of Vice-Presidents and their number has been based more on political and geographical considerations rather than on the volume of work and business of the bank. It should be pointed out, however, that the Bank has so far not had more than three Vice-Presidents at any one time.[9]

Staffing Problems

In Article 37(5) of the Agreement establishing the ADB, provision was made to the effect that the President, apart from securing competent technical staff 'shall pay full regard to the recruitment of personnel among nationals from African countries, especially as far as senior posts of an executive nature are concerned'. This indicates at the outset an awareness of the potential conflict between the desirability of recruiting Africans and the need to secure professionally competent persons. The need to appoint Africans to the most senior positions conforms to the idea of establishing an African institution which would reflect the Pan-African aspirations of member states. As early as 1963 in a Khartoum conference, a bitter argument ensued in which the UAR strongly held the view that the senior staff and advisers of the Bank should be exclusively Africans.

Thus at the early stage of the Bank's career, two separate problems emerged. The first was the recruitment, at the highest level, of personnel who could barely be spared from their domestic assignments. The second problem was that the middle cadre of Africans who sought posts in international agencies preferred the attractions of a European or American metropolis and such agencies were quick to accept suitable African personnel to maintain or make up the continent's quota. The UAR, which had a handful of qualified people, insisted that staffing should be proportionate to subscription. This further attracted more resistance to Egyptian recruitment than would otherwise have been the case.

The need to appoint Africans to the most senior position conforms with the idea of establishing an African institution which reflects the identity of the socio-political and developmental aspirations of member states.

These considerations explain the initial appointment of four Vice-Presidents from Nigeria, Kenya, Tunisia and Mali – an arrangement which reflects a clear geographical balance. Under this arrangement there was a presumption that the technical aspects of operation would be undertaken by a professional class supplied from technical assistance programmes. A number of factors vitiated this presumption.[10] First, there was the problem of recruiting even the few Africans considered suitable for the key positions in order to provide a counterpoise to the anticipated non-African professional personnel. Second, the technical assistance offered to the Africans is often phoney or inappropriate. The final point is the resultant loss of self-confidence, which kept management suspicious of any offer of technical assistance. The suspicion relates to the possible infringement of management's functions and the ultimate imposition of an alien style on the operations of an African institution. The difficulty in recruiting suitable Africans created the additional problem of securing an African commitment to a bank that is essentially subsidiary to both the bilateral sources of aid and to the World Bank that is primarily dominated by developed nations. This problem of staffing lingered on and almost crystallised into a permanent situation. This could quite easily have been remedied by a more imaginative recruitment policy. Such a policy, for example, could be pursued along the lines of the recruitment of non-Africans, with clearly defined and fixed terms of contract which allow sufficient time for scouting out competent African replacements.

Instead, the bank took up an offer made by the United Nations Special Fund at the Khartoum Conference. Under the agreement signed in 1967 between the Bank and the United Nations Development Programme (UNDP), the latter was to establish and staff a pre-investment unit within the Bank. Under this arrangement the UNDP was also to provide, over a five-year period, $2 700 000 out of an estimated cost of $4 900 000, which represents 55.1 per cent of the total cost. Such an arrangement was attractive and offered a prospect of providing an intervening period for training African staff. The UN regarded the arrangement as simple technical assistance which implied the training of African counterpart staff.

The UN therefore demanded this requirement to be met. A paradoxical situation thus arose in which a severely limited bank staff was depleted to augment non-African staff in the pre-investment unit. The unit came to dominate the operations of the Bank and frustrated the intentions of both the bank and the UN. Moreover the difficulty of recruiting appropriate staff through the UN system led to the appointment of mixed groups who were neither suitable nor committed to the delicate and difficult operation of institution-building. A non-African character began to emerge in the bank. As

White put it, 'The creative, if still unrefined unimplemented ideas of the early years had given way to the narrow technocratic approach'.[11]

The institution assumed the character of a highly foreign-dominated institution in the absence of a broad spectrum of African staff professionally qualified or otherwise. The domination seemed to have arisen in an invidious way through the injection of technocratic habits, ways of thinking which invoke conventional professional criteria devoid of indigenous political guidance. In a bid to secure international respectability the institution unwittingly drifted from the fundamental political concepts which animated it. (A similar problem also confronted the ECA for many years; see chapter 2.)

Although there was a general consensus among governments with regard to the purpose of the Bank as a useful instrument for promoting and accelerating the economic and social development of member countries, there was considerable divergence of views regarding the financial structure of the Bank. To make all necessary governmental and other contacts regarding the establishment of the bank, the Nine-country Committee decided to carry out consultations through its members which divided into three teams, each to visit a specified number of the 29 member countries of ECA together with its four associate members.

Membership, Capital Subscription and Voting Rights

Most of the countries consulted held the view that the Bank's capital should be subscribed by African countries. A small but vocal minority questioned the wisdom of such an approach and advised that a more flexible interpretation of the 'African character' and ownership should be adopted. These more cautious countries agreed that the control of the bank would still be African if the share capital of non-Africans was limited to 20 per cent of the total.[12] Some of the governments even expressed the view that a limited non-African participation would be valuable as a means of inspiring confidence in investors. Indeed, others thought that if non-African countries were unwilling to support the bank in no other way, a more imaginative approach would be to permit them to subscribe to the share capital.

The question of capital subscription was easily the most contentious one. The smaller countries favoured subscriptions related to economic capacity, but having equal voting rights. The larger countries, on the other hand, were in favour of a smaller differentiation of subscription levels, but weighted voting rights.

Three main issues were involved. In the first place, the Francophone countries were rather sceptical about the whole idea of an African Bank. While consultations about establishing the Bank were going on, a meeting of the Francophone countries in Libreville confirmed that the proposal represented an 'unrealistic' approach to the solution of African development problems. This attitude was attributed to disapproval by France and this was later confirmed by French officials in Paris. Moreover, it became evident that most governments were interested in the proposal because it would provide an additional avenue for channelling the increased flow of funds from developed countries. If to this we add the divergent views of members regarding non-African participation, the complexity of the problem can be appreciated.

The Nine-member Committee had a task that was by no means easy. Apart from sounding the opinions of the various member-countries about all facets of the proposal, it also had to take soundings regarding the extent to which the Bank could count on the developed countries for financial and technical support. These two functions were clearly mutually conflicting. On the one hand the developed countries were to be told that the membership of the Bank was to be entirely African and on the other they required non-African collaboration. But at the same time, the important aspect of the functions of the Committee was to establish good-will for the proposed Bank as an independent venture. In discussions with colonial and ex-colonial powers it was important to assure listeners that the proposed Bank was in no way intended to interfere with existing bilateral and multilateral relations, particularly those between Francophone states and France. Often members of the Committee took as their main theme the virtue of the Bank as an exercise in self-help. They explained in detail their perception of the Bank's role and its operational methods, and asked for suggestions about possible lines of collaboration. In a number of places visited by the teams of the Committee, they seemed to be seeking answers to questions which were imprecisely formulated. Members of the team unofficially admitted that they deliberately refrained from formulating their proposals precisely in the hope, never realised, that the developed countries would readily offer their own proposals. The results were disappointing.

One team was sent to Western Europe and the other to the Soviet Union and the USA. The West European team received the characteristic polite hearing. The Scandinavians welcomed the proposals but made it clear that they had rather limited resources. The Scandinavians, it would appear, had expected a lead from other, larger developed countries. The West Germans, on the other hand, needed evidence of the Bank's progress before taking a decision. The British, the French, the Belgians and the Dutch maintained varying degrees of acceptance. The Americans responded with some enthusiasm and made clear suggestions. They indicated that the exclusion of the developed countries could present problems. Finally, the Russians exercised some caution and on the issue of non-African membership insisted on equality of voting rights.

There was a definite danger in involving the proposed Bank in the ideological dispute between Russia and the USA. This strengthened the conviction that the membership of the institution should be restricted to African countries. It became clear that the Bank could not be established with American help. It was already well known that to secure the full participation of Francophone countries, French approval was important. The bitterness between France and the USA was particularly strong and the French would have frustrated any proposal that depended on American initiative.[13]

The irresistible conclusion to be drawn from all this was that the African countries would have to establish their own working institution with an international image or reputation which would attract the support of developed countries. Two problems arose from this. If the Bank's claims for external resources were to be justified from its operational records, how would it acquire such records? Moreover, if the Bank had to function in a way as to secure the approval of developed nations, what would be the impact of this on the Bank? These two issues seemed to prescribe a recipe for extreme parsimony and extraordinary efficiency to enable the bank carve out an image of international creditworthiness.

It would have been a surprise if the negotiation for the establishment of the Bank has been easier than it was. Considering the general nature of the African environment and the historical association of many African countries, the climate for the discussions was clearly predetermined.

The initial problem was that three groups of countries, Francophone, Anglophone and Arabic-speaking, were involved in the negotiations and there were only two prizes to share, namely the bank's headquarters and the office of the President.[14] At some point some people suggested a swap in which the Anglophone countries could have Mr Beheiry of Sudan as President if the French-speaking members accept Abidjan as headquarters. The whole proposition was thrown out and in fact withdrawn as improper.[15] Abidjan was however ultimately chosen as headquarters by the Board of Governors and Mr Beheiry was appointed President.

The location of the Bank's headquarters in Ivory Coast was a political decision which ignored technical considerations. Initially the following criteria were to be taken into account: communication facilities, central geographical position, existence of a large urban centre capable of providing amenities and services at reasonable cost, existence of financial institutions and, if possible, of a money market, availability of adequate staff and training facilities, availability of good housing, and office accommodation, 'political stability', freedom of movement of the Bank's funds, etc.[16]

It is thus interesting that none of these considerations became a factor in the choice of location of the headquarters. The Ivory Coast, which had not previously applied to host the Bank, was chosen by the Board of governors of the Bank. This was a compromise solution intended to placate and win over the Francophone countries to give firm support to the new institution. It should be remembered, that as indicated earlier, they had declared the establishment of the Bank as an unrealistic approach to the solution of the developmental problems of the African subregion.[17] The decision to locate the Bank's headquarters in the Ivory Coast created future difficulties and placed the Bank in a weak bargaining position in so far as the host government was concerned. Whenever the Bank made requests which the host government considered 'unacceptable' it never hesitated to show its resentment. When, for instance, the Bank made requested a financial contribution towards the erection of the Headquarters building or for a more liberal system of privileges and immunities for Bank officials and staff, the government had no qualms in retorting that it did not invite the Bank to Abidjan.[18] With the government in the position of a harassed host and the Bank an unwanted guest, relations between them were bound to be sour.

The question of capital subscription by member countries posed serious problems. As already indicated, the aggregate capital stock of the ADB was to be US $200 million and this was decided having due regards to the ability-to-pay or economic capacity of African countries as reflected by their populations and national income statistics.

The thorny problem that arose was whether subscription should be equal for all members or whether there should be variations and to what extent. The Committee of Nine ultimately recommended that 'subscriptions should be allocated on the basis of each member's economic capacity' and 'in order to avoid extreme differences between members' subscriptions. . . . There should be minimum and maximum limits equivalent, respectively, to US $1 million and US $30 million'.[19] In deciding on these, the Committee followed the practice of other international organisations like the World Bank and IMF and decided that the solution of the subscription problem should be based on a combination of factors: population, national income, export and tax revenues of the states concerned. Some of these indices posed serious difficulties; national income for example, is widely accepted as a general criterion of economic capacity or ability to pay, but statistics for its computation are not usually available for African countries. Choice of criteria apart, there was the question of the principle of allocation of subscriptions. Three options were open – equal, progressive or proportional assessment.

The principle of proportional assessment was finally adopted because, 'other things being equal, a country would subscribe in direct proportion to its capacity to pay'.[20] The principle of progressive assessment was rejected because the range of per capita incomes of Africans was considered insufficiently wide to warrant its application. Similarly, the principle of equal assessment was rejected on the grounds that it would place a severe burden on many countries and would be inequitable since countries with greater ability to pay might actually pay less.

By 31 December 1973, thirty-two African countries had had their allocations of the Bank's capital stock on the basis of an integrated scale up to a total of US $200.004 million adjusted for the 'floor' of US$1 million and the 'ceiling' US$30 million established by the Nine-country Committee. By 30 June 1974, the subscriptions of members had reached a total of 259.40 million of units of account and the paying members had risen to thirty-nine with their voting powers clearly determined and specified as follows.

In determining the voting powers of members' states two considerations were dominant. One group thought that for the sake of African solidarity, the principle of 'one flag, one vote' should apply while the other thought that it would be more equitable if the number of votes for each country equalled the number of its shares in the capital stock of the Bank.[21] The two views had to be reconciled. An acceptable formula or voting system would be such that 'members which need most assistance from the Bank should not be outvoted by those who can contribute larger shares to the Bank's capital resources, while ensuring that the latter would not be outvoted by the former – if for no other reason than that their own resources and continued expansion serve, and must be made to serve, the development of all members'.[22] Thus a pattern of weighted voting was evolved by which the smaller member countries were assigned more than a proportionate share of the voting power. Under this formula a 'minimum voting power of 625 votes was allocated to each member regardless of its initial subscription, plus one extra vote for each share of 10 000 units of account subscribed by it.' This formula is also used in multilateral lending organisations such as the Inter-American Development Bank, the IBRD and the Asian Development Bank. The system has the advantage of simultaneously taking into account the weaknesses and strengths of member countries in the allocation of voting rights. The goal of this technique is to achieve a more balanced distribution of voting power among members in the spirit of African solidarity and political equality.

The Bank opened its doors for business on 1 July 1966 and signed its first loan agreement in August the next year. The loan was of $2 300 000 was for upgrading two roads on the Kenya-Uganda and Kenya-Tanzania borders. By 1968, the Board of Directors had approved the financing of four projects at a cost of $5 400 000. The projects included the National Development Bank of Sierra Leone, irrigation schemes in the Medjerda Valley in Tunisia, a study of urban water supply and sewage in Uganda, a gas turbine plant in Liberia and the East African Development Bank.

It will have become evident that in the establishment of an African Development Bank, the issues that emerged were essentially political. Primarily they consisted of first, how to devise an adequate institutional base for African cooperation; second, how to allay the fears of the smaller countries that cooperation will lead to domination by already relatively advanced countries. Finally there was the issue of how to devise in the context of African development problems, a style that is appropriate to the peculiar circumstances of African dependence and political divisions. It is not surprising that these problems arose at every stage of African regional negotiations for the promotion of political aims or economic progress. In the immediate post-independence era, most African leaders concentrated on one variant or the other of these problems and the limits of their achievements were either set by their inability to tackle the complex reality of each of these problems or an admixture of all.

The Initial Resource Problems of the Bank

By excluding developed countries from participation in the share capital of the bank, the promoters of the Bank had placed unwarranted reliance on its slim resources and soon began to recognise its need for additional external resources for its operational activities.

In 1973, after the Bank had functioned for seven years, it was realised that its operational activities would come to a halt if it did not mobilise additional financial resources. The greatest initial difficulty which the Board of Directors noted was the difficulty of recovering initial subscription capital stock of the Bank. This default did not undermine the application of the voting powers already allocated to the erring countries. Arrears on capital subscription had become a constant feature of the Bank's balance sheet. By 1974, total arrears outstanding had reached US $19.81 million. This must be considered an improvement compared with the figure of US $41.73 million arrears in 1969. By 1974 Egypt and Ethiopia alone were accountable for well over 80% of the arrears outstanding.[23]

The relatively poor performance of the Bank in collecting subscriptions of member states was particularly damaging to the image of the institution. No doubt this possibility had been a source of concern to the Board of Directors long before arrears of subscription became a definite threat. The first President had demonstrated a measure of impatience with the defaulting members in the Opening Address at the Third Meeting of the Board of Governors. This situation, apart from being a poor reflection on the creditworthiness of the Bank, had given rise to an attitude of hesitancy or mistrust on the part of potential lenders to the Bank. More particularly, it seemed to reflect a clear manifestation of a serious lack of any real conviction on the part of African countries that the Bank can develop to a position of any central significance in African development process.

After many recriminations and the consideration and rejection of sanctions on defaulting members, a more workable formula was agreed on for collecting the arrears of subscriptions.

A new timetable for payment of arrears was drawn up and defaulting members were to pay their arrears in five instalments, the first of which must be 10% of the total; two half-yearly payments, each representing 20% of the arrears were to be paid a year later. The remaining two instalments comprised 50% of the total arrears and should be paid the subsequent year in two equal instalments. This payment carried an interest of 5% on all sums not paid in accordance with the timetable set out in the payment agreement.[24]

The response in payment of arrears under this arrangement was satisfactory but much had yet to be done to put the Bank's finances on a satisfactory footing.

Increase in the Ordinary Capital Resources of the Bank

The most difficult function which the authors of the Bank's Agreement had to perform was that of further increasing the capital stock of the Bank and the mobilisation of additional resources generally, especially from external sources. Failure to keep up payment of capital stock arrears was a factor in this. The constant mention of this failing in the balance sheets of the Bank proved especially damaging to its image and credibility.

Moreover, the African Development Bank depended solely on the guarantees from callable shares of member countries, who in any case were developing countries, and were therefore unlikely to provide adequate guarantees to satisfy potential lenders. Efforts by the Bank to secure financial assistance from non-member external sources yielded no satisfactory results. This failure was the more remarkable in that it came from Western capital-exporting countries and Socialist and Arab oil-exporting countries. It became apparent that for some time African resources must provide the only source of additional financial resources until other non-African sources have been thoroughly explored and reasonably certified.

To prevent too-early financial frustration, the Board of Governors called for a voluntary increase in capital subscription. This appeal for voluntary subscription attracted sizeable contributions from the richer member countries like Nigeria, Libya, Zaire and Algeria who paid 25 900 000; 20 000 000; 17 000 000; and 15 500 000 units of account respectively. The actual increase volunteered by all the members amounted to US $109.54 million, far exceeding the $60.6 million limit set by the Board of Governors. Encouraged by this response, the Board decided to increase its share capital from 320 million units of account to 400 million units of account.

This increase naturally raised again the question of voting rights, but this seemed easily resolved by reference to the provisions of Article 6(2) and (3) of the Agreement establishing the Bank. With regard to a voluntary increase in capital, a member shall have the right to subscribe 'a proportion of the increase of stock equivalent to the proportion which its stock therefore subscribed bears to the total stock of the Bank'.[25]

This provision did not resolve the conflict between the need to mobilise as much as possible of internal African resources and permitting the relatively richer African countries to contribute as their wealth permits. The provisions were also rather concerned with the maintenance of proportional and equitable voting rights consistent with regional balance and non-dominance of the richer members.

Perhaps a more practical way of circumventing the problem of voting powers, was for the richer members to make their additional contributions in the form of loans and grants which would not augment their voting powers. It was perhaps to permit a more general increase in capital resources that the establishment of the African Development Fund was contemplated.

The African Development Fund

The establishment of the African Development Fund was an attempt to solve, on a long-term basis, the financial problems of the institution. It had become obvious to the founders of the Bank that even if the outstanding subscriptions of the members were fully paid in, these would not be enough to meet the massive development requirements of the Bank and would certainly need additional external financial resources. Moreover, the Bank has been constrained by its limited resources to confine its loans and investments in member countries to directly productive projects which could sustain the demands of conventional lending conditions. It was also obvious that with no source of soft finance, the Bank could not invest in socially beneficial projects even though it is statutorily empowered to make such investments.

In April 1966, the Board of Governors of the African Development Bank adopted a resolution to establish an African Development Fund to be administered by the Bank. Non-African countries were invited to participate in financing the Fund. The African Development Fund was intended primarily to be an effective instrument for cooperation between African and non-African countries and other agencies interested in African economic and social progress.

Several factors complicated the initial attempts to establish the Fund.[26]

1 The greatest impediment was the plan to link the size of the Fund to the magnitude of the equity of the Bank. Some non-African countries saw this as something sinister and inconsistent with the declaration that the Bank would be run as a purely African institution. On the one hand, they were precluded from subscribing to the equity capital of the Bank with the concomitant rights and obligations; and, on the other, they were wooed by the back door to make an equivalent sacrifice in terms of contribution to the Fund. They argued that the questions of equity participation and Fund creation were interwoven and deserved simultaneous treatment.

2 Another vexing issue was the minimum contribution set for the Fund. Some non-African governments held the view that in no circumstance would they feel able to contemplate the suggested contribution of $10 million considering that they subscribed a much smaller amount for full membership of the Asian Development

Bank. The authors on their part argued that the amount was well within the reach of individual capital-exporting countries and this would give them some representation on its Joint Administrative Council.

3 The suggested management and operational arrangement of the Fund was equally contentious and unacceptable for the non-African governments. Typically, these problems were again satisfactorily resolved and the most attractive and equitable provision of the Fund agreement was 'that regional members of the Bank and the non-regional participants in the Fund shall participate on a 50:50 basis in exercising control over the utilisation of the Fund's resources and in the decision-making process designed to achieve its objective'.[27]

At the close of November 1972 the Fund Agreement was signed and on 30 June 1973, the Agreement establishing the African Development Fund entered into force. It is instructive to note that the signatories contributed a total of 90 659 050 units of account, with Canada and Japan contributing 15 million each followed by Italy with 10 million units of account.

Performance of the Bank

Several difficulties beset the measurement of the performance of development finance institutions. The difficulties are more complex when the institution is of a regional variety like the ADB which serves individual states that execute projects in varying socio-political and economic settings. For a national development finance institution several indices of performance are conceivable. Some of the known approaches in performance evaluation are the development approach, the employment approach, the income generation approach, the income distribution impact, the profitability approach, the aggregate investment approach and balance of payments approach. Each of these approaches can be used to judge the performance of an institution provided that account is taken of its special defects.[28]

The most general and perhaps the most important problem with all the measures is statistical, since the statistics for computing these magnitudes can hardly be found in anything like a sufficient amount in an African environment. A notable exception is the aggregate investment made by financing institutions. The mere enumeration of the value of investments and number of projects financed is barely a rough index and does not indicate the efficiency of the investments.

However, it does show how much finance has been mobilised and channelled into profitable investments in member countries. The guideline provided for the Bank's operations was that preference should be given to projects that benefit two or more countries and would be capable of stimulating inter-African cooperation.[29] The ADB itself has not tied itself to any particular definition of multinational projects or programmes. It classified projects, however, by whether:

(a) the geographical area of at least two countries is necessary for its implementation.
(b) although implemented in the geographical area of a single country, it concerns or affects another country or countries.
(c) it does not require a physical installation in a particular country, but two or more countries participate in its operations.[30]

As at 30 June 1974 the Bank had made investments totalling 23 300 000 units of account in various projects, mainly in transport and public utilities. Thirty-eight per cent of the 1974 loans went to the West African region, 28% to North African states, 23% to East Africa and 11% to Central Africa. The geographical distribution of the loans from 1967 to 1974 presents a different picture. Twenty-eight percent went to West Africa, 26% to North Africa, 26% to East Africa, and 14% to Central Africa; multinational organisations like Air Afrique received 6%.[31]

In 1977 the African Development Fund granted loans totalling almost $142m which was 77% higher than the $80m granted in 1976 and 52% higher than the 1975 loan of little over $95m. By 1977 the Fund had committed well over $360m in financing about ninety projects in twenty-seven African countries.[32]

In accordance with the ADB group lending policy, greater emphasis was given to agriculture from 1977 and the ADF committed more funds for agriculture by more than $35m over the 1976 total of $15m.

In 1978 the cumulative loans granted by the Bank group was $1380m as against $958m in the previous year. While the number of projects in 1977 was 258, that of 1978 was 328, an increase of nearly 30%.[33]

Several multinational projects benefited from the loans of the ADB. Such projects are the Liptako Gourma telecommunications scheme, the Accra-Abidjan highway and the Ghana/Ivory Coast power interconnection. The Bank co-financed nine projects with other major development and finance institutions to the value of $760m. The African Development Fund (ADF) co-financed 11 projects, totalling $262m. The Bank co-financed projects with the World Bank group (such as the International Development Agency) more than any other group of institutions did. It also co-financed with major institutions such as Saudi Arabian Fund, Kuwait Fund, European Development Fund, the European Investment Bank and bilateral agencies as USAID, Caisse Central de Co-operation Economique, the United Kingdom, West Germany and others.[34]

The most remarkable achievement was the 1979 loans of more than $516m granted for 68 projects in most of the member states of the bank. The important role played by the bank in the development of OAU countries is clearly reflected in the fact that the cumulative loans and credits of the ADB group in 1980 was nearly $2000m for about 400 projects spread through the African continent and many islands in the Indian and Atlantic Oceans.[35] The various development projects financed by the Bank group have helped in creating better living standards, employment opportunities, new techniques and expertise in member states.

Other Achievements in the Bank

The question of admitting non-Africans to the membership of the African Development Bank had become a recurrent and hotly debated issue since the Bank's inception. At the Ninth Annual Meeting of the Board of Governors in 1980, a vote was taken on the proposal to admit non-Africans and it was marginally defeated. Thus while the fate of the Bank hung on the preservation of its mythical 'African character', resources steadily proved inadequate for its expanding activities and it was becoming increasingly unable to carry out its African mission.

At its Fifteenth Annual Meeting on 18 May 1979, the proposal was again put to vote and it was accepted by a majority of the Governors. Thus the ADB owned by 48 member states of the OAU opened its doors to non-African members. This was a very significant achievement in the history of the Bank's evolution and would determine the scope for future performance. By this action, the capital stock rose from $1.4 billion to $6.3 billion. To maintain the 'African character' and independence of the Bank, the regional members would subscribe two-thirds or $4.2 billion of the authorised capital and non-regional members $2.16m. Twenty-five per cent would be paid-up and the rest callable. Of the 18-member Board of Directors, 12 would be Africans and 6 non-Africans.[36] This was a significant breakthrough and an opening of a financial floodgate into the Bank's resource pool.

Quite naturally, members of the African Development Fund opted to become members of the African Bank. These countries are:

Argentina, Austria, Belgium, Brazil, Canada, Denmark, Finland, West Germany, Italy, Japan, South Korea, Kuwait, the Netherlands, Norway, Saudi Arabia, Spain, Sweden, Switzerland, the United Kingdom, the USA and Yugoslavia.

At a period when negotiations between developed and developing countries are breaking up in frustrated disagreements in Brussels over the Lome convention and in Manila over UNCTAD, it is gratifying for African countries to record a fruitful agreement over the long-debated issue of non-African membership of the Bank.

Prospects

This account of the establishment and activities of the African Development Bank reflects less than fully the problems, paradoxes and unresolved dilemmas in an African experiment to create an institution committed to providing a developmental focus in an economically backward environment.

Immediately the first step in establishing the Bank was taken, the first set of problems emerged sharply. The initial problem was one of the long-term inadequacy of African financial resources and the need to solicit and accept non-African participation in the capital stock of the Bank and at the same time maintain the essentially 'African character' of the institution. The resource problem increased during the process of establishing the Bank and after. In its early stages, resource limitations precluded the Bank from experimenting on alternative strategies for African development. It therefore supported investments in which considerations of profitability were paramount and the potential returns certified through conventional investment appraisal. The demands for competent personnel needed for conducting adequate feasibility studies and investment appraisal conflicted with the maintenance of the 'African character' of the institution, for that implied the employment of predominantly African personnel, which was in chronically short supply. To remedy this shortage the Bank entered into an agreement with the UN for staffing a preinvestment unit in the Bank where African counterpart staff could be trained. The unit came to dominate the operations of the Bank through the employment of mixed groups uncommitted to the ideals of the Bank. This domination also took the form of the injection of technocratic habits and procedures based on professional criteria but which lack political direction.

Fear of partial loss of independence, and mutual suspicion, pervaded the discussions of the Bank. This is reflected in the appointment of multiple governors, and Vice-Presidents without clearly defined functions.

In all these difficulties the Africans seemed to have emerged successfully, but the solution to each problem generated a new problem and the institution has progressed in a kind of unstable equilibrium. There are features of the African environment to which the Bank has had to address itself. There is the shortage of skilled manpower, especially of economic and financial experts, which has led to the inexorable reliance on whimsical offers of technical assistance, often reflected, at least at the early stages, in the Bank's staffing. The prospect of the Bank making any real and lasting impact in its sphere of operations will depend on the effective use of a core of well-trained indigenous personnel committed to the African mission. This would involve special training at all levels for many promising Africans who would execute their functions in the true African spirit.

Instead of actually doing this, the governments devoted a disproportionate amount of attention to the mobilisation of internal and external financial resources through equity subscription and the establishment of general funds. The most frustrating aspects of the African environment were the the pattern and channel of flow of financial assistance and its inadequacy. But this was an area in which developed countries could have mitigated the shortage about twelve years ago through equity participation. The future success of the Bank evidently depends on how prudently and expediently it handles offers of financial participation in its projects.

The prospects of the Bank undeniably depend also on how clear the Bank is about what it wants. It is clear that the behaviour, philosophies and orientation of member countries, long predetermined by their historical experience, had generated genuine developmental objectives and ideals. But these proved difficult to realise as the problems of implementation unfolded themselves. The problems arose from the determination to maintain a mythical 'African character'. While the member countries cherished the ideals of material progress for their citizens, they flagrantly repudiated the obvious means by which the ideals could be more rapidly and easily achieved – participation by non-Africans as partners in progress on clearly defined conditions.

Finally a spirit of commitment and cooperation must pervade the negotiations and deliberations of member countries for more fruitful operations in the future. There seems to be an inadequate appreciation among members that their membership consists of numerous small and financially weak countries highly dependent on single bilateral assistance and on the benevolence of former colonial masters. Nevertheless, the inability of some of these states to pay up arrears of their capital subscription should be viewed sympathetically as reflecting resource limitation rather than lack of commitment to the course of African development.

The smaller members themselves make the problems more complex by expressing fears, which may well be groundless, about the possibility of domination by big member countries. They therefore insist on equality as a condition for their continued membership. Such postures may not always be helpful in an atmosphere which requires mutual understanding and cooperation.

So far the African Development Bank has performed relatively well and can do more if given strong support and recognition by member countries as an institution of central significance in Africa through which some important financial transactions may be channelled for development purposes. The Bank has provided a unique example of a successful experiment in international problem-management in an environment of bewildering complexity and for which there can be no analogue.

The full and spontaneous participation of capital-exporting countries of the world in the Bank's capital subscription, provides the strongest testimony of the Bank's current relative success indicates its potential. The Bank has fitted into a global institutional pattern which can be central in negotiations for development assistance from developed countries. No doubt a regional development bank in Africa must unavoidably be seen essentially as a political instrument for resistance, to, or for mitigating, the domination of developed countries of the framework of African international economic relations. The satisfactory performance of this role cannot, however, lie in the maintenance of postures that may lead to the hardening of negotiating attitudes and impede the steady flow of development and technical cooperation from the industrialised countries while the need lasts.

Notes

1 See *ECA: Consideration of Commission Resolution 52 (IV)*, a paper prepared as a basis of discussion by the participants at the First Meeting of the Nine-country Committee on the establishment of an African Development Bank, E/CN.14/ADB/1 of 12 June, 1962, p. 1.

2 A comprehensive account of these banks and their performance is given in John White, *Regional Development Banks* (London: Overseas Development Institute, 1970).

3 Ime Ebong, *Development Financing under Constraints*, (Research Institute of the Friedrich-Ebert-Foundation, 1974), p. 5.

4 White, *op. cit.*, p. 92 (see note 2 above).

5   Ebong, *op. cit.*, p. 17 (see note 3 above).
6   *Ibid.*, p. 18.
7   White, *op. cit.*, p. 124 (see note 2 above).
8   *Report of Team A2 on consultations with African Governments*: E/CN/.14/ADB/6/Add. 2, p. 3 and Annex VI p. 3. Their view seemed to have been influenced by the recommendation of the Panel of Experts.
9   *Report of Team A2* E/CN.14/ADB/6/Add. 3, p. 2.
10 Article 3.
11 White, *op. cit.*, p. 94 (see note 2 above).
12 *Ibid.*, p. 94.
13 For a detailed discussion of all this see John White, *op. cit.*, p. 96–102.
14 White, *op. cit.*, p. 28.
15 Summary Record E/CN.14/ADB/28, p. 84.
16 Ebong, *op. cit.*, p. 22 (see note 5 above).
17 *Resolution of Council of Minister of OAMCE*, (Libreville, 1 September 1962) in E/CN.14/ADB/6 Annex I, pp. 1–2.
18 Ebong, *op. cit.*, p. 22.
19 *ECA, African Development Bank: Allocation of Capital Subscription, Notes by the Executive Secretary to the Preparatory Meeting, Conference of Finance Ministers on the Establishment of an African Development Bank*, Khartoum, 16–17 July 1963, E/CN.14/FMAB/11, p. 6.
20 *Ibid*.
21 *ECA: Report of Team A3 on Consultations with African Governments concerning the Establishment of an African Development Bank, Committee Nine*, Douala 24–7 September 1962, E/CN.14/ADB/6/Add. 3, p. 4.
22 *Explanatory Outline of a Charter for African Development Bank*, Document E/CN.14/ADB/12, p. 33.
23 Ebong, *op. cit.*, p. 55.
24 See *Summary Record of the Seventh Annual Meeting*, p. 124.
25 See also *ADB: Report of the Board of Directors on the Implementation of Board of Governors' Resolution 9–72 concerning the mobilization of Additional Financial Resources for the African Development* ADB/BG/LX/12/Corr. 1, pp. 7–99.
26 Ebong, *op. cit.*, p. 64.
27 *Ibid.*, p. 71.
28 For a detailed discussion of these see I. Diaku, *Industrial Finance in Nigeria: A Study of Sources, Method and Impact of Industrial Development Financing in a Developing Economy*, (Longman Nigeria Ltd, forthcoming).
29 *ADB: Statement of Policy and Procedure*, p. 5.
30 *Ibid.*, p. 9.
31 *West Africa*, 26 May 1975, p. 593.
32 *West Africa*, 17 April 1978, p. 745.
33 *West Africa*, 21 May 1979, p. 884.
34 *Ibid*.
35 *West Africa*, 12 May 1980, p. 833.
36 *West Africa*, 11 June 1979. See also *Central Bank of Nigeria, Annual Report*, (Lagos) 1979 and 1980.

4 An African Common Market or African Free Trade Area: Which Way Africa?

Ralph. I. Onwuka

The call for economic cooperation in Africa is general and emphatic. African leaders themselves have duly accepted the recommendations, both from within and outside the continent, that African economic integration is a rational strategy for the development of the area. It was against this background that there emerged the *Lagos Plan of Action* of 1980 which looks forward to an African Common Market (ACM) by the year 2000.

The intention of this chapter is to confront the question posed in its title, in the light of the prevailing African political economy: a search for a realistic approach to African economic integration. It does not appear that an African Common Market can be achieved by the year 2000; this study therefore suggests an African Free Trade Area (AFTA) as a more realistic integration design. Let us first examine the grandiose hope found in the *Lagos Plan of Action* which encapsulates the OAU's desire to set up an African Common Market by the year 2000, in an attempt to diagnose the two systems of economic cooperation in Africa.

1 The Emergence of the *Plan of Action*

The *Plan of Action* seems to be a logical climax of a series of rhetorical exercises at various UN, and OAU Conferences on the issue. Before the findings of the UN Conference on Technical Cooperation among Developing Countries held in Buenos Aires in 1978, there theoretically existed an Inter-African Convention providing for a technical Cooperation Programme signed in Kampala in 1975 by the Heads of State of the OAU. And in 1979, at the Arusha Ministerial Meeting of the Group of 77 a decision was taken to form a 'short-term' programme of action for global priorities in ECDC. In the same year the OAU had organised the Monrovia Symposium on the future development prospects of Africa towards the year 2000. The symposium, in general but pedagogic terms, articulated its new approach towards international cooperation between countries suffering from the same ills as 'a means of cultivating a development mentality based on collective self-dependence.'[1]

The Arusha Ministerial Meeting and the OAU's Monrovia symposium supplied the intellectual fillip for a higher theoretical phase that culminated in the *Lagos Plan of Action*. It is wrong to assert that the *Plan of Action* was a climax of various conferences, symposia, and resolutions. It was an anti-climax, rather, because apart from the Monrovia symposium there had been equally convincing OAU resolutions and declarations on economic development adopted in Algiers in September 1968, in Addis Ababa in August 1970 and 1973, and in Libreville in 1977 when economic integration was emphatically adopted as a viable strategy for continental development. As early as January 1965, the African States had, perhaps glibly, mentioned a plan for an African Common Market and large-scale integration of trade and industries.[2] Much more positive mention of an African Economic Community was made at the Eleventh Extraordinary Session of the OAU Council of Ministers held in Kinshasa, Zaire in December 1976 when the Council recommended to the OAU:

> to establish an African Economic Community; an objective which should be attained within a period of 15 to 25 years and in successive stages.[3]

The African Heads of State and Government approved the Council's recommendation in July 1977 in Libreville. Similarly motivated was the OAU Declaration of Guidelines and Measures for National and Collective Self-reliance in Social and Economic Development for the Establishment of a New International Economic Order adopted in Monrovia in July 1979. In their ensuing Monrovia Declaration the African heads of state firmly rehearsed their earlier belief in 'an eventual establishment of an African Common Market leading to an African Economic Community.'[4]

Thus the Monrovia Declaration prefaced the Lagos OAU Summit of April 1980 when the *Plan of Action* was adopted.

2 The Plan for an African Common Market

The *Lagos Plan of Action* consisted for the most part of guidelines and schemes for the implementation of the Monrovia Strategy for the Economic Development of Africa. The affirmed measures are *inter alia* those 'for the establishment of subregional organisations and the strengthening of existing ones towards the establishment of an African Common Market'.[5] The Draft Protocol on African Common Market prepared by the Council of Ministers spells out, in four pages, most of the obvious doctrinaire issues without due regard for the circumstances of the region. First, the Protocol is committed to the creation of an African Economic Community by the year 2000. Second, members of the planned Community shall be the OAU States. Third, in a language similar to that in the Monrovian Declaration, the aims and objectives of the Community are said to be:

> to promote development, co-operation and integration among its member states, in all economic, social, and cultural fields for the purpose of fostering closer relations among its member states towards accelerated collective self-reliant and endogenous economic, social and cultural development of the African continent to raise the quality of standard of living and dignity and respect of its people.[6]

The statement of the objectives of the Community maintains the language of the previous rhetoric of the OAU declarations. They all remain vague and pedantic in their respective pledges, aims, commitments or convictions. In only one page of the draft Protocol are attempts made to translate the avowed objectives into action: the orthodox prcedure for establishing an African common external tariff, and a common commercial policy towards non-members is to be adopted by first eliminating tariff and non-tariff barriers among the participating states. Towards the desired objectives two sets of pledges are made, one for the 1980s, the other for the 1990s. The former group of pledges are aimed at strengthening subregional and sectoral economic integration structures, while the latter, a logical follow-up, involves the introduction of further subregional and regional economic activities in six distinct stages:

(a) the fostering of sectoral integration at all levels in many fields including food and agriculture, industry, transport, science and technology;
(b) the abolition of obstacles to free movement of persons, ideas, services and capital between the member states;
(c) the harmonisation of development strategies, policies and plans and the promotion of joint projects particularly in the economic fields;
(d) the harmonisation of financial policies and monetary integration among the member states with the ultimate objective of adopting a single unit of currency by the member states.

(e) the establishment of a Common Development Fund for cooperation, compensation, guarantee, and development; and
(f) such other activities that would promote the grand objectives of the Community as may be decided upon.

The above taxonomies of the intended African Economic Community are to be implemented within the framework of the OAU's Economic Commission not the UN's ECA, and thus it was Edem Kodjo and not A.A. Adedeji who was assigned the responsibility of preparing the Community's Treaty and Protocol for its operational framework modalities. Five major functional institutions to be created within this structure are an Assembly of Heads of State, a Legislative Assembly, Conferences of Ministers, Specialised Commissions and the Secretariat. Let us examine how feasible these ideas are within the desired period.

3 A Feasibility Analysis of the Plan

In carrying out a feasibility assessment of the Plan to erect an African Common Market by the year 2000 four questions quickly present themselves:
Will the African political economy pass through radical changes?
Will the nature and content of Africa's external dependence on capital and technology change to allow for an autonomous and self-reliant mode of production in the continent?
Will the response of the African States towards cooperation arrangements be sufficiently positive to disallow dissent or disintegration dysfunctional to an African Common Market?
Will it be easy for members of the existing subregional common markets to transfer their loyalties and if necessary the present structures to a continental superstructure? Let us treat the issues embodied in the above questions.

(a) African Political Economy Pyramided on External Dependence

Both Ali Mazrui[7] and the *Plan of Action*, in different circumstances, have adduced evidence to show that the continent of Africa is the most 'brutalised' by poverty, ignorance and colonialism and yet is one of the wealthiest in natural resources. Ali Mazrui has taken great time and effort to deliberate on this paradox without offering any prescriptive diagnosis. The OAU has ambitiously articulated the search for a diagnosis in its *Plan of Action*. The continent is the poorest in the world as the Plan acknowledges: 'Africa has 20 of the 31 least developed countries in the world'.[8]

Africa's Gross Domestic Product is merely 2.7 per cent of the world's and per capita income in the continent averages US$166. Economic forecasts indicate no change. Amidst this economic decay there are huge natural resources in the continent. The *Plan* continues:

> Our Continent ... has 97% of world reserves of chrome, 85% platinum, 64% of world reserves of manganese, 25% of world reserves of uranium and 13% of world reserves of copper without mentioning bauxite, nickel, and lead (and gold); 20% of world hydro-electrical potential, 20% of traded oil in the world (excluding US and USSR), 70% of world cocoa production; one third of world coffee, and 50% of palm production.[9]

The African situation of extreme poverty amidst vast natural resources is rooted in past colonialism (and its advanced stage of neocolonialism) and in the absence of technology and capital in the area. The dependence-relationship between developed and developing countries based on unequal exchange is well articulated by Samir Amin.[10] Most African resources are either in the control of the apartheid system or tied to the economic and strategic interests of the developed world, including the transnational corporations. In the UNITAR-sponsored book, *Multinational Co-operation for Development in West Africa*[11] the author has graphically shown the vast logistic, administrative and financial support offered by such world bodies as UNESCO, ITU, IBRD, and IMF in multilateral efforts to implement diverse projects in the subregion. Because the multilateral aids are designed to be inadequate for African development needs, the unbridgeable gap is partly filled with bilateral aids and financial activities of the transnational corporations. An African Economic Community that operates under the present world economic order would be fragile, purely dependent on and directed by external decision-makers. This is well demonstrated by the foreign-orientated nature of the African Development Bank, the Fund of ECOWAS, and the *Banque Centrale des Etats de l'Afrique l'Ouest* (BCEAO). An ACM Cooperation Fund will be bedevilled with similar helplessness, able only to stare its obligations in the face without the financial resources to satisfy them self-reliantly.

On the question of technology, the member states of the OAU have recognised its role in development without making coordinated and adequate provisions for technological planning. The *Plan of Action* presumes that the class system will be restructured, and the leadership reorientated in such a way that the economies will be better managed and large-scale corruption minimised. No mention was made of ways of curbing the extroverted-consumer attitude of most African people.

(b) Economic Inequality, and Low Intra-African Trade

Mainly because of the prevailing poverty of the area, the varying degree of economic capability and the large number of states involved in the proposed African Economic Community, the question of distribution of cost and benefit will be keenly contested. Experience at the subregional level has shown that African leaders have varying and conflicting perception of what constitutes acceptable costs and expected benefits in such development integration. One is therefore hesitant to accept that there will emerge an African Common Market that is not cumbersome to operate and generally accepted by the African States.

Cost and benefit issues would be less controversial if the level of endogenous development were high in the region; and a robust intra-African trade would be a necessary condition for such development.[12] But the present state of intra-African trade is far from encouraging. According to the 1980 issue of *African Trade* published by ECA, between 1971 and 1978 intra-African trade was both disappointing and erratic in its trend and content. In 1967 intra-African trade shown as percentage of total trade was abysmally low at 5.6, and by 1978 the percentage had fallen to 3.9. The highest percentage ever achieved between 1967 and 1978 was 5.9 in 1968. It would seem that as the continent grows older, African states increase the volume of their business with the developed countries and decrease those with their African neighbours. This is mainly because

> Many African countries are still conditioned by strong attachment to pre-independence colonial economic ties whatever the rhetorics giving the contrary impression may be.[13]

Thus there is a dire need for a campaign to 'delink' the existing pre-independence economic ties with the major world trading centres as part of a general endeavour to boost intra-African trade. The OAU's scheme for establishing a Common Market is ambiguous and faulted on one major ground. The *Plan* has not, like the previous Declarations or Schemes, specifically committed the African states. It is an intention to integrate expressed in a very vague manner. Such expressions as 'interested countries', 'African states should endeavour', 'should grant', for 'should be assisted' portray an absence of definite commitment. The prevailing paralysis of will to bridge the gap between theory and practice is yet to be overcome in contemporary African politics both at regional and subregional levels.

The Future of Subregional Common Markets in Africa

Although adequate thought was given to the future of the existing subregional economic communities in the general scheme there was a naive hope that these subregional communities will automatically transfer their allegiance to a continental community. The *Plan* expects four subregional communities to emerge or grow from the existing structures:

> It is hereby proposed, taking into account previous analyses, to divide the African region into four subregions corresponding respectively to West Africa (Economic Community of West African States), East Africa (East Africa Community), Central Africa (Union of Central African States) and North Africa (Economic Community of North Africa).[14]

In acknowledgement of the geo-political situation in East Africa the Report envisages a new East African Community that will embrace not just Uganda, Kenya and Tanzania but also Zambia, Malawi, Ethiopia, Somalia, the Malagasy Republic, Mauritius, Seychelles, Comoros, Botswana, Lesotho, Swaziland, Mozambique and Zimbabwe, and later Namibia and South Africa. The demise of the former East African Community membered by only three states was due to what A. Hazlewood calls below 'a multiplicity of ailments ... which were too much for the body to bear.'[15] These 'ailments' still persist in all the subregions of the continent. In West Africa, for example, the implementation of the first phase of the ECOWAS Protocol on Free Movement of People has aroused 'some latent chauvinisms' across the area. Also, the survival of both the Economic Community of the Great Lakes and the Southern African Customs Union has been determined by the apartheid policy of South Africa. A customs union not directly referred to in the Plan was the *Communauté Economique de l'Afrique de l'Ouest* (CEAO) formed by the Francophone States of Ivory Coast, Mali, Mauritania, Niger, Senegal, and Upper Volta. Another is the Mano River Union formed by Liberia and Sierra Leone later joined by Guinea. By mid-1981, the Mano River Union had broken down tariff barriers between member states in its bid to erect a common external tariff wall against non-members. Because of the diverse geo-political problems in the continent it was suggested that

> If the Organisation of African Unity dreams of a continental common market by the year 2000 is to have any hope of reaching reality, it will be as a (form of) collaboration of regional common markets rather than as a linking of all the states of the continent.[16]

Such 'horizontal' instead of 'vertical' regional integration is best implemented under a Free Trade arrangement.

4 An African Free Trade Area – A Realistic Approach

An African Free Trade Area (AFTA) would lead to the suppression of tariffs and quantitative restrictions between the participating units (states or subregions) in Africa. An African Common Market, on the other hand, would eventually involve not only the elimination of restrictions on tariffs in trade but also the suppression of all barriers 'on commodity and factor movement with some degree of harmonisation of national economic policies'.[17] This, as a higher level of economic integration, would involve the African states in greater structural, economic and administrative adjustment than would be the case in an African Free Trade Area. Thus an African Free Trade Area would allow the individual subregional common market to move at its logical pace. Such an arrangement would be similar to the Latin American Free Trade Association (LAFTA) created in 1961 by the Treaty of Montevideo[18] or the European Free Trade Association (EFTA). LAFTA embraces both the members and non-members of the Andean Pact, in the way that an African Free Trade Area will comprise all the members of the existing and future subregional common markets.

When the European Free Trade Area (EFTA) came into force in 1960 a number of objectives[19] were set out in Article 2 of the Stockholm Convention achievement:

(a) to promote in the area of the association and in each member state a sustained expansion of economic activity, full employment, increased productivity and the rational use of resources, financial stability and continuous improvement in living standards;

(b) to secure that trade between member states takes place in conditions of fair competition;

(c) to avoid significant disparity between member states in the conditions of supply of raw materials produced within the area of the association;
(d) to contribute to the harmonious development and expansion of world trade and to the progressive removal of barriers to it

The terms of the Stockholm Convention laid down a timetable for 'the reduction of import duties on industrial goods traded between member states'. In both EFTA and LAFTA timetables for gradual reductions of restrictions on intra-region trade are formulated based on prevailing conditions.

Africa can learn from Europe and Latin America in the experience of Free Trade Area arrangements. The Preferential Trade Area (PTA) of Eastern and Southern Africa will lay the foundation for an African Free Trade Area. The idea of PTA originated from the 1978 Lusaka Declaration of intent and commitment on the establishment of the PTA as a logical first step towards the creation of an African Common Market. The treaty establishing the area was signed in December 1981 by nine of the original eighteen states, mainly the Southern African Development Coordination Conference (SADCC) countries that negotiated the Protocols. The treaty was signed by Comoros, Djibouti, Ethiopia, Kenya, Malawi, Mauritania, Somalia, Uganda and Zambia. By the provisions of the PTA Protocols only seven member states are required to sign and ratify the Treaty for the Organisation to be operational. The PTA's twelve Protocols provide, among other things, for re-exporting within the area, removal of tariff and non-tariff trade barriers, easing of transit trade and the establishment of clearing and payments arrangements among member states.

The mode of integration of AFTA would be based on three major instruments, namely:
(a) trade liberation schemes;
(b) joint industrial schemes; and
(c) principles of reciprocity.

The dynamics of these machineries of integration would be spelt out in the various instruments. The liberalisation of trade would be between member units who should agree on a common schedule for such liberalisation. Agreements are necessary on the following issues: (i) institutional arrangements, (ii) the necessary transitional period, (iii) the rules of origin, (iv) margin of preference to be granted, (v) the method of sharing benefits, (vi) reciprocity of benefits.[20]

It would also be necessary to give certain concessions to such less-developed African countries as Sudan, Chad, Niger, Mali, Gambia,

Guinea, Upper Volta, Benin, Central African Republic, Uganda, Rivanda, Burundi, Ethiopia, Somalia, Malawi, Tanzania, Botswana, Lesotho and Comoros.

A Joint industrial programme is necessary for the joint development of specific industries. One would expect this to be carried out through complementarity agreements. The *OAU Plan of Action* has already recognised the need for joint action in such areas as energy, telecommunications, and transportation generally. Specifically, there is the established desire for the construction of an integrated road, rail and maritime transport system. There is also the intention to develop African rivers and lake basins in order to boost agricultural production. Complementary agreements should direct the nature of joint industrial programmes. In some cases, inter-country specialisation could be organised vertically or horizontally. In the former, all stages of industrial production take place in a country while in the latter case, production is located in each country under certain laid-down rules. The principle of reciprocity, like a complementarity agreement, provides for mutually agreed incentives, balanced industrial growth and facilitated trade within the free trade area. The principle of reciprocity allows a country to grant preferential treatment to its neighbours if it receives similar preferential treatment in return. Thus if Nigeria accords certain trade preferences to Cameroon and thereby forgoes the advantages of being able to buy cheaper goods from Britain, Cameroon should accord similar treatment to Nigeria. Although the principle is not accorded formal recognition in the Treaty of Rome as in that of Montevideo, the principle of reciprocity remained an important factor in the development of both the EEC and LAFTA.[21]

Institutional arrangements must be responsive to political conditions in Africa. Both the Montevideo and Stockholm treaties have far less flexible arrangements than the EEC for inter-governmental agreements on common plans and policies. The Standing Executive of LAFTA and the Council of EFTA do not have a power of decision comparable with that of the Council of Ministers of the EEC. Thus the prime institutions of the African Free Trade Area would more closely resemble those of LAFTA or EFTA than those of the EEC, primarily because the major focus of a free trade is that of watching over the systematic reduction of trade barriers. The African condition does not require a sudden jump to supranationality. Through AFTA every participating State would maintain its sovereign political rights and yet through committees, meetings or schedules intra-African trade barriers would gradually be removed. In EFTA, for example, there are a number of committees (e.g. customs, trade, agricultural review and budget) that assist, and advise the Council on their respective functional areas.

Advisory committees of government expect to consider such problems as statistics, transport, definition of origin, industrial development, customs questions and monetary questions. LAFTA seems to be more *ad hoc* than EFTA in its institutional provisions, reflecting the contrasting levels of political stability in Europe and Latin America. Africa is certainly much less developed and less stable than either Europe or possibly Latin America. An African Free Trade Area would set up various 'standing', 'permanent' and *ad hoc* committees relevant to the development needs of the continent: such areas as transport and communication, agricultural production, trade, energy and joint industrial projects.

The prevailing financial institutions in Africa are to be utilised in easing the monetary transactions, financing development projects, and compensating the more deprived and less-developed members of the Free Trade Area. The structure of the four subregional banks in the continent, namely the East African Development Bank, the West African Development Bank, the Development Bank of West Africa, and the Development Bank of the Great Lakes, explains their sectional missions. These subregional banks should, side by side with the African Development Bank, strengthen the monetary base of the area and ensure that the available capital is rationally and equitably utilised. The African Development Bank, along with the Central Banks of the member states is to be responsible for creating regional 'systems of compensation and payment so as to break down current payments barriers on inter-African trade'[22] and for other duties prescribed by the integrating free area.

The principle of reciprocity operating within the framework of an African Clearing House (possibly an enlarged West African Clearing House) would reduce the tension of multilateral trade in Africa. This would facilitate trade liberalisation and ease balance of payments problems of member states of an African Free Trade Area. It would be important to ascertain that, as in EFTA, the benefits which might be derived from the removal of tariffs and quantitative restrictions were not nullified by government aids and subventions.

Problems of External Dependence, Multinational Corporations, Uneven Development and Complex Rules of Origin

In this analysis I have opted for an African Free Trade Area as a viable beginning and perhaps alternative to an African Common Market. Although AFTA is a less ambitious and thus a more realistic arrangement, there remain critical issues of external linkages mainly through transnational corporations, uneven development in the area, and the complex rules of origin that usually characterise a Free Trade Area.

These issues are better handled under AFTA rather than the ACM scheme in a politically volatile continent such as Africa. The institutions of an AFTA would be more flexible and could more easily adjust to the political dynamics of African cooperation movements. Several committees, commissions, boards and numerous *ad hoc* agencies are usually created to deal with these integration issues. They are survival issues which would be faced under AFTA in a functional and gradual manner, rather than in a strictly constitutional and supranational way. A quantum leap to an ACM would generate disloyalty in defence of the economic sovereignty of individual states. A Free Trade Area would be conducive to gradual socialisation and integrational behaviour, leading to a gradual and systematic confrontation of the survival issues.

The external economic linkages with the world capitals are founded on colonialism and the prevailing paucity of capital and technology in the African continent. The transnational corporations (TNCs) profit from both situations. But while appreciating the role of foreign enterprise in Africa, effort is to be made within the integration framework to harmonise the various national policy guidelines that determine and direct the activities of the TNCs. The situation in Latin America is perhaps less frustrating than that in Africa where low-level domestic production renders foreign investment readily acceptable. The first step would therefore be to explore business areas of (a) exclusively African enterprise and (b) selected areas of joint ventures between domestic and foreign enterprises. The Nigerian and Ghanaian governments, for example, have differing devices and 'schedules' aimed at increasing the participation of their respective domestic industries. African countries should not compete for direct foreign investment; this would allow the TNCs to play off one African state against another easily, in order to obtain increased incentives (e.g. tax holidays, privileges of duty-free imports, equipment and raw materials). Through integration planning no domestic entrepreneurs should be accorded inferior investment treatment than that allowed non-African investors.

In Africa inter-country differences in the treatment of foreign capital are more 'a question of comparative strength of industrial enterprise' than of differences in ideology. This is quite evident in

Guinea, Tanzania or Zimbabwe, where Western capital is embraced side by side with socialism or Marxism. But as LAFTA advised, so also should AFTA act:

> By planning cooperation with foreign enterprises LAFTA countries can ensure that while foreign capital achieves reasonable security and a fair return, the main gains from regional integration stay within the region, and help to provide resources for still further expansion.[23]

The resources of the Area should be utilised in order to generate even development. The most liberal attention and indeed concession, should be accorded the sixteen lowest-income states while the greatest sacrifice should be borne by the OPEC states of Algeria, Angola, Congo, Libya and Nigeria. The less-developed countries properly so characterised, would receive special or preferential concessions from the other members of the Area. Such dispensation would encourage them to expand in certain productive areas. The Treaty of Montevideo[23] has made such provisions for such countries as Bolivia, Paraguay and Ecuador. In making provisions for the weaker African states to 'catch up' with the others a two-tier preference system may be adopted. The weaker states could also reduce their 'import duties charges and other trade restrictions less rapidly than is required of the others.'[24] Positive and direct aid could be given to the low-income states to enable them to remedy any balance of payments problems. Finally, direct technical assistance accorded these least-developed areas would aid them in their productive activities.

The need to have extensive and well-defined 'rules of origin' provided for in the African Free Trade Area does not diminish the merits of the Free Area. As in both LAFTA and EFTA, rules of origin are necessary in order to ensure that only goods which have undergone certain processes of production within Africa benefit from tariff reduction. Goods that do not wholly or substantially originate from the continent would be excluded under the tariff-reduction scheme. It would sometimes be necessary to further adopt a 'process rule' to clearly define the nature and content of process that goods should undergo in order to qualify for tariff reduction under the AFTA system. A 'percentage criterion' would also be used to ensure that 'non-Area materials' used in the production do not exceed a certain percentage (say fifty per cent) of the export price of the goods. In addition, conditions would be set out for the abolition of quantitative import restrictions within the framework of the general supression of trade restrictions in Africa. Finally AFTA is recommended because it is an economic cooperation arrangement that will allow within the time envisaged for gradual but cohesive measures to be taken towards foreign investors in Africa. Besides, AFTA has more favourable integrative potentials and perceptual conditions than ACM. On the other hand the ACM could by constitutional arrangements adopt radical measures towards an autonomous development in the region, without allowing for enough time for member states to orientate themselves fully to the integration process. The ACM if created in less than twenty years is likely to collapse in the absence of (a) political stability, (b) cohesive economic planning and (c) favourable integration mechanisms.

Conclusion

The study acknowledges the need for continental economic integration, but doubts the feasibility of the projected African Common Market by the year 2000. The *Plan of Action* is elaborate but does not seem workable in the time allowed. An African Free Trade Area would be a more realistic approach in the light of the prevailing political economy of the region. Such a Trade Area should make clear and careful provision for the problems of the less-developed member states, the operations of the multinational corporations and rules of origin.

Notes

1 *What kind of Africa by the Year 2000? Final Report of the Monrovia Symposium on the future development prospects of Africa towards the Year 2000*, Monrovia-Liberia, 12–16 February 1979, (Addis Ababa: OAU), p. 27.
2 *West Africa* (London), 30 June 1980, p. 1174.
3 *OAU Document*, ECH/ECO. 8(XIV) Rev. 2, Add. 1.
4 *Monrovia Declaration of Commitment of the Heads of State and Government of the OAU on Guidelines and Measures for National and Collective Self-reliance in Social and Economic Development for the Establishment of a New International Economic Order* (Monrovia – Liberia), July 1979.
5 *Draft Protocol on the African Economic Community*, OAU Doc. ECM/ECO. 8 (SIV) Rev. 2 Add. 1.
6 *Ibid.*, p. 2.
7 A. Mazrui, *African Condition; Reith Lectures* (London: Heinemann 1980).
8 OAU Document ECH/ECO/9 (XIV) Rev. 1, p. 6.
9 *Ibid.*, p. 4.
10 S. Amin, *Unequal Development: An Essay on Social Formations of*

Peripheral Capitalisms (New York: Africana, 1976).

11   John Renninger, *Multinational Corporations for Development in West Africa*, (New York: Pergamon Press, 1979)

12   *West Africa*, 26 May 1980, p. 937.

13   *Ibid.*, 6 August 1979, p. 1411.

14   *Report of the Secretary General on the Stages of the Integration of African Economies and the Establishment of an African Common Market* ECM/ECO/8(XIV), p. 25-6.

15   A. Hazlewood, 'The End of the East African Community. What are the Lessons for Regional Integration Schemes?', chapter 10 in this anthology.

16   Editorial, *The Times* (London), Saturday, 25 July 1981.

17   Bela Balassa, *The Theory of Economic Integration* (London: Unwin University Books, 1973).

18   Sidney Dell, *A Latin American Common Market*? (London: Oxford University Press, 1966), pp. 2, 3.

19   *The European Free Trade Association* (EFTA) (London: Central Office of Information, 1968).

20   *Ibid.*, pp. 185-6. See also H. Liesner, *Atlantic Harmonisation Making Free Trade Work*, (London: Trade Policy Research Centre, 1968), p. 7.

21   ECM/ECO/8/(XIV) p. 33.

22   S. Dell, *op. cit.*, p. 194 (see note 18 above).

23   Article 32, Treaty of Montevideo (LAFTA).

24   S. Dell, *op. cit.*, pp. 42-3.

Part Two

Regionalism in West Africa:
Problems and Prospects

5 ECOWAS/CEAO: Conflict and Cooperation in West Africa

S.K.B. Asante

Introduction

The parallel existence of the sixteen-nation Economic Community of West African States (ECOWAS for English-speaking and CEDEAO for French-speaking) and the six-nation Francophone CEAO (Communauté economique de l'Afrique de l'Ouest) as regional economic cooperation experiments in West Africa, and the resulting interlocking relationships, as member states of the latter grouping are also signatories to the former, have been a subject of continuing debate in recent years among scholars as well as keen observers of the West African economic integration process.[1] Generally, the debate is centred on the extent to which the two organisations (ECOWAS and CEAO) are compatible, particularly in the area of trade liberalisation now being implemented by both groupings. It is predicted that as the two schemes reach an advanced stage in their respective developments, a degree of incompatibility would be a potential source of conflict.

It must be pointed out, also, that CEAO is not the only regional economic grouping which is co-existing with ECOWAS in West Africa. The subregion has been a fertile ground for regional economic cooperation experiments especially since the early 1960s. Besides ECOWAS and CEAO, there are several multilateral, bilateral and special arrangements. As the Executive Secretary of ECOWAS recently remarked: 'Today, ECOWAS member-states belong to nearly 30 intergovernmental organizations whose main objectives are economic cooperation either at sectoral level or on a broad and all-embracing scale'.[2] Basically, these groupings have the same objectives as ECOWAS.

But whereas such groupings as the Mano River Union or the Cape Verde/Guinea Bissau Free Trade area can only help to develop the new all-embracing ECOWAS, the CEAO (comprising Ivory Coast, Mali, Mauritania, Niger, Senegal and Upper Volta) is in many respects a miniature ECOWAS, and may thus be less easy to accommodate. Consequently, the co-existence of CEAO and ECOWAS in the sub-region has posed a number of challenging questions. What differences are there between ECOWAS and CEAO? To what extent does a competitive situation arise from the parallel existence of the two subregional economic groupings? How is CEAO a positive threat to ECOWAS? Do the treaty goals represent a contradiction between them? Can the double membership of the CEAO members lead to a weakening of both cooperation experiments? Which undertaking has the greater chance of success?

It is not the purpose of this chapter to offer positive or sufficient answers to these crucial questions mainly because of first, the short existence so far of the two nascent organisations and second, the paucity of reliable information about the current developments of the CEAO particularly. What I intend to do here is to examine critically the extent to which the existence of the two schemes in the subregion could lead to a conflict in the near future or an effective cooperation which would be mutually beneficial to both of them. The chapter is divided into five sections. The first section focuses attention on the birth of the two groupings stressing, *inter alia*, the major aims and objectives as well as institutional structures. In section 2, the major differences between the two organisations are briefly analysed. Section 3 concentrates on the current development efforts of CEAO and ECOWAS respectively. In section 4, efforts at cooperation between the two organisations are analysed, while section 5 attempts to examine aspects of the two experiments which are likely to lead to a conflict between them. Finally, I attempt briefly to look into the future of ECOWAS and CEAO.

Birth of CEAO-ECOWAS as Rival Groupings

Like the erstwhile East African Community, both CEAO and ECOWAS have a varied background. The former is the latest of the experiments at regional cooperation by the Francophone West African states, and the latter the latest of the various schemes combining the Anglophone and Francophone countries of the subregion. However, CEAO is older than ECOWAS, having been created next after UDEAO (Union douanière des états de l'Afrique de l'Ouest) set up in 1959 and revised in 1966, but unanimously admitted by the Heads of State (in the preamble to the Treaty of Abidjan) to have been a failure. Specifically, CEAO dates from a protocol of 21 May 1970 in Bamako and its confirmation on 17 April 1973 by the Treaty of Abidjan. It began to function on 1 January 1974.

On the other hand, the direct negotiations leading to the formation of ECOWAS began in April 1972 when the Heads of State of Nigeria and Togo decided to revive the idea of an economic community which would cut across linguistic and cultural barriers. The series of meetings and intense diplomatic manoeuvres[3] that followed the Nigeria-Togo initiative culminated in the signing on 28 May 1975 of the ECOWAS Treaty at Lagos by fifteen heads of state and government of the West African subregion; Cape Verde has since joined as the Community's sixteenth member. The Treaty came into effect on 23 June 1975 after seven states had ratified it. In operational terms, however, the Community got started during the first quarter of 1977 when two top officials – the Executive Secretary and Managing Director of the Fund – assumed duty in January of that year.

Significantly ECOWAS and CEAO initially emerged as rival groupings in the subregion. The Nigeria-Togo initiative of April 1972 was followed a few weeks later, on 3 June 1972, by the initiating of the preliminary agreements announcing the formation of the CEAO. Nigeria saw this development as a direct attempt by France to nip in the bud the Nigeria-Togo effort and to postpone once again the 'creation of a bigger and more positive economic grouping' in the subregion. The Federal Government was convinced that France, which had previously sabotaged a 1968 project for a West African Economic Community, was once more 'through the back-door and with the aid of puppet leaders' postponing regional cooperation in the sub-region as envisaged in the recent Nigeria-Togo agreement.[4]

However, France was not the only country interested in the creation of a new French-speaking community as a rival grouping to the Nigeria-Togo efforts during this period. For various reasons, the EEC also fully backed the newly created CEAO. Efforts of the EEC at the time were determined by two major goals. First, to create an alternative for the Francophone countries to the West African Community projected in Monrovia in 1968. And second, to establish a *fait accompli* in Francophone West Africa before Great Britain's entry into the European Common Market because 'the likely structural change caused by the expansion of the EEC was also bound to affect the relations between the EEC and Africa which until then had been dominated in definition and practical terms' by French economic and political goals.[5]

The six Francophone CEAO states were not unaware of French and EEC interests in their embryonic community. They were, however, convinced, as President Ould Daddah of Mauritania told the press on signing the CEAO Treaty, that the CEAO was 'a step towards a larger West African grouping', and that the new community was a 'subregion' which should take its place eventually in a broader economic entity. It was even suggested by President Diori of Niger that to be successful the community needed to take account first of geographical factors, 'relegating language, political and even monetary considerations to the second place'.[6] These references to the possibility of enlarging the new community to include English-speaking neighbours were favourably received in Guinea, a non-member state of CEAO. In Guinea's view, it was patently to West Africa's advantage that its countries would emerge from their colonialist structure and take account of geographical realities as well as their people's interests.[7]

There is much evidence to suggest that nearly all the member states of CEAO were aiming at a West African-wide economic cooperation. Their common objective was that such a grouping should emerge out of the embryonic CEAO, and not from outside their Community. Hence after the Abidjan meeting of 16–17 April 1973, the six Heads of State of CEAO were fully confident that 'a point of no return' had been reached in the march towards regional economic cooperation and a more rapid and balanced development of the totality of their countries. President Senghor then called the new Community the 'first step towards the creation of a vast regional entity stretching from Mauritania to Angola'.[8] To go beyond this first step, President Diori of Niger, in his capacity as chairman of CEAO, toured Nigeria, Benin, Togo, and Ghana in May 1973, to investigate the possibility of enlarging the CEAO. He declared in these four countries that the CEAO was 'not a war machine directed against Anglophone states, or a family affair between Francophone states'. The CEAO, he said, was only a stage in West African development, and was open to all West African countries.

The tour was a dismal failure. It should be recalled that it was during this very period (July–August 1973) that a Nigeria-Togo official delegation was making a similar tour of the West African states in respect to the projected ECOWAS. Despite the cold response to the Diori tour, the member states of the CEAO were persistent in their campaign for the 'widening of the CEAO'. With an obvious reference to the ECOWAS project proposed by Nigeria and Togo, President Lamizana, chairman of the inaugural ministerial meeting of CEAO held in Ouagadougou, Upper Volta, in March 1974 (exactly one month after the jurists and experts had met in Accra to draft the ECOWAS Treaty), declared that it would be logical that 'Third World countries from our region should ask to belong to the organisation (CEAO) by stating eventually the changes they would like to see in the Treaty, instead of abandoning an organisation to join another which would be founded on the same principles'.[9]

Thus at the initial stages in the formation of ECOWAS, West Africa was confronted by two similar sub-regional economic groupings each campaigning for an enlarged membership. Neither organisation was prepared to give up the initiative it had taken, in favour of the other. The development, to some extent, resembled the early period of negotiations towards the formation of the EEC when Western Europe witnessed the emergence of two blocs – the Common Market or European Economic Community on the one hand, and the European Free Trade Association (EFTA) on the other. However, whereas EFTA ceased to exist or became moribund after Britain's entry into the EEC in January 1973, ECOWAS and CEAO continue to operate independently as separate organisations. At the beginning, the CEAO member states underestimated the enthusiasm of Nigeria and Togo for their kind of arrangement. There was a failure on their part to appreciate what Nigeria and Togo were hoping to achieve. However, despite that, the member states of the CEAO agreed to join ECOWAS while retaining their membership of the CEAO; this was due principally to the changing economic status of Nigeria as the dominant economic power in the West African sub-region and also to the relentless diplomatic offensive of General Yakubu Gowon, Head of the Federal Military Government of Nigeria, and his able team, including in particular, Dr Adebayo Adedeji, the Nigerian counterpart of Raul Prebisch of Latin America or Jean Monnet of France. Realising the growing economic importance of the country in the subregion, the Federal Government quickly and restlessly threw the full weight of Nigeria behind the new initiative.

Interestingly enough, in terms of aims and objectives, institutional structures and decision-making processes, there is not much difference between ECOWAS and CEAO. Briefly, the ECOWAS Treaty, containing 64 articles arranged into 14 chapters, has as its central objectives the promotion of

> cooperation and development in virtually all fields of economic activity, particularly in the fields of industry, transport, telecommunications, energy, agriculture, natural resources, commerce, monetary and financial questions and in social and cultural matters, for the purpose of raising the standard of living of its people, of increasing and maintaining economic stability, of fostering closer relations among its members and contributing to the progress of development of the African continent. (Article 2)

There are perhaps seven principal objectives discernible from the foregoing all-embracing, if not fuzzy, set of objectives. These can be listed as: elimination of customs duties; abolition of quantitative and administrative restrictions on trade; establishment of a common customs tariff and a common commercial policy; the abolition of obstacles to the free movement of persons, services, and capital; the harmonisation of agricultural and industrial policies; the establishment of a fund for cooperation; and the harmonisation of monetary policies. The Treaty provided some specific goals and specific provisions for realising these declared objectives. These are in the areas of trade, monetary cooperation and industrialisation. The Treaty also provides for a lengthy transitional period for all of the goals to be realised. For example, it is envisaged that the establishment of the customs union would take a transitional period of fifteen years after the Treaty has come into force. Within this period all existing customs and other barriers to free trade would have been gradually whittled down and finally eliminated, giving way to common customs, tariffs and nomenclature for the Community against outside countries.

In almost similar phraseology, the Treaty of CEAO is arranged under six titles and contains 22 chapters divided into 51 articles. Supplementing and annexed to the Treaty are 10 protocols, containing 106 articles, and an appendix of definitions.[10] The apparatus is thus much more impressive than that of its predecessor, the UDEAO.

Like ECOWAS and other regional organisations in the developing countries, the main objectives of CEAO are first, to improve the infrastructure of the area as a whole by cooperation in the development of transportation and communication; second, to promote and accelerate the joint industrialisation of the member states; third, to facilitate trade among members in both manufactured products and raw materials; fourth, to create a unified regional common market which is to be regulated by a progressive customs tariff and a common fiscal system to regulate the commercial relations with third party countries; and finally, to compensate for any shortfalls in revenue derived from goods imported by the affected member states, particularly in respect of industrial goods produced within the zone of the special preferential system. Briefly stated, these objectives were designed in all respects to attempt to overcome the shortcomings of both the UDEAO and UDEAC.

The CEAO objectives were to be implemented by the Community institutions whose powers and responsibilities are detailed in title IV of the Convention. The supreme organ is the Conference of Heads of State and Government, the 'Acts' of which require a unanimous vote. These acts are concerned with the appointment of the top officials of the Community, approval of the budget and, more generally, any question of importance or under dispute. Subordinate to the conference is the Council of Ministers, the composition of which varies according to the subject under discussion. The third most important institution of CEAO is the General Secretariat which is responsible for preparing the decisions of the higher organs and carrying them into execution. It consists of a number of organs and *ad hoc* study groups and two important components are the Community Bureau for Industrial Development (BCDI) and the Community Trade Promotion Office (OCPE) and their subordinate offices such as (a) an inter-state statistical service, (b) a Community bureau for agricultural development, (c) a Community cattle and meat office, (d) a Committee of experts for transport and communications cooperation, (e) a committee of experts for customs cooperation and (f) a Community bureau for fisheries products. Finally, the CEAO provides for the establishment of an Arbitration Court responsible for settling disputes, particularly in respect of interpretation of the Treaty.

In many respects, the institutional pattern of the CEAO is the same as that of ECOWAS, which also has provided for the Authority of Heads of State and Government as the highest decision-making organ of the Community charged with administering and directing the integrative movement of the Organisation. Like the CEAO, the (ECOWAS) Authority of Heads of State and Government is assisted by another political body, the Council of Ministers charged with the responsibility of keeping 'under review the functioning and development' of the Community in accordance with the ECOWAS Treaty as well as making recommendations to the Authority on the harmonious functioning and development of the Community. Again, as in CEAO, the third most important institution of ECOWAS is the Executive Secretariat of the Community established in Article 8 of the Lagos Treaty. It is the bureau headed by an Executive Secretary who is appointed by and is directly responsible to the Authority and who can be removed from office by the Authority on the recommendation of the Council of Ministers. There are four technical and specialised Commissions in ECOWAS, namely the Trade, Customs, Immigration, Monetary and Payment Commission; the Industry, Agriculture and Natural Resources Commission; the Transport, Telecommunications and Energy Commission; and the Social and Cultural Affairs Commission. Each of these Commissions is made up of experts from all the member states and their duty is to draw up programmes in their relevant fields of competence and assess the implementation of such programmes. There is a provision for the creation of any other specialised and technical bodies should the need arise. Taking advantage of this provision, the Community has recently established a

Defence Commission. Finally, like many other economic groupings, the ECOWAS Treaty makes provisions for setting up a Tribunal.

Unlike the defunct East African Common Market, neither the CEAO nor the ECOWAS Treaties have provisions for a Development Bank. Instead, the ECOWAS Treaty, for example, establishes under Article 50 a Fund for Cooperation, Compensation and Development. Capital in the Fund will be used to finance projects in member states, provide compensation to members where necessary, guarantee foreign investments in member states, and help develop the poorer member states. This Fund will be established from contributions by member states based on their economic strength, assessed as a factor of GNP and population; from the income of the Community enterprises; and from receipts from bilateral, multilateral and other foreign sources and subsidiaries and contributions of all kinds from all sources.

Similarly, the CEAO Treaty provides for a Community Development Fund (FCD) which, according to Moussa N'gom, is the CEAO's most important feature – and a highly dynamic one in that it 'has carefully countered' the main criticisms of the earlier customs unions.[11] The CEAO Fund is to finance development projects to the extent of one-third of the shortfall in tax revenue to be compensated. It is also to be used to subsidise state budgets, to establish enterprises in member states on their request and to help those states which have suffered from the negative economic and social impact of the creation of the Community. The sources of the Fund are to be revenues collected from importations by each member state and also from external aid. The fund will also take advantage of any other financial sources made available to it by the Community, including loans which the Community may issue or contract.

It is significant to note that the institutional structures of the CEAO and ECOWAS are not generally different from those of other regional economic groupings in Africa. For example, in making the Authority of Heads of State and Government (or the Conference of Heads of State) the supreme organ of the grouping, both the ECOWAS and CEAO Treaties are merely adopting the practice of the defunct as well as the existing economic, and even political, cooperation schemes in Africa. It is often considered necessary in the continent to involve the highest level of political representation, usually the heads of state and/or government at the highest decision-making level. Under the UDEAC Treaty, for instance, the executive functions are carried out by the Council of Heads of State, which is the supreme organ of the organisation and thus has wide powers and responsibilities in the formulation of policies for the attainment of the treaty objectives. The Council has the power to determine customs and economic policy and to make decisions regarding the payments to be made to the Joint Solidarity Fund and the distribution of such funds to the member states. Similarly, the East African Community's Authority was the supreme organ of the defunct East African Community and was composed of the three presidents of Kenya, Uganda, and Tanzania. This organ of EAC was responsible for the general direction and control of economic decisions in accordance with the provisions of the treaty.

On the other hand, unlike African systems of economic cooperation, none of the economic regional groupings in Latin America involves the Heads of State and Government in the institutions' machineries responsible for administering and directing the affairs of the movement. The Andean Common Market, for example, has at the top of its institutional structure, the Mixed Commission, an inter-governmental body resembling a diplomatic conference, which meets three times a year. Similarly, the Latin American Economic System (SELA) established in October 1975 has as its supreme body the Latin American Council which is composed of one representative (not head of state of government) of each member state. This, however, does not make these organisations completely insulated from political pressures. The Andean Common Market, for instance, has not been able, despite its unique organisational machinery, to insulate the decision-making process from the politics of national interest. The Mixed Commission is sensitive to national priorities, and it has frequently modified technical proposals of the Junta, an independent secretariat of supranational officials.[12] Perhaps the only significant difference here is that the African regional economic schemes, such as ECOWAS or CEAO, have more direct political involvement in their operation than those of Latin America.

Ostensibly, both CEAO and ECOWAS were to be actual customs unions. The two treaties also provide for free trade and free mobility of persons, as well as a common external tariff. Critically studied, however, the two groupings can be distinguished in certain important respects.

ECOWAS-CEAO: How Dissimilar?

The first major distinction is the participation of the 'regional superpower', Nigeria, in ECOWAS as well as the fact that the former colonial powers did not initiate cooperation but had to react to it. This, in many respects, distinguishes ECOWAS from CEAO. Nigeria is no doubt one of the foremost of the new 'middle powers' that are assuming an increasing importance in world affairs. Because of her power, enormous wealth and size, Nigeria's 'presence in ECOWAS has certain advantages'. John Ravenhill has recently observed that an effective regional scheme would appear to:

> require the leadership of a strong 'core' state, willing and able to provide the necessary side-payments to weaker members of the partnership in order to sustain existing integrative arrangements and allow their extension into new areas of cooperation.[13]

In neo-functional terms, therefore, Nigeria is playing the role of a strong 'core' state. Increasingly, Nigeria is 'becoming a diplomatic, financial, and administrative centre for the entire West African area'.[14]

Second, whereas ECOWAS was inspired mainly by African political leaders, and was created and being administered by African technocrats and bureaucrats, the contrary is the case in respect of CEAO. For not only was the creation of CEAO inspired by France and the EEC; the CEAO Treaty, like that of UDEAC, shows the overpowering influence of Jacques David, a former French customs officials in the colonial administration, who is now an official of the EEC in Brussels. A technocrat who feels that the EEC provided a model for Africa, Jacques David offers this approach as a 'recipe for economic prosperity' and finds it quite natural that 'African governments, so concerned with their economic development, should seek means of transferring and adopting techniques and processes which have given very encouraging results in Europe'.[15] The CEAO states, like those of the UDEAC, are harnessed to the French system to a degree that makes them collectively depend on France, and hence deserving of the latter's support.

Third, and closely related to this, the CEAO as well as such other African regional groupings as UDEAO, UDEAC and even the East African Community (EAC) have their origins in the colonial period. The Fedération de l'Afrique Occidentale Française gave rise to the UDEAO and then the CEAO (without Guinea and Benin). In central Africa, the UDEAC is simply the extension of the former Fedération de l'Afrique Equatoriale Française (without Chad). ECOWAS is unique in the sense that first, it does not have its origins from the colonial period and, second, it extends beyond the geographic framework set up by the colonial powers. This should not suggest, however, that ECOWAS would be any less susceptible to external (or ex-colonial power) interests; it does suggest that ECOWAS would seem to possess a larger potential and opportunity than CEAO for breaking out of the ex-colonial enclave.

Third, two German economists, Kuehn and Seelow, have recently argued that 'there is greater solidarity of CEAO than ECOWAS' because the former organisation has fewer members, common language and currency as well as common colonial background. Hence, in their view, the cooperation attempt by the six Francophone nations has a somewhat better chance for success.[16] It should be pointed out, however, that there were differences of opinion among the signatories of CEAO. Benin, Niger and Togo, for example, felt that CEAO 'would not be viable if Nigeria were excluded'. The Upper Volta felt the same way about excluding the Anglophone countries in general and Ghana in particular. Since the early years of CEAO formation, Benin and Niger have been aware of the fact that they are too far away from the Ivory Coast and Senegal and that their economic interests lie more with Nigeria, their immediate neighbour, which is also West Africa's economic giant. These disagreements, together with tensions between the landlocked and coastal states, in part 'delayed the formal signing of the final treaty by over a year after the preliminary agreements had been initialled in Bamako on 3 June 1972'.[17] Besides, Mauritania, which is the strongest link between Arab Africa and Africa south of the Sahara, more and more 'must look northwards towards the Arab League and the Muslim world'. As Yansane has noted, Mauritania is compelled to lean in that direction 'by the flow of petro-dollars from which it benefits, and the backing extended by Arab states to support its national currency'.[18] Mauritania is the only CEAO member which has withdrawn from the franc zone.

CEAO-ECOWAS: Achievements So Far

While the CEAO has been in effective operation since January 1974, ECOWAS began functioning from early 1977. Thus, although the two organisations are still in their evolutionary stages, the CEAO is more advanced than ECOWAS, particularly in the fields of organisation and promotion of inter-state trade, and operation of the community fund, as well as in the area of economic cooperation within the Community.[19]

Organisation and promotion of inter-state trade within CEAO are intended to lead to the 'creation of a Community market with a common external tariff in a twelve-year period'. The founding fathers of the CEAO were careful to be less ambitious than their predecessor organisations like UDEAO, by not even providing for a complete free trade area. Since the CEAO Treaty came into force, two categories of products have dominated inter-state trading relations. First, the only goods which 'may circulate freely without liability to any taxes or duties', are raw produce which is unprocessed, unworked and entirely local. The second category of products is 'industrial products originating from the member countries'. Unlike unprocessed products, industrial products are subject to duty, but at a preferential rate. The effect is that the product once accepted is 'given favourable fiscal treatment which strengthens its competitive position'. This is effected through the Taxe de Coopération Régionale (TCR), which, as Mamadou Bathily has noted, is a single tax collected once only and calculated case by case in such a way as to provide maximum tax revenue but maintain a preferential status.[20] It is collected by the tax authorities of the consuming country.

By the end of 1976, inter-state trade in industrial products had expanded considerably, with Ivory Coast and Senegal accounting for about 20 billion francs CFA out of a total of 20.8 billion francs CFA. Significantly, too, by December 1978, some 618 industrial products which were subject to TCR were produced by 175 enterprises or companies (of which 94 were located in Ivory Coast, 56 in Senegal and none in Mauritania).[21]

While the CEAO inter-state trade is showing some remarkable progress, the activities of ECOWAS in this area are very much in the rudimentary stage. The Community has, however, completed a comprehensive trade liberalisation and promotion programme, whose implementation will cover a ten-year period (May 1978–May 1989). The programme provides for complete elimination of all trade barriers, thus creating conditions favourable to the development of intra-community trade. It will culminate in the establishment of a free trade area in the subregion in May 1989 and is destined to regulate on a gradual basis the vast potential ECOWAS market 'which now consists of some 150 million consumers, and which ... will expand to cover no less than 200 million souls in the year 2000.[22]

The first phase of the ECOWAS liberalisation programme was completed in 1981. This phase placed emphasis on setting up structures, procedures and customs documents and fiscal measures required at the national level for the smooth implementation of the programme. To this end, some important decisions directed to the implementation of the liberalisation scheme were taken by the Community in 1979 and 1980. First, a definition of traditional handicrafts as well as a list of the products which would enjoy the Community's preferential tariff have been drawn up by an *ad hoc* committee on trade liberalisation. Second, a list of priority industrial products eligible for accelerated liberalisation 'on account of their vital role' not only in the development of intra-community trade but also in promotion of industrial co-operation within the Community has been established. Third, for an effective and smooth implementation of the trade liberalisation scheme, the Community introduced for use from January 1981, such important customs documents as the ECOWAS Certificate of Origin, the ECOWAS Movement Certificate, Common Statistical Standards and Definitions, and ECOWAS Rules and Procedures for the Verification and Proof of the Community Origin of Products from member states.

Another area of interest to both the CEAO and ECOWAS is the operation of the respective community funds. In this field too, CEAO is far ahead of ECOWAS. For example, the resources of the CEAO Fund which are realised from the annual contributions of member states – as determined by the magnitude of their participation in the Community's trade in industrial products – have been growing progressively: 1047 million francs CFA in 1975 and 2280 million francs CFA in 1976. Between 1979 and 1980, the resources of the fund increased from 4203 million francs CFA to 6760.0 million francs CFA. The resources of the Fund have been utilised partly to compensate those states which had lost customs revenue as a result of the introduction of the TCR, and partly to carry out feasibility studies of possible Community projects to be located in the less developed CEAO member states. The total resources of the fund for 1975 were, for, example, earmarked for feasibility studies of thirty-five agricultural and industrial development projects in some member states of the Community. In 1979 and 1980 some 2802 million francs CFA and 4506.0 million francs CFA respectively were set aside 'for compensation of those member states whose economies had been dislocated as a result of the creation of the Community'.[23]

Besides, at the Third Conference of CEAO Heads of State and Government held at Abidjan in June 1977, a 'Solidarity Fund' was created. It began to operate two years after in June 1979. The resources of the Fund, which were initially fixed at 5 million francs CFA for the years 1977 and 1978, were later reduced to 1.5 million for the year 1979 but increased to 8 million for 1980. The purpose of the Fund was to guarantee loans for all profitable projects. The four less-developed states of the Community (Upper Volta, Mali, Mauritania and Niger) have reasonably benefited from the Solidarity Fund.[24]

On the other hand, the ECOWAS Fund based in Lome has not been able to make a similar impact. The Fund was established with an authorised capital of $500 million, and called-up capital of $50 million. By 31 August 1979, the Fund had collected $31 084 128 or 62 per cent of the initial called-up capital, leaving $18 915 872 or 38 per cent unpaid. This amount has been invested in banks in Europe and Togo. Member states' contributions to the Fund have not been encouraging. Of the ECOWAS members, it was Benin, Guinea, Niger and Togo which had by the end of 1979 paid their complete quota. Guinea Bissau, Ivory Coast, Senegal and Sierra Leone had paid 95 per cent while Nigeria and Liberia had paid 67 per cent and 32 per cent respectively, and Cape Verde 50 per cent. Upper Volta and Ghana had paid 15 per cent but Mali, Mauritania and the Gambia had not paid any amount whatsoever.[25] By the end of 1981, however, the Fund had been able to finalise the policy measures which are vital to its smooth operation. These include outlines of general policies relating to loans, investments, guarantees and subventions.[26]

To this point in our analysis, it is quite obvious that as far as the initial implementation of treaty objectives is concerned, the CEAO as an 'organised trade zone and an area of concerted development' has done better than ECOWAS. This apparent success in early take-off is generally due to the longstanding common historical, administrative, colonial and economic experiences of the member states of the CEAO. After all, unlike ECOWAS which has no real predecessor regional grouping, CEAO directly replaced UDEAO; its institutional pattern is the same as that of its predecessor organisation. It is not surprising, therefore, that after overcoming the differences of opinion during the negotiating stages of the Community, the six CEAO member countries individually and collectively professed to expand their national markets through the progressive elimination of tariff barriers to inter-state trade within the Community and to initiate a new active regional policy of economic cooperation in the areas of industrial, commercial, customs and transportation development.

On the other hand, in view of its diversity and size, ECOWAS was preoccupied during the first four years with staffing as well as complex administrative problems. The Treaty itself was lacking in detail: only broad outlines were contained in the documents. This was done perhaps to make it possible to achieve consensus and enable the Heads of State to sign the Treaty. To make ECOWAS institutionally operational, therefore, efforts were directed during the early period to establish an effective administration, to improve and to complement basic documentation, to collect basic information upon which the technical work of the Community was to be built, and to formulate regional policies and programmes. By May 1980 when the fifth summit of the Heads of State and Government was held in Lome, the 'conceptualisation phase' and the establishment of the functional structures of the institutions of the Community had been completed. This summit took some far-reaching decisions which marked the end of the period of formulating the major Community policies and measures that were required to 'give practical form to the framework for cooperation' as defined by the ECOWAS Treaty. By May 1981, the Community had been able to make some appreciable inroads into its top priority areas such as trade and customs cooperation, transport and communications, immigration matters, and industrial and agricultural cooperation.

As indicated above, the trade liberalisation scheme had already commenced. The coming period will call for an effective monitoring system to ascertain compliance with the programme and ensure success of the use of the harmonised documents. Undoubtedly, effective implementation of trade liberalisation can give a valuable stimulus to investment, stimulate measures of cooperation in production, and generally assist to develop other measures to expand production. Along with the trade liberalisation programme is the compensation scheme which also became operational on 28 May 1981. The operation of this mechanism will demand an improvement in the quality of trade and fiscal data from member states. There is the problem of whether or not to merge or reconcile the ECOWAS compensation scheme with that of the CEAO which has already made some significant achievements.

One other area of interest is the Telecommunication and Transport Programme. This is indeed the first Community project to be funded with Community funds. The investment is in itself important as it will not only test the capacity of the member states to invest in joint projects, but also the suitability of the procedures, loan conditions and guarantee mechanism devised by the Fund. This is a challenge to the political will and the extent of commitments of member states of the Community to ECOWAS, as the implementation of the project will involve extensive cooperation among the ECOWAS countries who would be required to coordinate the various national transport systems, and improve the access of the land-locked member states to the sea. To this may be added the importance of the recent ratification of the free mobility-of-persons provision for the promotion of the ECOWAS idea. This appears to be the only provision of the ECOWAS Treaty which attempts to involve the man in the street. The Community citizens would now be able for the first time to travel freely across national boundaries to seek gainful employment where the opportunities at home were few and far between. Consequently, this is an operational feature with which trade unions at national and local levels are particularly concerned.

On the whole, therefore, while CEAO has much to its credit in terms of practical achievements, ECOWAS has also initiated some extensive and laudable schemes for its take-off. In some areas actual implementation has reached fairly advanced stages in the two Communities. But can the two organisations continue to co-exist or cooperate harmoniously? What are the possible areas of future conflict?

CEAO-ECOWAS: Cooperation or Conflict?

Since ECOWAS became operational in 1977, the Secretariat in Lagos has been working consistently towards the creation of 'an efficient cooperation framework' for all the economic cooperation institutions operating within West Africa, in particular the Francophone CEAO. The rationale behind this effort is that if the policies and programmes of the intergovernmental organisations in the subregion are not co-ordinated, there would be duplication, unnecessary competition among them and dissipation of the meagre resources of the subregion.

The effort of ECOWAS towards this end 'yielded encouraging initial results' at the first meeting of Heads of intergovernmental organisations in West Africa held in Monrovia on 17 and 18 January, 1979. At this meeting, remarked the Executive Secretary of ECOWAS, 'the modus operandi' was agreed upon.[27] Specifically, a programme for cooperation between ECOWAS and other intergovernmental schemes in West Africa was prepared. Within the framework of this programme, ECOWAS undertook, in collaboration with other organisations, to prepare specific projects capable of ensuring better cooperation as well as greater efficiency in the operation of the organisations of the subregion. The meeting also decided to establish close links of cooperation aimed at fostering the coordination and harmonisation of development actions of the organisations. To this end, the heads of the organisations resolved to set up the following bodies:

(a) A Council of Heads of Intergovernmental Organisations charged with defining and orientating cooperation between the organisations;

(b) An Experts Committee of Intergovernmental Organisations responsible for studying and proposing to the meeting of the heads who will prepare all the actions aimed at promoting and strengthening cooperation;

(c) ECOWAS was to be the subregional coordinator charged with ensuring the permanent follow-up of the programme of co-operation defined by the Council.[28]

Subsequent meetings were held at Ouagadougou and Freetown

between officials of ECOWAS and those of CEAO and Mano River Union with a view to examining the different fields in which the harmonisation of programme and policy measures was necessary. This was followed by a series of meetings at the level of Chief Executives of the three organisations in Lome on 24 and 25 November 1980; Freetown, on 11 and 12 February 1981: and Lome again on 9 and 10 March 1981. By the end of the second Lome meeting, all the three institutions 'were satisfied that all the problems that had been brought up for discussion had found an acceptable solution', except for the issue of the derogation from Article 20 of the ECOWAS Treaty,[29] which is discussed below.

These efforts notwithstanding, the cooperation between ECOWAS and CEAO is not likely to continue undisturbed, particularly as the two organisations attain maturity. There are certain elements which seem to contain the seeds of future conflict. In the rest of this chapter, therefore, I attempt to highlight aspects of the two experiments which are likely to act as obstacles to a harmonious co-existence of ECOWAS and CEAO.

In the first place, it is envisaged that the CEAO would mature into a customs union by 1986 while the fifteen-year teething period envisaged for ECOWAS places its maturity into a customs union at 1990. Thus CEAO as a customs union would precede ECOWAS as one. There appears therefore to be room for a conflict of loyalty between the two in those countries (Francophone) that belong to the two bodies. One is left wondering how such a conflict could be resolved. For example, would the six Francophone countries continue to support ECOWAS and remain loyal to it after their international trade and economic development interests have come to be catered for by CEAO?

Second, and perhaps more seriously, one other major problem confronting ECOWAS is the evident incompatibility of some of the provisions of both the Community and CEAO treaties, particularly in the area of trade liberalisation which, as noted above, is being implemented by both groupings. The relatively advanced stage of the CEAO trade liberalisation scheme would seem to pose crucial problems for the development of ECOWAS. For instance, though the CEAO's ultimate goal is the establishment of a customs union with a common external tariff over a period of twelve years (as compared to fifteen years of ECOWAS), it does not envisage a general free trade area within the customs union as was the case for ECOWAS. The CEAO trade liberalisation scheme calls for a preferential trading area through the use of the TCR. A free trade area will exist only for goods which are raw produce.

The implication of the co-existence of the two liberalisation schemes of ECOWAS and CEAO becomes evident in practical terms after the ECOWAS and CEAO customs unions have been established. The same produce, as for example, canned beer, would be traded within CEAO countries under the TCR preferential treatment, and be subjected to the agreed TCR import duty rate; while in ECOWAS, it would carry no import charges as long as it meets the ECOWAS origin requirement.[30] This would no doubt result in an unsatisfactory situation within ECOWAS. To avoid such an unpleasant development, some commentators have gone so far as to suggest a dissolution of both CEAO and the Mano River Union so that provisions of the ECOWAS Treaty can be implemented without any impediment.[31] This point is discussed in chapters 6 and 8.

Closely related to this is yet another contradiction between the CEAO and ECOWAS treaties. Under the ECOWAS scheme, the rights and obligations of members deriving from previously signed contracts (which includes the CEAO Treaty) are not affected. On the other hand, ECOWAS members (including the CEAO members) are obliged to remove all provisions (discriminations) from prior treaties 'which are not compatible' with the provisions of the ECOWAS Treaty, and not to enact new ones. This in turn means that according to the ECOWAS Treaty (reciprocal grant of most favoured status) CEAO members would be obligated to expand all preferences granted to each other to all of ECOWAS. In other words, the customs union of CEAO logically has to cease to exist at some time in the future and to merge with ECOWAS.

This complicated issue has, not least, disturbed the CEAO which has been making persistent requests to ECOWAS for a 'derogation from Article 20 of the ECOWAS Treaty' which, as indicated above, requires that 'Member States shall accord to one another in relations to trade between them the most-favoured-nation treatment.' The request for 'derogation' would allow the CEAO member states to keep among themselves the preferential treatment afforded by their respective liberalisation programmes. This tricky issue of 'derogation' has still not been resolved. The information supplied by the CEAO on this subject, as requested by ECOWAS, was found to be fragmentary and insufficient to enable the Lome meeting of heads of institutions in March 1981 'to come to a final decision'. It was argued that the recommendation by the CEAO officials 'would need to be re-examined in the light of a more comprehensive analysis of the problem'.[32]

All the evidence would seem to point to a possible conflict between the CEAO and ECOWAS in the near future. Key issues to emphasise are the CEAO members' absolute confidence in, and strong regard for, their organisation 'as a possible alternative to an integrated wider community', and their stubborn unwillingness to transfer 'complete allegiance and legitimacy' to ECOWAS because of (i) uncertainty of benefits they are likely to derive from ECOWAS, and (ii) the fact that CEAO 'is built on a strong mutual political identification'[33] which is vigorously supported by France in particular and the EEC in general. During the negotiation stages of ECOWAS, for example, some CEAO members were not only dragging their feet about ECOWAS, they were also criticising aspects of the Lagos Treaty. Barely a month after signing the ECOWAS charter, a Senegalese diplomat, M. Yousouph Sylla, was arguing in the weekly newspaper *L'Ouest Africain* that a customs union of the kind proposed by ECOWAS, involving the abolition of all tariffs, was incompatible with the CEAO's preferential system.[34] And during this same period, President Senghor made it plain in Lagos that Senegal, for one, was placing her hopes on CEAO which had already set up its regional taxation scheme and cooperation fund, and which had already embarked on its first projects.[35]

Conclusion: The Future of ECOWAS and CEAO

At the present state of regional cooperation no final judgement can be passed as yet on the prospects for ECOWAS and CEAO. However, the urge to contemplate the future relationship between the two organisations is compelling. It would seem that, to some extent, the routes of effective cooperation between them are littered with some discouraging factors. And if I may engage in dreams for a while, I can see the immediate future punctuated by a series of misunderstanding, and perhaps tensions. CEAO activities since the creation of ECOWAS reflect the view consistently put forward by President Houghouet-Boigny, and later advocated by Senghor, former President of Senegal, that unity among Francophone states would be the first major step towards a wider West African Unity.[36] Can ECOWAS, then, dilute the Francophone-Anglophone distinction and actually help to gradually unshackle Francophone West African states from the grips of France and the EEC through the Lome Convention? Much would depend on 'patient and skilful diplomacy' on the part of especially Nigeria, the 'regional superpower', and to some extent Togo (the two principal actors in the move towards formation of ECOWAS), directed at reassuring the members of CEAO of the 'positive need to change its status and to become a unit operating under the aegis of ECOWAS', and not a competitor. The CEAO members should be thoroughly convinced of the greater potentials for ECOWAS and, by implication, the 'near irrelevance' or superfluity of the continued operation of their organisation. The success of such efforts would depend on two crucial factors. First, the weakening of the ties between France and her former colonial territories. This special position is likely to decline in importance as the weight of Nigeria continues to increase and French capital is directly challenged on its special 'hunting grounds' by foreign competition. Second, the willingness of the primary members of the CEAO – Senegal and Ivory Coast – to end the incompatibility between ECOWAS and CEAO. This in turn would in practice 'depend on their regard for ECOWAS as a body for solving economic problems associated with CEAO'.[37] It is not being suggested, however, that in the foreseeable future, one can realistically imagine that the prerequisite for the survival of ECOWAS 'will necessarily hinge' upon the disappearance of CEAO.

Notes

1 See for example, Rainer Kuehn and Frank Seelow, 'ECOWAS and CEAO: Regional Cooperation in West Africa', *Development and Cooperation*, 3/1980 (May/June), pp. 11–13; and Ralph I. Onwuka, 'Independence Within ECOWAS: I', *West Africa*, 10 October, 1977.

2 Aboubakar Diaby-Quattara, 'ECOWAS and Regional Economic Cooperation', unpublished address to Nigeria's principal representatives abroad, Lagos, 27 July, 1979.

3 For details, see Olatunde J.B. Ojo, 'Nigeria and ECOWAS' *International Organisation*, 34(4), Autumn 1980, pp. 579–603.

4 Text of a commentary broadcast by Radio Kaduna, Nigeria, on 18 July 1972. For details see Colin Legum (ed.), *Africa, Contemporary Record 1971–1973*, p. 238.

5 Kuehn and Seelow, *op. cit.*, p. 12 (See note 1 above).

6 Legum *op. cit.*, pp. 238–40 (see note 4 above).

7 Text of a commentary broadcast by Radio Conakry, Guinea, 7 June 1972.

8 Legum *op. cit.*, pp. 241–2 (see note 4 above).

9 *Ibid.*, p. 194.

10 Mamadou Bathily, 'The West African Economic Community: A development Community', *The Courier*, 34 (November–December 1975), p. 56.

11 Moussa N'gom, 'CEAO: The West African Economic Community', *The Courier*, 44 (July–August 1977), p. 50.

12 William P. Avery and James D. Cochrane, 'Innovation in Latin American Regionalism: The Andean Common Market', *International Organisation*, 27(2), Spring 1973, p. 203.

13 John Ravenhill, 'Regional Integration and Development in Africa: Lessons from the East African Community', *Journal of Commonwealth and Comparative Politics*, November 1979, p. 243.

14 John P. Renninger, 'The Future of Economic Cooperation Schemes in Africa, with Special Reference to ECOWAS' in T.M. Shaw (ed.), *Alternative Futures for Africa* (Boulder, Colorado: Westview Press, Inc., 1982), p. 172.

15 J. David (ed.), *L'Afrique sans frontières*, (Bory, Monaco, 1965), p. 5. Cited in M. Diouf, 'Approaches to Economic Integration in Black Africa: Assessment and suggestions', paper presented at an international seminar on Planning Economic Integration: Experiences, Policies, and Models, held in West Berlin, November 1979.

16 Kuehn and Seelow, *op cit.*, p. 12 (see note 1 above).

17 Ojo, *op. cit.*, p. 581 (see note 3 above).

18 Aguibou Yansane, 'The State of Economic Integration in North West Africa, South of the Sahara: The Emergence of the Economic Community of West African States (ECOWAS)', *African Studies Review*, XX (2), September 177, p. 73.

19 In this section on the achievements of CEAO, I have drawn heavily on the scholarly and highly documented study of Professor W.A. Ndongko, 'Regional Economic Integration of French-Speaking Countries in Africa: The Case of the West African Economic Community (CEAO)', paper presented at the International Conference on Law and Economy in Africa, Ife, Nigeria, February 1982.

20 Bathily, *op. cit.*, p. 57 (see note 10 above).

21 Ndongko, *op. cit.* (see note 19 above).

22 ECW/CM/IX/2/Rev. 1, *Annual Report of the Executive Secretary of ECOWAS, 1980–1981*, Lagos, May 1981.

23 Ndongko, *op. cit.* (see note 19 above).

24 *Ibid*.

25 F-BD/CA-5-79-2, *Report on 5th meeting of Board of Directors of ECOWAS Fund* held in Lome, October 1979.

26 ECW/CM/IX/2/Rev. 1, *Annual Report of the Executive Secretary of ECOWAS, 1980–1981*.

27 ECW/CM/VI/2, *Report of the Executive Secretary to Council of Ministers*, (Dakar, November 1979).

28 F-BD/CA-5-79-2, *Report of the 5th Meeting of Board of Directors of ECOWAS Fund*, Lome, October 1979.

29 ECW/CM/IX/2 Rev. 1, *Annual Report of Executive Secretary, 1980–1981*.

30 Diaby-Quattara, *op. cit.* (see note 2 above).

31 *Ibid*.

32 ECW/CM/IX/2/Rev. 1, *Annual Report of the Executive Secretary, 1980–1981*.

33 Ralph Onwuka, 'Independence within ECOWAS: I' (see note 1 above).

34 *The Times* (London), 30 June 1975, Special Supplement on West Africa, p. iv.

35 For President Senghor's continuing hesitations, see *West Africa*, 26 May 1975 and 14 February 1977.

36 Eniola O. Adeniyi, 'The Economic Community of West African States Within the Framework of the New International Economic Order', paper presented at the International Conference on ECOWAS, Lagos, August 1976.

37 Onwuka, 'Independence within ECOWAS' (see note 1 above).

6 The Future of the Central African Customs and Economic Union – UDEAC

Wilfred A. Ndongko

Introduction

In the early 1960s when colonial rule ended in the greater part of the African continent, several independent states emerged within the boundaries established during the colonial era 'by a combination of historical chance, diplomatic and military manoeuvre between the European powers and political administrative convenience'.[1] These boundaries, which were classified by many as 'artificial', maintained and defended by those who inherited political power, soon posed grave problems both to the independence and economic growth of the new states.

This situation was the same in such areas as Equatorial Africa which had had a loose federation prior to independence. Despite the opportunity to achieve full independence and status,[2] at the departure of their colonisers each of the territories had gained autonomy, and political power transferred to the individual territorial leader and not to a supra-territorial unit. Problems were not long in coming. Within the inherited and maintained boundaries, and given their small sizes, poverty in human and financial resources, limited natural resources, in short their economic nonviability, the new states could hardly satisfy their economic expectations. Willing as they might have been to undertake their development programmes, they were handicapped by this lamentable situation as well as by inexperience. Reliance on the former colonial 'masters' was inevitable in this case.

Such reliance, however, was not to be, unfortunately for these newly independent states, on a charitable basis. The colonial masters naturally continued not only the exploitation but also the domination of the young nations – a state of affairs for which they had been strongly criticised prior to independence by the emerging African elite and by Pan-Africanists, especially. They had to eliminate, or at least, reduce such exploitation and domination. They had to confirm their 'liberty', break the dependence links, defend their dignity as well as their personality. But how could this come about? How could these new states assure their political and economic independence vis-a-vis the industrialised states?

To the United Nations Conference on Trade and Development (UNCTAD), the Economic Commission for Africa (ECA), most economists and theorists, the Pan-Africanists and politicians, for whom the development and progress of these 'poor' nations was and is still is a concern, the solution could only be found in concerted efforts. These efforts, Bela Balassa holds, would 're-establish the decomposed economic area into national units, into larger viable economic units – through integration'. Economic integration, he continues, 'will remedy distortions in the location of productive activity caused by the decomposition of an economic area into national units.'[3]

Reginald and Seidman for their part believe that:

> The only way to achieve the economic reconstruction and development essential to fulfil the aspirations, needs and demands of the peoples of Africa is through a substantial shift to continental planning, so as to unite increasingly the resources, markets and capital of Africa in a single substantial economic unit.[4]

Whatever the differences of approach advocated, regional or continental, the principles and aims seem to be the same and have long won general acceptance. But to what extent and with what success has the principle of integration, generally accepted as the only means by which viable economic units can be created, been applied in the 'balkanised' states of Africa?

Far from remaining merely aims and principles, which in themselves are empty of content unless sustained by performance, the acceptance of concerted efforts as the only means of consolidating the political and economic independence of the African states and thereby their overall position vis-a-vis that of the developed countries, especially the former metropolitan powers, is evident in the many existing and planned regional groupings in Africa.

The purpose of this chapter is to critically examine the viability and future stability or otherwise of the UDEAC, with particular emphasis on those integrative factors or forces which influenced its creation and have continued to determine the extent to which its various goals and specific objectives have been accomplished. An understanding and appreciation of the importance of these forces on regional economic integration efforts in Central Africa requires an examination of the historical background to the UDEAC.

Historical Background to the UDEAC

The initial effort to regroup the Central African Countries into a single regional unit has its beginnings in the colonial era. For purposes of easy administration, France by a decree of 15 January 1910 created the 'Afrique Equatorial Francaise – AEF', which comprised the Central African Republic, Chad, Gabon and Congo. The various federal services established for the grouping ranged from coordination of financial policies and transport and economic affairs, to scientific research and techniques.

In 1958, when the member states of AEF opted for individual self-government, their leaders accepted to jointly operate the various services which had been set up in 1910. To this end, they established a customs union through the signing of the Brazzaville Treaty on 23 June 1959. The union was called the Equatorial Customs Union – Union Douanière Equatoriale (UDE). The UDE Treaty was later modified by another Treaty signed on 7 December 1959 at Libreville, Gabon. The objectives of the UDE included: the establishment of a common external tariff and import duties, the harmonisation of the fiscal systems of the four member states and the coordination of the economic and social development plans.[5]

Because Cameroon, under French trusteeship, had the same administrative economic influences, it became gradually absorbed into the UDE, which by 1961 had become Union Douanière Equatoriale et du Cameroun. In December 1964, the Presidents of the five Central African States decided to create the UDEAC – the Equatorial Customs and Economic Union – by signing the Brazzaville Treaty, which called for the elimination of restrictions on commodity movement between member states, the setting up of a common external tariff against third countries and the removal of barriers to factor movements including some degree of the harmonisation of national economic policies, particularly in the areas of industrial, investment and transportation development.

For the running of the Union, three institutions were created: the Council of Heads of States which is the supreme organ of the UDEAC, the Management Committee responsible for examining various UDEAC problems and making proposals to the Council of Heads of States for final decisions, and the General Secretariat headed by a Secretary-General whose role is limited to general administration and implementation of the decisions of the Heads of States. In addition, a Solidarity Fund was set up to help reduce the existing economic and social disparities between the more developed member states like Cameroon and Gabon and the less developed ones like the

Central African Republic and Chad.[6]

However, by 1968, it became clear that membership in the UDEAC involved too much sacrifice for the two inland states – Chad and the Central African Republic. As a consequence, early in 1968, Chad and the Central African Republic withdrew from the UDEAC to form a new regional economic union with Zaire (Union des Etats d'Afrique Centrale – Union of Equatorial African States). By the end of 1968, only Zaire and Chad remained in the new economic grouping because the Central African Republic withdrew to rejoin the UDEAC. Up till 1983 UDEAC was still made up of Cameroon, Central African Republic, Congo and Gabon and eighteen years in existence. Its survival can be explained by a number of integrative and sustaining forces.

The Role of Integrative Forces

If in most of Africa, excluding perhaps East Africa, the Maghreb and some regions of West Africa, integrative forces are limited, the Central African States are convinced that there exist in their region enough forces that could pull them together into a single unit. Before we proceed, however, some terminological clarifications seem necessary. The term 'internal' is used in this chapter to refer to the area within the frontiers of the member states of UDEAC considered as a unit. Internal integrative forces are therefore those forces whose influence comes from within the integrating states of the Union. The term 'external' on the other hand, refers to forces outside the territory of the Union. External forces therefore are those that come from outside the Union.

Amongst the most important internal factors is population distribution. Communities can unite and pursue common goals more successfully if they are geographically linked to one another. Transactions between the member-states are easier when the distances to be traversed are shorter and therefore less costly. Within such a geographical unit with similarity in population, tastes are more likely to be similar. Furthermore, 'it can be argued that it is easier for a firm to establish distribution channels in adjacent countries, since the cost of supervision and communication increases with distance.'[7]

In the Central African region, the geographical proximity of the UDEAC states is an asset for an economic integration arrangement. The states share common boundaries and thus offer the linkage that is necessary for the success of such regional goupings. Although the prevailing geographical affinity is not complemented with a good network of communications (which has been and is still one of the reasons for the Union's slow progress) it is almost certain that the efforts of the uniting states will be directed towards overcoming this obstacle.

The importance of this factor comes out in the Union des Etats d'Afrique Centrale (UEAC), the operation of which had long been rendered impossible by the withdrawal of CAR which provided the necessary link between Chad and Zaire. Since the withdrawal of the Central African Republic (CAR), UEAC has been reduced to a symbolic existence only.

UDEAC is further blessed by the existence within its geographical territory, at least along the 'artificial' frontiers separating the states, of populations which can rightly be considered as homogeneous. This is particularly true of the regions along the Cameroon-Gabon; along the Cameroon-CAR borders, for example, there are the Baya in CAR and the Baya-Kaka in Cameroon. The Cameroon-Gabon border population is Fang extending from Ebolowa in Cameroon to Oyem in Gabon.[8]

Closely linked to the above asset is history. During the Scramble for Africa, France laid her claws on a greater portion of Equatorial Africa from Moyen Congo Gabon through Ubangui-Chari to Chad. By the Berlin Act of 1885, the French grip on these territories was confirmed. To these, which remained French colonies until independence, was added a greater part of German Kamerun.[9] From then, the whole region of the future UDEAC found itself under a common colonial master, whose influence was far-reaching in shaping the future of the region.

As the French authority gained ground, there developed a series of common characteristics which later influenced the establishment of UDEAC. Although derived from an external force, these common characteristics had been so deeply entrenched in the region before the creation of UDEAC that they could be considered internal forces. Culturally and socially these states developed great similarity. They had a common language – French – which served and continues to serve as a uniting force in Central Africa. An additional and very important force which remains a uniting factor in UDEAC is the monetary problem as they all belong to the Franc zone where the currency in circulation is the French CFA.[10] It presents neither exchange nor circulation difficulties as its circulation is free within the zone. It is evident that common elements such as history, monetary system and language, enabled these states to be aware of their common interests and hence more willing to coordinate their efforts. These were, however, not the only conjunctive forces.

The sizes of the states also contributed to the coordination of action in Equatorial Africa. All the four UDEAC states are small, geographically, economically and demographically. The territorial distribution of population over an estimated total area of 1 708 000 square kilometers ranges from a little above half a million in Gabon to about eight million in Cameroon. The global GNP (Gross National Product) in 1970 was only 461 500 million franc CFA. Whether size in this case is measured in terms of population or GNP, the UDEAC states are evidently too small to undertake any economic development programmes independently, although there is division of thought as to the effect of the size of a nation on its economic growth and its efficiency. However, convinced that 'by joining hands, and pooling what they have of bargaining power they can together gain for themselves consideration which they could not have got individually,'[11] the Central African leaders sought to coordinate their efforts in the Customs and Economic Union of Central Africa. The establishment of the Union, they were convinced, was to re-establish the continuity of economic flows hitherto disturbed by national boundaries. There were, however, wider hopes. Such subregional groupings formed a necessary stage in the search for continental unity.

Indeed the last point in the preamble of the Treaty creating UDEAC expresses the intention of the UDEAC countries not only to create a common market within the Central African region but also the hope that such a union would eventually lead to the creation of a true African Common Market. Although it is agreed that preambles merely express general intentions and *ipso facto* are not binding on the signatories of a treaty, the leaders of Equatorial Africa seem to be holding tight to the above point as though it were one of the major goals of UDEAC. The Union, although economic, will provide a base on which the political union of Africa would be achieved. At least this is what the leaders seem to have maintained and continue to maintain as the only way to unity in Africa.

Within this same region, where other subregional economic groupings exist and in which the UDEAC states also participate, the leaders are also of this opinion.[12] This idea thus played a great role in drawing the states together and continues to play this role in keeping them in the Union. After the economic foundation is firmly established, they hold, it will be possible to work for a political union from the common and concrete base. As experience has shown, this is more of a hope than a reality. Nevertheless, the consequences of history and geography, in the birth of UDEAC cannot be neglected.

The foregoing factors played a limited role in the formation of the UDEAC, but a more important part must be attributed to the willingness and determination of the leaders of the region to unite. This was probably the single most important factor in the creation of UDEAC.

The UDEAC leaders had some common characteristics, the combination of which was able to produce the mutual understanding so vital in any union. Their shared characteristics included their age group, their past educational background under the French system, and common past experiences either in these colonial schools, as representatives of their territories in the French National Assembly or even at conferences.[13] These elements generated some mutual feelings among the leaders and determined the extent to which they could agree on joint projects which they considered as serving the interests of their people. Within this atmosphere of understanding integration was thus possible and progress was achieved.

No single factor seems to exert as much weight as the political force in its contribution to UDEAC's establishment and maintenance. Even the negotiating stages were observed to have been dominated by politics. Andre Anguile[14] and Jacques David[15] who had taken part in the negotiations for the creation of the Union remarked, '*nous courrons le risque de voir les aspectes politiques dominer ... les aspectes économiques de cette évolution.*'[16] Where they ran such risks and where politics dominated and tended to bring deadlock or halt the progress of the negotiations, as Anguile agrees, recourse was had to the political leaders who found an acceptable solution to the impasse.[17]

Furthermore, it is evident that when the Union was faced with the danger of dissolution which ended with a partial split in 1968, the solution was found in this way. It was the political leaders' will and determination that has kept UDEAC still operating to this day. This leads some authors like Mutharika to conclude that, 'the decision-making machinery of the African states, lies in the hands of the political leaders even with regard to purely economic matters.'[18]

From the last days of colonial rule and the immediate post-independence years, the internal factors discussed above were already pulling the Equatorial African countries towards the creation of an integrated unit. Although these could in themselves lead to the birth of UDEAC, external forces came to exert further influence and together facilitated the establishment of the Union. A discussion of these forces will now be attempted.

French influence has been a persistent factor in French-speaking Africa. It played and continues to play a determining role in whatever these former colonies do. This is true of what happens both within the states, among them and even in their relations with other countries of the world. The constitution of regional groupings among former French territories is no exception. They are, as in the English-speaking or even Arab-speaking countries, highly influenced by their colonial past. However, the colonial past was not the sole external integrative force in the creation of UDEAC.

The United Nations also influenced the formation of regional groupings in the Third World through some of its specialised institutions. The United Nations Conference on Trade and Development (UNCTAD) and the Economic Commission for Africa also played a role in the establishment of UDEAC. In the Final Act of UNCTAD, held in Geneva from March to June 1964, we read:

> Regional economic groupings, integration or other forms of economic cooperation should be encouraged among the developing countries as a means of expanding their intra-regional and extra-regional trade and encouraging their economic growth and their industrial and agricultural diversification ... [19]

Also as quoted in Hazlewood's *African Integration and Disintegration*:

> The delegates at the Fourth Meeting of the ECA rested their unanimous view that increased cooperation among the African states was required in order to promote intra-African trade, industrialisation and economic development in general.[20]

Both these international bodies, with identical views on the approach to the economic development of developing countries, contributed ideally to the emergence of regional groupings in Africa and Latin America.

The Economic Commission for Africa considers that single African states are too small for industrial development and that the African continent as a whole is too large a unit for such development at the present time.[21] To facilitate the growth of regional economic groupings, it has divided the continent into subregions. It also hoped by this division to assure a more efficient distribution of its resources for the undertaking of regional projects within the subregions. The UDEAC states fall within one of these ECA subregions. If these states wish to continue to benefit from ECA assistance, which for the present at least they do need, they have to hold on firmly to the Union they have established. This same argument holds for the aid-policy adopted by some industrialised countries, like France and USA.

Due to the unfortunate economic situation in which a majority of the African states found themselves after independence, most of them, including the UDEAC states, depend a great deal on external capital both public and private for the realisation of a greater part of their development plans.[22] As a result of this dependence, the policies of these states are likely to be influenced by those of the donor countries. We will examine the aid policy of one of the countries on which the UDEAC states depend most – France. Joseph Nye maintains that:

> French governmental support has played an important role in the organisations of ex-French African States such as the Joint African and Malagasy Organisation (OCAM), Union Douanière et Economique de l'Afrique Centrale (UDEAC), and Conseil de l'Entente.[23]

French support is based on the findings and recommendations of the Jeanneney investigations and report tendered, at the French Government's request, as early as 1963. On regional cooperative institutions the team held the opinion that:

> the existence of such cooperative institutions is so important for the development of the states of our former Empire that France should continue to reward [them], in its offers of cooperation, ... France ought to favour everything which contributes to the cohesion of the aided countries among themselves. To this end it ought to give preference to assistance which, channelled through multinational institutions created by aided countries, would contribute to the realisation of regionally harmonized projects.[24]

In spite of the existence of bilateral agreements between France and its former colonies, the Jeanneney Report recommended that aid to regional groupings or multinational institutions should be given preference over the bilateral aid programmes.

Finally as an integrative external force we will examine the influence of the European Economic Community (EEC) on the Central African states and the establishment of UDEAC. According to some writers on integration theory, 'the heavy coat of European theory needs alteration before it can be worn in African climates.'[25] While application of theories might not be possible in Africa, many are of the opinion that the principle itself and the European initiative and success in regional economic integration had a great impact on the evolution of similar groupings elsewhere in the world.

This is the view held by Lynn Mytelka and Anguile and David with regards to the evolution of UDEAC. As a moving force to the creation of the Customs and Economic Union of Central Africa, Mytelka argues that:

> As the European reconstruction took off in the late 1950s and

spectacular growth appeared somehow related to the existence of a common market, leaders in Equatorial Africa, as well as elsewhere in the Third World, came to believe that the solution to the economic problems of their countries lay in the transfer of integrative processes and institutions to their region.[26]

Anguile and David, the authors of *L'Afrique sans Frontières*, the first of the books to be written on UDEAC, appear also to have considered this factor as one of the most important determining factors in the establishment of UDEAC.

We have in the foregoing discussion examined the many integrative forces, the many forces of cohesion and unity within Equatorial Africa that gradually drew the five (today four) states to finally sign the UDEAC Treaty in Brazzaville on 8 December 1964 which came into force on 1 January 1966. We have also, through a few examples, seen that these forces long present in the region could unite the states only after the political 'barrier' had been broken. Even after the Union had been established, politics continued to play a significant role in its sustenance, as is evident especially in its third year of operation in 1968, and in the crisis the Union faced in its fifth year.

Conclusion

It is evident that the base for economic integration, closer inter-state cooperation and joint economic development has been set up in Central Africa. The UDEAC states, in effect, have realised that joint efforts to combat 'under-development' are necessary. Besides, the world situation seems to favour unity. Europe, for instance, is evolving not only towards economic unity but also towards political unity. In short, the world has been shrunk to a point where the policies of 'live and let live' or 'isolationism' are no longer possible.

To the extent that the UDEAC states are willing to bind themselves by means of treaty in order to effect certain joint projects and programmes, it represents a major leap forward in the direction of concerted development. To the extent that these endeavours are already yielding some fruits, it cannot be denied that economic integration in the region is on a relatively smooth path. The UDEAC states are determined to face the battle of development in unison. However, in spite of their determination and the existing integrative forces in the region, these attempts are checked by several obstacles – economic and especially political.

These political forces have played and continue to play an

important role in the integration process not only in Equatorial Africa but in most of the continent. Thus Joseph Nye warns that scholars studying integration in Africa must remember the primacy of politics and not be misled by assumptions natural to 'developed societies'. In effect, political forces can be singled out as the main causes for failure of most UDEAC projects to materialise.

Of these forces we note among others, domestic instability. Most, if not all, the member states are fragile. Because their own states are poorly integrated internally, the leaders turn their attention inward in order to achieve internal cohesion or integration, hence partially neglecting regional demands. Next, there is the continuous dependence on foreign public and private sources for development capital due to the financial weakness of UDEAC. The union, therefore, remains an instrument of dependence, particularly on the former colonial power which naturally tends subtly to exert the control lost at the political level. This results in some form of domination from the exterior.

Besides, there is the inequality in the levels of development of the member states which is itself due, in part, to what Yondo refers to as *'le leg colonial'*. In addition, we note the creation of UEAC, that provided the most serious challenge to UDEAC. It prevented UDEAC's expansion and brought rivalry in the region. Finally these are further complicated by the persistence of nationalism and the institutional weakness of the Union. National planners are always nationally orientated and never extend their views positively to the other member states. Under these pressures it appears unlikely that UDEAC states, like most Third World states, would be able to completely break the bonds of underdevelopment, despite their own efforts. Evidently something must be done, if the Union is to provide complete satisfaction to the members and the world at large.

To combat the problems resulting from dependence on foreign sources and the traditional ties with some industrialised countries, courage, obstinacy and determination are necessary since it seems only radical measures can remedy the situation. As long as these foreign 'partners' do not contribute positively to the progress of the Union, the ties that link them should not only be reviewed but changed completely. New agreements on the basis of equality and effective reciprocity should be concluded. Only such a change might rid the Union of external domination.

As to the problems of nationalism and institutional defects in UDEAC, only a revision of the present structure might remedy the situation. UDEAC certainly needs a strong and an effective institutional machinery. The establishment of such an institution, supranational in nature, is essential for successful coordination of development policies. The leaders must demonstrate their willingness to yield to this supranational body; they must be prepared to take appropriate measures to ensure that the decisions taken by the organ they create are fully supported both morally and materially. This is likely to mean a lot of sacrifices but it is needed if anything concrete is to be established at the subregional level.

The establishment of a supranational body, endowed with both decisional and administrative powers, would, it seems, provide the best answer to the problems that the coordination and harmonisation of plans and industrial policies in UDEAC face. Unless this approach is accepted and applied, the existing organs will remain, as they have proved to be, no more than debating forums, where decisions might well be taken but not implemented in the long run.

Notes

1   Arthur Hazlewood (ed.), *African Integration and Disintegration: Case Studies in Economic and Political Union* (London: Oxford University Press, 1967), p. 3.

2   After the failure of the proposed Union des Républiques d'Afrique Centrale (URAC), mentioned already in the introductory chapter, a political Union of the four ex-AEF territories was suggested and the Constitution presented to the UN. According to this the four states had to attain independence as a whole. The Constitution provided, for instance, a common nationality for the four territories, a common flag and an anthem. Gabon opposed it, considering political unity as secondary to economic problems. See André Anguile and Jacques David, *L'Afrique Sans Frontières* (Monaco: Paul Bory, 1965), pp. 28–35.

3   Bela Balassa, *The Theory of Economic Integration* (London: Allen & Unwin, 1965), p. 39.

4   Reginald, H. Green and A. Seidman, *Unity or Poverty? The Economics of Pan-Africanism* (Harmondsworth: Penguin Books, 1968), p. 22.

5   Louis Sohn (ed.), *Basic Documents on African Regional Organisation* (New York: Oceanic Publications Inc., 1971), pp. 263ff.

6   UDEAC: *Traité Instituant Une Union Douanière et Economique de l'Afrique Centrale*, Brazzaville, 1964, Articles 1 and 2.

7   Bela Balassa, *The Theory of Economic Integration*, pp. 39–40.

8   For a more detailed study of the populations of the region, see for example Victor T. Levine, *The Cameroons from Mandate to Independence* (Berkeley: University of California Press, 1964), pp. 5–14; William A. Hance, *Population, Migration and Urbanization in Africa* (New York: Columbia University Press, 1970); Roland Oliver and Anthony Atmore, *Africa Since 1800* (Cambridge: Cambridge University Press, 1969), pp. 42–53.

9 The spelling here is in reference to Cameroon as a German Protectorate. The form used throughout this paper will be the English form – Cameroon. Cameroon ceased to be a German protectorate when it was divided on 14 March 1916 between France and Great Britain, both of whom received the League of Nations Mandate to govern the territories as from 1922. See J. De Dreux-Brèze, *Le problème de régroupement en Afrique Equatoriale, Du régime colonial à l'Union Douanière et Economique de L'Afrique Centrale* (Paris: R. Pichon et R. Durrand-Auzias, 1968) and H. Brunschwig, *Mythes et Réalités de L'impérialisme colonial Français, 1871–1914* (Paris: Armand Colin, 1960).

10 Franc CFA: Formerly Communauté Financière Africaine it became Coopération Financière Africaine since the Brazzaville Accord of November, 1972. For more on the Franc Zone see, for example, Xavier de la Fournière, *La Zone Franc* (Paris: PUF, 1971)

11 Gunnar Myrdal, *Economic Theory and Under-Developed Regions*, (London: Duckworth, 1957), p. 69. While Mutharika sees the small domestic markets as posing 'a serious obstacle to the application of technological innovations of modern economies,' Pierre Tchangue, Secretary-General of UDEAC, advises as a remedy regionalism as 'de tels regroupements offrent de meilleures perspectives à l'application de la science et de la technique moderne dans le domain du developpement économique et social', Annuaire Officiel de l'Union Douanière et Economique de l'Afrique Centrale (Brazzaville, 1972), Introductory Note.

12 Within the Chad Basin Commission (Chad, Nigeria, Niger and Cameroon) Hammani Diori, President of Niger during the last session of the commission's meeting in Yaounde, is quoted as saying that 'it was through economic "unities" such as the Lake Chad Basin Commission that Africans could easily defeat their present economic situation and then work for African Unity.' (ACAP, 5 December 1973). The translation is of the ACAP. Tombalbaye of Chad, then still in OCAM, is also of the same opinion: '*Le but,*' he declared, '*demeure encore une fois, de constuire tous ensemble tout le continent.*' These illustrate to what extent the leaders are all convinced of the future unity of Africa through small regional groupings.

13 The conferences include those attended by the members of the Brazzaville bloc and the Monrovia bloc. Massamba Dabat and Tombalbaye are said to have developed and strengthened their friendship during these conferences.

14 André G. Anguile was Gabonese Minister of Finance and Economic Planning during the negotiating years of UDEAC. He participated in meetings of for instance, UDE, OAMCE, EEC and OAU. He signed the UDEAC Treaty for the Gabonese President in 1964. See *Journal Officiel de l'UDEAC* (1ère Année), 1 January 1966.

15 Jacques E. David, whose services in the AEF date back to 1946 when he was the Assistant Federal Director of Customs, was Technical Adviser to Gabonese Minister of Finance and Economic Planning (Anguile) during the same period the latter held that office. He participated with Anguile in the several meetings and conferences mentioned above. They were thus well

informed of the problems of the various phases in the formation of UDEAC.

16 *Ibid.*, pp. 82–4.

17 Mutharika, B.W.T. *Toward Multinational Economic Cooperation in Africa* (New York: Praeger Special Studies, 1972).

18 Miguel S. Wionezek, 'The Latin American Free Trade Association' in *International Political Communities, an Anthology* (New York: Doubleday & Company, Inc., 1966), p. 301.

19 Quoted in Hazlewood, *op. cit.*, p. 25. Based on the economic, social and political conditions in Africa in the early 1960s, the ECA recommended the division of the continent into four sub-regions, one each for East, Central, West and North Africa. See Mutharika, op. cit., pp. 34–8 (see note 17 above.)

20 Immanuel Wallerstein, *Africa: The Politics of Unity* (New York: Vintage Books, 1967), p. 143. The Central African ECA sub-region includes the following countries: Cameroon, CAR, Chad, Equatorial Guinea, Gabon, Rwanda, Burundi and Zaire. Its headquarters is in Kinshasha.

21 See *Europe – France – Outremer*, Special, No. 509, June 1972 for the Development Plans of the four states.

22 Joseph Nye (Jr.) 'Comparing Common Markets: a Revised Neo-Functionalist Model,' in Leon W. Lindberg, and Stuart A. Scheingold (eds), *International Organisation*, Vol. XXIV, No. 4 (Autumn 1970), p. 811.

23 Wallerstein, *op. cit.*, p. 133 (see note 20 above).

24 See Nye, *Pan-Africanism and East African Integration* (Cambridge: Harvard University Press, 1966), pp. 18–19.

25 Lyn K. Mytelka, *Bargaining in a Third World Integrative System: l'Union Douanière et Economique de l'Afrique Centrale*, (unpublished manuscript, 1972), p. 1.

26 *Ibid.*

7 ECOWAS Defence Pact and Regionalism in Africa

Tom Imobighe

In an attempt to optimise African security and defence efforts, African statesmen addressed themselves to the problem at the continental level. Early debates on the subject were centred on Kwame Nkrumah's idea of an African High Command which he first advanced in November 1960, and later presented in many Pan-African fora as a concerted plan of action for peace and security in Africa.[1] These debates about a continental defence arrangement went on for more than a decade before attention was directed towards a regional approach to the problem. Thus, as far as Africa is concerned, regionalism in defence terms as distinct from continentalism did not receive serious attention until the 1970s.

However, at the global level, it could be said that since the end of the Second World War there has been a growing tendency on the part of states to move towards some degree of regionalism not only in economic but also in defence spheres. Such regional defence systems as the North Atlantic Treaty Organisation (NATO), the Warsaw Pact, the South-East Asia Treaty Organisation (SEATO), the Baghdad Pact and the Arab Defence Council were early manifestations of regional defence arrangements. This increasing drive towards regionalism emanates from the general realisation that universalism in defence terms is unrealistic, ineffective and unreliable. The woeful failure of the collective security arrangement under the League of Nations and the inability of the United Nations which succeeded the League to improve upon it in terms of effectiveness and reliability foredoomed further efforts towards universal defence arrangements.

In this chapter, an attempt will be made to look at regional defence arrangement as a means of achieving relative, if not optimum, security and examine the position of the ECOWAS Defence Pact within the global subsystemic security equation. The study will proceed from there to take a critical look at the ECOWAS Defence Pact not only in terms of structure, relevance and effectiveness, but also in terms of its place in the African continental security equation. It is hoped that this will help to throw some light on the whole question as to whether optimum continental security in Africa could best be achieved through regional defence arrangements.

Achieving Optimum Security through Regional Defence Arrangements

States have two principal choices in trying to deal with their security problems. They could either rely on their individual self-efforts or pool resources with some other states either on a bilateral or multilateral basis. Reliance on individual self-effort, though honourable, could at times be very expensive if one is faced with a formidable opponent. Hence at times, it is nice to succumb to the attraction of some joint defence arrangements. However, deciding on some measure of joint action still confronts a state with a number of options. These range from deciding on a universal collective security arrangement, to adopting some bilateral arrangements.

As has been noted earlier, the classic form of collective security by which states assume defence commitment on a global scale, is entirely unreliable. For it is hardly possible to expect sovereign states within the present global system to exhibit any identity of interest in any particular conflict that would commit them to a joint enforcement action. Interests can be more easily aggregated for a common action within a smaller organisation. Thus to a certain extent, the smaller the group coming together for purpose of collective defence, the more reliable it will be in terms of commitment to a joint enforcement action.

However, the distinction must be made between the commitment to joint action and the effectiveness of the ensuring action. That a group exhibits a high commitment to a joint action does not automatically guarantee that it would actually take an effective action against its opponent. Effectiveness of action is usually determined by the institutional and infrastructural arrangements and the means at the disposal of the group *vis-à-vis* the opposing group, as well as the efficient handling of the available means. Thus while it is more likely to expect a greater sense of commitment to joint action in an organisation of five members than in one with ten member states, it does not also follow that when the various interests are reconciled and a joint action is taken in each case, that the organisation with five members will be more effective than the one with ten.

The important point in favour of smaller units of international organisations whether for defence or other purposes is the relative ease with which consensus could be arrived at for a joint enforcement action. Interests are more easily reconciled in a smaller group than in an unwieldy collection of states. The point to emphasise here is that unlike a universal defence arrangement, a collective defence arrangement could be based on the proximity of members to one another which makes them susceptible to a common security problem. It could also be based on idological compatibility in which case they

Table 7.1 Organisation of Joint Defence Arrangements

Multilateral Defence System		Bilateral Defence System
Collective Security System	Collective Defence System	
This is a more or less global security arrangement, of the kind which was experimented with under the League of Nations and the United Nations. It has not been very successful.	More or less a new name for alliance systems embracing all the multilateral defence arrangements outside the United Nations, sometimes given the general name of regional organisation. The main types are: *Intercontinental* i.e. deriving its membership from more than one continent e.g. NATO and the Warsaw Pact. *Continental* i.e. spreading its membership over one continent, e.g. the arrangement under the OAS and the one being planned under the OAU. *Regional* i.e. limited to a section or sub-section of a continent, like the ECOWAS Defence Pact.	Involving only two states

share an identical interest to preserve their common values against an opposing ideology. There are two essential factors in a collective defence set-up, namely, some identity of interest and the perception of a common threat. The stand taken in this study is that these two factors are more easily aggregated in a small organisation than a large one, hence, in a regional organisation than a global one.

However, discussing a regional defence arrangement could be misleading if the particular one in question is not put in its proper perspective. For instance, all multilateral defence arrangements outside the United Nations collective security arrangement are sometimes referred to as regional organisations. This type of classification can hardly be adequate with reference to the ECOWAS Defence Pact, and any future defence arrangement under the OAU. If one were to take the present arrangement under the OAU as a regional defence organisation, then the ECOWAS Defence Pact would lie for a subregional defence organisation. In order to remove the confusion, joint defence organisations have been examined in most of the existing literature, and a table is provided opposite which clearly shows the context under which the ECOWAS Defence Pact is being addressed (Table 7.1).

The ECOWAS Defence Pact

The ECOWAS Defence Pact occupies a mid-way position in a graded defence arrangement ladder usually undertaken by states which comprises the following components: unilateral, bilateral, regional, continental and global defence arrangements. Judging from a general pattern of multilateral defence arrangements, it could be said that the ECOWAS Pact stands a relatively good chance of being a viable defence proposition in that being a regional pact, it took care of some of the inadequacies in the unilateral and bilateral arrangements while shedding the idealism in the global arrangement. Nonetheless, the viability of the ECOWAS Defence Pact must still be measured against the two factors governing joint defence efforts which we mentioned earlier in this study, namely, community of interests and the perception of a common threat.

Community of Interest

Though geographically ECOWAS states belong to a closely-knit region, their recent history was completely bereft of any form of cohesive development as a group. Foreign intrusion polarised the region into two principal colonial cultures, the French and the British. Throughout the period of colonial administration the Francophone countries developed in their separate compartment while the Anglophone countries developed in theirs. The two sides had very little interaction. Even most of the interactions within each colonial group were vertical interactions between each colony and the imperial power. Only in the French areas was there some form of horizontal interaction between the colonies, though not with the same intensity as the interaction between each of the colonies and metropolitan France. This is mainly the result of the French assimilation policy under which French Equatorial Africa was administered as one political unit with the sole aim of making the people French.

On the other hand, the British policy of indirect rule emphasised the separate development of the various colonies. It provided little or no room for horizontal interaction. Unlike the experience in the French West African colonies, the British colonies did not have the benefit of a supra-national political and economic structure and activity in the sense which allows for maximum economic and political activities between the various colonial entities.

While the above diversities within ECOWAS are worth mentioning, some of the integrative features of the colonial period, especially in the area of defence, must be recognised. During the process of the so-called pacification of this region the colonial powers were compelled to use security forces drawn from one community to pacify another. Thus with time, these forces recruited from various communities became the nucleus of each of the colonial armies. This formed the background of a tradition of common defence efforts within each of the two principal groups of colonies (the British and the French) in West Africa. For instance, in Gambia, Ghana, Nigeria and Sierra Leone, the British established the Royal West African Frontier Force which represented the joint defence instrument for the maintenance of security in the area until these states attained independent status.

It could thus be seen that there was an element of centralisation of military efforts within British West Africa even though indirect rule emphasised separate development. The whole arrangement followed the British organisational and command structures while British military schools serviced the training of the officers. In cases where initial training for potential officers had to be done locally, these were centrally organised within the region like the Teshic Military School near Accra which provided preliminary training for officers from British West Africa.

The integration of defence efforts was even more extensive in the

French possessions in West Africa. The *troupes coloniales* were seen as a reserve army loyal only to France. As a group, the French colonial army was made up of units with no particular territorial affiliations. Thus in Francophone West Africa, the French had a large military establishment which enjoyed centralised training and promotion arrangements. Even though after independence the French military superstructure was broken into territorial forces, the tradition of joint defence effort was not completely abandoned. It was to a certain degree carried into the post-independence era with France acting as the connecting cord through the series of bilateral defence agreements with these states.

Granting that the Portuguese territories of Guinea-Bissau and Cape Verde are inconsequential to the general pattern mentioned above, it could be said that the problem of integrating the ECOWAS forces is a minor one. In fact in terms of reconciling the diverse defence traditions of these states, the two principal military cultures, the French and the British, are not diametrically opposed, and the two groups of colonies carried their inherited colonial tradition into the post-independence period. Where there were slight changes as in the case of Guinea, Nigeria and a few other former British colonies, there was more diversification which incorporated some elements of the Soviet system rather than a complete break with the inherited system. Perhaps only Guinea rejected the inherited colonial tradition and adopted its own pattern whereby the role of the Guinean Armed Forces embraced not only defence, but also a wide range of developmental activities like roadbuilding, farm projects and minor construction work.

The foregoing does not however denote the presence of a community of interests among the ECOWAS members. It shows, however, that their so-called diverse military traditions, which constitute a familiar argument against the viability of the ECOWAS Defence experiment, are not irreconcilable. What is important to emphasise here is that by agreeing to form a common economic community, the ECOWAS states have demonstrated that they share common economic and social goals.

In other words, they are aware of their many disabilities which they feel could best be redressed through economic integration. For instance, most of the states suffer from the disability of smallness and are therefore incapable of establishing viable industries without some form of partnership. On the other hand, no less than eight of the sixteen ECOWAS states suffer from the disability of a mono-crop economy while about five of them depend on only two crops for over 60 per cent of their foreign exchange earnings. This situation makes the economies of ECOWAS states very vulnerable to the fluctuations in the world market. Besides, eight of the world's thirty-seven poorest countries are from this region, which according to R.I. Onwuka, 'is persistently a region that does not feed itself.'[2] In fact, most of the states rely on external powers to balance their budgets. It is obvious from the above statistics that they could not find economic and social salvation in their mode of separate development which has turned them into client-states of the developed economies of others outside the continent.

Among ECOWAS priorities are a progressive development of a customs union and common tariff on imported goods from third countries;[3] and harmonisation of policies in the areas of transport, communications, energy and mineral resources for rapid industrialisation.[4] All these mean that these states want to generate maximum economic and social interactions among themselves and to wrest control of their economic destiny from the hands of foreign exploiters.

Defence Implication of ECOWAS Economic Imperatives

The establishment of an economic union by a group of states usually has defence implications which transcend territorial borders. The protection of joint services, industrial and economic ventures jointly owned cannot be left in the hands of the individual states, especially in the case of ECOWAS where some of its members are too weak to protect themselves. Under such circumstances common security arrangements are necessary to protect such collective ventures. It is in this sense that economic union usually advances a state's defence focus beyond its borders. The need for a defence component becomes even more imperative if the collective, though legitimate, actions of the group are bound to invite hostilities from different quarters.

Examples are many in history where international economic organisations logically developed a defence component. For instance, NATO provides the defence umbrella for the European Economic Community (EEC) even though a principal member of NATO (the United States) is not in the EEC. NATO was a product of the post-war integrative effort in Europe which saw its genesis in the Marshall Plan. Also the Organisation of American States (OAS) which was basically a forum for joint economic assistance has its defence component as embodied in the Lima Accord. In Eastern Europe, the Warsaw Pact also forms the defence umbrella over the COMECON.

The Arab League also has its defence component in the Arab Defence Council. Even in the EEC's economic association with Africa, there was the tendency by France to give it a defence backing. In January 1978, the former French President, Valéry Giscard d'Estaing, proposed a pact of solidarity which would include defence provisions between the EEC countries and Africa.[5]

From the foregoing it could be said that the ECOWAS Defence Pact emanated from a general concern by its members to protect shared interests. According to Togo, one of the leading exponents of the Pact, if economic integration and cooperation are to be meaningful then they have to be accompanied by a defence and security arrangement.[6] Senegal also gave a similar impression in the proposals it submitted the same year for the creation of a defence component for ECOWAS.[7] This point was further emphasised by President Senghor of Senegal on 28 May 1979 at the ECOWAS Summit in Dakar when he said:

> There is hardly any need for me to demonstrate the fact that development cannot be secured in a climate of insecurity. This being so, we must among ourselves, establish a genuine West African solidarity pact to guard against external aggression.[8]

Perception of Threat within ECOWAS

The need to add a defence component to the ECOWAS Treaty became imperative not only because ECOWAS ideals conflict with those of the powers with imperialistic interests in the region, but also because the area has been the object of previous external violations. For instance, in November 1970, the Republic of Guinea experienced an attempted invasion by Portuguese-led mercenaries. Also, in January 1977, the Republic of Benin experienced another mercenary assault on the region. Besides, the numerous French military interventions and the presence of French troops in and around the ECOWAS region to promote its imperialistic designs in the area pose a lot of security worries for some of the ECOWAS member states.

A number of these states are worried about these threats, the more so because if the high hopes of ECOWAS materialise, the neo-colonial powers lurking around in the region will find the situation rather uncomfortable and may decide on hostile action against selected targets. One is not trying to underestimate the problems ECOWAS is facing and will continue to face for some time in its economic programmes. In fact, these problems are compounded by the fact that they depend on some measure of cooperation from the industrialised states through the release of finance capital, technical and other aids for a number of ECOWAS projects to materialise. Nonetheless, it is worth mentioning that if the ECOWAS industrialisation programme should materialise, the raw materials and minerals produced in the region will be increasingly utilised within the region. This will obviously rob the present importers of ECOWAS minerals and raw materials of a vital source of cheap supply of these commodities. Also the generation of intra-Community trade will deprive these powers of their traditional markets for the disposal of their manufactured goods. Of course, the increasing prosperity of the region will also mean less dependence of ECOWAS states on the exploitative external forces who will not take kindly to that.

These hostile forces could react in various ways. They could use mercenaries as they have done in the past to hit at selected targets; they could engineer coups to topple detested governments, and if necessary use subtle means to undermine the security of the region like economic sabotage and diplomatic blackmail. In this regard, one must say that ECOWAS countries are very vulnerable since these external forces have strategic information about ECOWAS states within their easy reach. After all, they supply and even instal all the security gadgets of these states. Besides, they can stop supplies when it serves their interests to do so.

Another source of threat which should not be disregarded is apartheid South Africa. Even though remote from the region, it has developed long-range capability which diminishes the crippling effect of the distance between her and West Africa. Thus South Africa could feel that the increasing prosperity of this region will lead to more positive support for the freedom fighters from the latter. She could, thus see ECOWAS success as a big threat to her apartheid institutions and as a result decide on a preemptive action on selected ECOWAS targets.

From the above analysis, it is clear that the main conditions for collective defence arrangements (i.e. community of interest and perception of common threat) are fulfilled in the ECOWAS defence experiment. This does not necessarily mean that the defence pact as it is envisaged at the moment is viable. To determine this, a content analysis of the Protocol is necessary.

Content Analysis of the ECOWAS Defence Pact

The analysis here will be carried out under four principal provisions which are classified for analytical convenience only.

1 *Non-aggression Provision*: This is contained in the preamble to the Treaty and is virtually a restatement of the OAU and United Nations provisions. However, unlike the case of the OAU, the Treaty contains no institutional or procedural provisions for the peaceful settlement of disputes. It can thus be assumed that the members would adopt the OAU *ad hoc* mediation and conciliation techniques with all their weaknessess.

2 *Enforcement Provision*: The members declare in the Treaty that 'any armed threat or aggression directed against any Member State shall constitute a threat or aggression against the entire Community.'[9] They also resolve to 'give mutual aid and assistance for defence against any armed aggression'.[10] For purpose of enforcement action member states are expected 'to place at the disposal of the Community, ear-marked units from the existing National Armed Forces' which 'shall be referred to as the Allied Armed Forces of the Community (AAFC)'.[11]

There is also a provision for specific emergency situations warranting Community action. These are two, namely external aggression and an internal armed conflict which is 'engineered and supported actively from outside' and which is likely to endanger the security and peace of the Community.[12] Since it is often too easy for rulers to attribute their predicament to outside machinations, this provision is likely to involve the ECOWAS in defence commitment of unknown dimension since it is too easy for a hard-pressed regime to cite external involvement as a reason for ECOWAS action against even a popular internal revolution. The implication of this provision is that ECOWAS might be so bogged down with quelling internal revolutions as to have little or no time to prepare for, and deal with external threats and aggressions.

3 *Institutional and Command Provisions*: Three principal institutions were established for the servicing of the ECOWAS Defence Pact. These include the *Authority of the Heads of State and Government* otherwise referred to as *The Authority*. It is the responsibility of The Authority to examine the general problems of peace and security within the Community and decide on the expediency of military action.[13]

The next Institution is the *Defence Council* which shall consist of Ministers of Defence and Foreign Affairs of Member States. In a crisis, the Council could be enlarged to include any other Ministers from member states. The ECOWAS Executive Secretary and the Deputy Executive Secretary in charge of military affairs are expected to be in attendance at Council meetings. The main responsibility of the Defence Council is to prepare the agenda of sessions of the

Authority dealing with defence matters. However, in an emergency, the Defence Council could consider the expediency of an enforcement action and the means of intervention.[14]

The third Institution is the *Defence Commission* which shall consist of a Chief of Staff from each member state. The Defence Commission is responsible for Examining the technical aspect of defence matters. Thus on the whole the Commission is the technical adviser to the Defence Council.[15]

The following command structure is provided for in the protocol.[16] There is a Deputy Executive Secretary (Military) at the ECOWAS Secretariat to be responsible for all defence matters. He shall be appointed by the Defence Council for a period of four years renewable only once and he shall be a senior serving military officer. The strength of his support staff will be determined by the Defence Council.

Finally, there shall be a Commander of AAFC to be appointed by The Authority 'on the proposal of the Defence Council', and shall act in accordance with the powers conferred on him by the Authority. He is expected to implement with the Chief of Defence Staff of the assisted state the armed intervention and assistance as may be decided by the Authority.

There are roles and positions that are not properly streamlined in the Protocol in regard to the institutions and command structure. For instance, there is an element of dual authority in regard to enforcement action especially in an emergency. It may be that giving the Defence Council the responsibility of effecting necessary action in an emergency is to ensure prompt response in aid of the victim of aggression. However, whereas there is an element of obligatory provision under Article 6, paragraph 4 of the Protocol, that 'decisions taken by the Authority shall be immediately enforceable on member states,' no such provision is made in the Defence Council decision in the said emergency situations. This means, though it is not so stated, that Council decisions will of necessity be submitted to the Authority for sanction in order to get them enforceable. This tends to negate the inherent benefit in the measure and thereby makes it unnecessary.

On the other hand, there is also a provision under Article 9 which by implication subjects the actions of the Commander of the AAFC to the so-called 'competent political authority of the Member State or States being aided.' This will certainly create some problems for the Force Commander, as well as bottlenecks which might in the end impede the effective prosecution of any enforcement measure. This is more so since, according to Article 14, paragraph 2, the Force Commander shall subject his force to the joint management of the

Chief of Defence Staff of the assisted country in the implementation of an armed intervention. The organisational structure of the ECOWAS Defence System is illustrated in Table 7.2.

4 *Financial Provision*: This is perhaps one of the weakest areas of the Protocol. There is nothing to show that the funding of the Defence Pact has been properly articulated. The only mention of funds is that the Deputy Executive Secretary (Military) 'shall prepare and manage

Table 7.2 The Organisation and Command Structure of ECOWAS Defence System

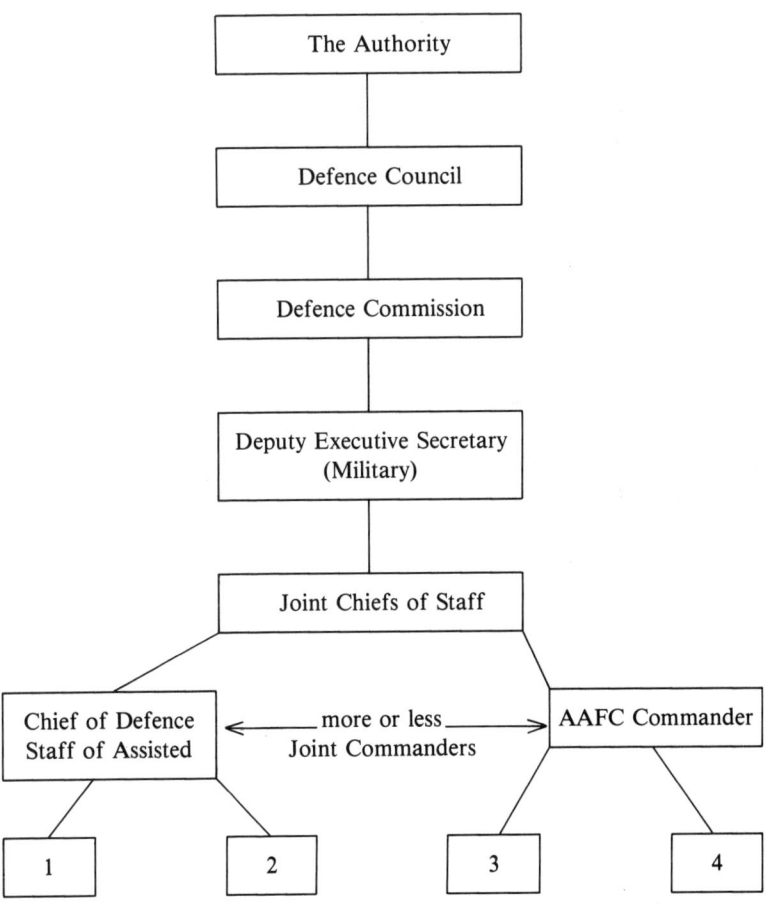

Note: 1–4 represent units of contributed troops including those of the assisted country.

the military budget of the Secretariat.'[17] Nothing is said about the types of funds to be kept, like 'a regular fund', for the normal administrative functions of the defence system or a 'special fund' for financing the armed interventions or the occasional joint military exercises. There is also no provision as to how members will contribute to the fund. The whole thing might boil down to *ad hoc* fund-raising as the situation warrants. It is very likely that, this being so, ECOWAS might be faced with aggression without being able to raise the money to finance any intervention. This weakness tends to minimise the merit of the whole arrangement.

ECOWAS Defence Pact within the Context of OAU Collective Defence System

The ECOWAS Defence Pact, as has been noted earlier, is based on the perception that the projected drive to improve the economic and social lot of the members of the Community can be done only in an atmosphere of peace and tranquillity at both the intra-community and extra-community levels. At the intra-community level, it was observed in the study that there is no adequate arrangement for the settlement of intra-community disputes apart from the provision for the interposition of ECOWAS troops between the disputants.

At the extra-community level, there is the question of the credibility of the Pact as a deterrent against external aggression. The content analysis of the Pact has shown that there are some gaps in the arrangement which need serious attention to ensure the viability and hence credibility of the Pact.

In another study the author has suggested that any collective defence arrangement in the Continent must reckon with African strategic realities.[18] On the basis of the proven inability of African states to carry out military deployment on a continental scale, a loose decentralised arrangement based on regional commands was suggested. This means solving Africa's defence disability through regional collective defence arrangements. It could be said that the ECOWAS Defence Pact has basically satisfied similar arrangements in the other regions of the Continent. When this is done, the task that will be left for the OAU will be to coordinate and integrate the regional arrangements at the top for purposes of overall continental defence.

There are two specific areas where the ECOWAS defence arrangement exhibited a good reflection of Africa's strategic realities. First, it did not make provision for a standing ECOWAS force in peacetime. This has helped to take care, in a way, of the perennial financial problems bedevilling African joint ventures. Under the ECOWAS arrangement, the maintenance of the ear-marked units of the AAFC during peacetime will be the responsibility of the individual states. The Community's financial problems will therefore be limited to raising funds to maintain the skeleton staff at the Command headquarters and for emergency situations, as well as for the occasional joint exercises. It is, however, unfortunate that the financial arrangement to meet with the ECOWAS defence functions even on this reduced scale is most inadequate.

Second, the ECOWAS Pact made provision for occasional joint exercises as may be approved by the Authority. This will have the effect of gradually integrating the armed forces of the member states and solve the problem of diversity in military traditions including the command systems of member states. While the arrangement is a good reflection of one of Africa's basic strategic problems, the form in which it is set out in the Protocol is not firm enough. There ought to be a firm standing arrangement on the number and manner, as well as the scope of such joint exercises within each year. Besides, there ought to be an arrangement for joint training, as well as exchange of military personnel.

Finally, because of the need to carry out the above-mentioned regular integrative activities, the Commander of the AAFC should not be appointed on *ad hoc* basis. He should be appointed on the same terms as the Deputive Executive Secretary (Military). Apart from commanding the troops during real emergencies, he should see to the effective conduct of the integrative activities referred to above. On the whole, the ECOWAS Defence Pact is a good experiment in regional defence arrangement in Africa. Admittedly, there are weaknesses here and there. These are not insurmountable. With a little bit of determination on the part of member states to make the arrangement succeed, most of the identified weaknesses in the arrangement will be solved in good time.

Notes

1　See T.A. Imobighe, 'An African High Command: The Search For a Feasible Strategy of Continental Defence' in *African Affairs*, Vol. 79, No. 315, April 1980, p. 241.

2　Ralph I. Onwuka, *Development And Integration in West Africa: The Case of ECOWAS* (Ife: University Press, 1982), p. 2.

3　*ECOWAS Treaty*, Article 12.

4   *Ibid.*, Articles 40 and 48.

5   Giscard d'Estaing made the proposition during his visit to Ivory Coast.

6   See Government of the Republic of Togo, *Proposals on Agreement on Non-Aggression and Assistance on Defence Matters Between The Member States of ECOWAS,* 1973, preamble.

7   See Government of the Republic of Senegal, *Proposals on Protocol of Assistance on the Defence of the Economic Community of West African States,* 1973, preamble. It is remarkable that the ECOWAS Defence Protocol was drawn up as a result of the harmonisation of both the Togolese and the Senegalese proposals.

8   President Senghor, *Welcome Address* to ECOWAS Delegations to the Summit in Daker, 28–9 May 1979.

9   A/SP3/5/81, *Protocol Relating to Mutual Assistance on Defence* (Freetown), 29 May 1981, Article 2.

10 *Ibid.*, Article 3.

11 *Ibid.*, Article 13.

12 *Ibid.*, Article 4.

13 *Ibid.*, Article 6.

14 *Ibid.*, Article 8, para. 2.

15 *Ibid.*, Article 11.

16 See Articles 12 to 18 for all the Command Structure.

17 *Ibid.*, Article 12, para. 6.

18 T.A. Imobighe, *op. cit.*, p. 252 (see note 1 above).

8 The Mano River Union: Politics of Survival or Dependence?

Amadu Sesay

.... I am convinced more than ever that our long-term salvation lies in cooperation among ourselves rather than in perpetual dependence on external factors beyond our control. We can achieve through economic cooperation the self-control needed, to prevent external manipulation of our internal policies.[1]

We believe in regional cooperation with equal fervour, because it is only after developing African states have coordinated their efforts and organised themselves at regional levels, that we can have the strength or purpose which will make people listen to us not only at the OAU, but also at the United Nations.[2]

Introduction

The Mano River Union (MRU) – a customs union between Sierra Leone and Liberia – was enlarged by Guinea's accession in 1980. (Since Guinea is still in the process of adjustment within the Union, most of the following analysis will be based on the experiences of the founders – Sierra Leone and Liberia – although where appropriate, mention will made of Guinea.) The MRU was not conceived in an environmental vacuum. Its roots could be traced to a myriad of factors – political, economic and socio-cultural both internal and external. These factors persuaded the Third World, including Sierra Leone and Liberia, to place great emphasis on collective economic cooperation at the regional and subregional levels.

The External Environment

The external environment within which the MRU was conceived is characterised on a global scale by extreme economic and technological inequalities between the developed North and underdeveloped South to which Africa and the Third World generally, belong. For example, out of the United Nations (UN) 25 least-developed countries in the world, Africa alone has seventeen which include two members of the MRU, Sierra Leone and Guinea. Besides that, most African countries are constantly under tremendous economic pressure due to their inability to pay for their import bills and chronic adverse balance of payments problems. This is because most developing states have mono-cultural economies; they depend on the export of raw materials to the developed North for foreign exchange to pay for their imports. However, in the past decade or so, the price of exports has dramatically fallen relative to that of imports. All attempts by the South particularly in Africa to improve their balance of trade, and so accelerate industrialisation and development, have been hampered by the restrictive trade practices of the developed countries. The North wants to retain its economic pre-eminence, and is thus reluctant to encourage industrialisation in the South. To discourage the South, the North has imposed high tariffs on processed or semi-processed goods from the developing countries. This in turn, has frustrated solo attempts by developing states – especially the very small ones – to diversify their economies so as to achieve some measure of self-sufficiency and independence *vis-à-vis* the developed North.

Attempts to rectify the economic imbalance between the North and South have led to various strategies by the UN and its agencies. These include:

(i) the UN development decades
(ii) the UNCTAD Conferences
(iii) GATT and related meetings
(iv) the negotiations for a New International Economic Order.

Besides these strategies, individuals – mainly from the North – have also come out with their own recipes for closing the gap between the rich North and the poor South.[3] And in Africa in particular, self-reliance strategies have been closely linked with the activities of ECA (Economic Commission for Africa) and the OAU (Organisation of African Unity). The most notable landmarks in that direction have been the Futures symposium organised by the ECA in Monrovia in 1979, and the OAU Lagos economic summit and *Plan of Action* in April 1980.[4] All these meetings stressed the urgent need by African countries to embark upon self-reliant economic development through collective economic cooperation at the subregional and regional levels.

The Domestic Environment

Apart from the hostile external environment, then, the domestic circumstances of Sierra Leone and Liberia also prompted them to reconsider their approaches to development. First, both states are very small even by African standards. With Guinea, their combined land area is merely 429 000 square kilometres. More important, Sierra Leone and Liberia are respectively the fifth and sixth smallest African countries. The total population of the three countries is again small, 10.5 million in 1979. Out of this figure Guinea, the largest and most populous, accounts for half, 5.3 million. Secondly, two of the members, Guinea and Sierra Leone are among the UN's least-developed nations or what the World Bank has called low-income countries, underdeveloped economically and technologically. This is reflected in their GDPs for 1979; $790 m., $94 m. and $1.504 m. for Sierra Leone, Liberia and Guinea respectively. All three states have mono-economies. They are dependent on the export of raw materials for their foreign exchange to pay for their imports; iron ore and rubber for Liberia, diamonds for Sierra Leone and pineapples, bauxite and iron ore for Guinea. Third, all three countries exhibit similar socio-political problems ranging from ethnic rivalries, threats to internal security, to outright violence and political instability.[5] Besides, they all suffer from high illiteracy and infant mortality rates, severe shortages of skilled managerial and administrative personnel and an almost total absence of indigenous technology. The combination of these factors means that the three states are perpetually dependent upon, and are at the mercy of the developed countries of the West for security, financial and technical assistance. The corollary of this has been their incorporation into the periphery of the capitalist economic and political systems.

The situation is enhanced by the smallness of their markets, which makes it impossible for large investment projects to be undertaken economically. Thus, individually, they cannot attract enough investment from abroad. This problem has been compounded by their inability to raise enough funds domestically to finance their development projects because of the prevailing low salaries and the related low level of savings in these countries. Finally, it has become obvious that the attempts hitherto made by the developing states to industrialise through the adoption of Western Northern growth models are not yielding the desired results. This is evident in the growth rates in Sierra Leone, Liberia and Guinea in the period 1970–78. These were: 1.3 for Sierra Leone, 0.2 for Liberia and 0.8 for Guinea.[6] It is not surprising, then, that leaders of all three states share the belief that they are victims of an oppressive international economic order which is heavily biased in favour of the developed countries of the North. They also believe that they could only alleviate their poor economic performance through policies of collective self-reliance and cooperation.

The Rationale for the Mano River Union

The rationale for the Mano River Union could be divided into two broad categories: economic and political.[7] Both Siaka Stevens and William Tolbert (the latter was killed in a military coup in 1980) hoped that the Union would accelerate the economic development of their respective countries, reduce their political and economic dependence on the West, and finally, ensure the survival of Sierra Leone and Liberia. Any assessment of the Union since its inception in 1973, must of necessity, therefore, relate to the answers to the following questions:

(i) to what extent has it been able to enhance the welfare of the citizens?

(ii) to what extent has the Union been able to implement its objectives?

(iii) to what extent has it merely served as a medium for the collective exploitation and incorporation of the members by the west?

The Mano River Union: Problems of Survival

From the performance of the Union since its inception, it is doubtful whether it has achieved many of its basic objectives. Indeed, in many respects, it has failed completely to do so. It has not promoted industrialisation or the acquisition of appropriate capital technology in member states. Indeed, the Union has so far not been able to 'formulate a clear and effective industrial and technological policy to ensure the establishment of self-reliant and self-sustaining industrialisation process'.[8] The net result of this situation is that the Union is unable to discriminate against aid and technology offered by external sources. On the contrary, it has been eager to 'accept and solicit any type of industrial investment within the Union. Industrialisation is therefore characterised by a proliferation of incoherent industrial establishment which contributes very little to the domestic economy'.[9] Besides that, agriculture has not received the right emphasis either. Although rice is the staple food in Sierra Leone and Liberia, the two countries have not so far achieved self-sufficiency in rice production. In fact, they are net importers of the commodity. For many years now, Sierra Leone has depended on either the United Nations Food and Agricultural Organisation (FAO) or, upon friendly countries such as Japan and the United States of America, for rice, to feed its people. Finally, the Union has not increased the political leverage of its members either individually or collectively. What is becoming increasingly obvious is that the Union has made it easier than before for the exploitation and incorporation of the members by the West and their multinational corporations (MNCs).[10] To support this broad conclusion, I shall trace briefly below some of the major landmarks in the Union's nine-year history.

Between 1973 and 1978, the following measures had been taken by the members; the harmonisation of customs law and control of vehicular traffic, harmonisation of 79 per cent of excise rates, excise regulations, customs and excise administration and procedure and the organisation of their customs and excise. In 1977, the two original states harmonised their tariffs with respect to third parties. Besides that, the two members also reached agreement on:
 (i) an export credit guarantee scheme;
 (ii) the creation of export promotion councils and
 (iii) a simplified drawback scheme for the export of manufactured goods.

Then finally in 1981, the members implemented the protocol on intra-union trade. With its introduction, the creation of the customs union had been completed. The impact of the harmonised external tariff and intra-union trade on the member states is glaring in several areas.

One of the most significant effects of the Common External Tariff (CET) was the reduction in the incidence of smuggling across the border between Freetown and Monrovia. The issue of smuggling has been a sensitive one in the relations of the two states. For Sierra Leone particularly, it was viewed with serious concern since the country's main foreign exchange-earner – diamonds – was involved. The harmonisation of the external tariffs made smuggling of the precious stones to Liberia less profitable but increased the risks of such adventure. Another effect of the CET is that it enlarged the markets of the two countries, by making both available to foreign investors. This made it more attractive to invest in either country since the bigger market also offered brighter prospects of profits from investments.[11] Finally, the CET was expected to enhance the leverage of both countries in negotiations with other parties such as the EEC or the Economic Community of West African States (ECOWAS). However, it is doubtful if this has actually happened. For instance, the negotiations for the second Lome Convention were carried out under the banner of the Africa, Caribbean and Pacific countries (ACP). In any case, at the time of the negotiations the Union had not distinguished itself to enhance its bargaining power as a sub-group within the ACP.

In West Africa, the Union has entered into discussions with ECOWAS on the following issues: 'treatment of categories of products such as handcrafts, under the different trade liberalisation programmes', 'consideration of the ECOWAS Statistical Standards and Definitions', and 'consideration of Customs Declaration Forms, Customs Codes and Certificate of Origin',[12] etc. It is doubtful, again, whether the Union has been able to get substantial concessions from the sixteen nation ECOWAS on such technical problems. Besides that, there is even the more fundamental question as to how long the Mano River Union would continue to exist side by side with the much bigger and potentially much more viable ECOWAS. Although there is at the moment no discernible pressure on the smaller sub-groups within ECOWAS to disband, when the sixteen-nation community becomes fully operational and leads the subregion towards economic and political integration, the Mano River Union and similar sub-groups will be forced to break up; see chapter 5 for more details on this point.

The Impact of Intra-Union Trade

The introduction of intra-union trade in May 1981 marked the final phase in the creation of a customs union as noted earlier, between Sierra Leone and Liberia. Like the Common External Tariff, intra-union trade is expected to bring a number of benefits to union members:

(i) provide goods of local origin with a large and protected market;
(ii) induce economic growth and development; and
(iii) stimulate industrialisation.

Disappointingly, however, trade between the members has not been affected in any significant way. There are many reasons for this poor start. First is the competitive nature of their economies, already mentioned. This is aided by the near-total absence of infra-structural linkages between the members. But this is to be expected. Each of the members had had a different colonial experience.[13] Historically, all the key linkages were between the colonial territory and the colonial metropole (e.g. telephones and telegraphic links). Besides, trade after independence has been conducted mainly with the developed countries in the North. This is particularly true for Sierra Leone and Liberia whose trade is with Britain and America respectively. In 1979 for instance, 86 per cent of all Liberia's exports went to the West.[14] Not surprisingly, then, trade between the Union members is minimal.[15]

Another important barrier to intra-union trade is the different currencies used in Sierra Leone, Liberia and Guinea. In Liberia where the US dollar is legal tender, there are no foreign exchange restrictions. This is however not the case for both Guinea and Sierra Leone which use local currencies – the inconvertible franc and the Leone respectively. This has hampered smooth and easy movement of capital within the Union, and consequently, the movement of goods and trade. The final obstacle to intra-union trade is the absence of the so-called Union Industries. This is due to the slow response by investors to the requests made by the Union for investment. At the time of writing all the Union Industries are still on the drawing board. Until they become operational, the trade between members will continue to be paltry. It is obvious by now that there is a very low propensity for trade between the members. This situation raises the question whether they would gain by forming the customs union. In his classic study of customs unions, Lipsey has argued that, 'countries which have a low proportion of trade with each other and [do not have] a high proportion of ... foreign trade are likely to lose if they form a customs union'. This seems to be the case with regard to the Mano River Union, at least in the short run. As we have noted, the intra-union trade has not had any noticeable impact on the Union. Besides that, the common external tariff has served to divert trade from the community to the developed countries in the North, their traditional trading partners. So far, the reduction of tariff on some imported items such as baby food and medical supplies has thrown the balance of advantage in favour of the developed countries. This situation is rather worrying, given Jacob Viner's conclusion that 'the balance of advantage and disadvantage in a customs union will depend on how much trade is created and how much is diverted'[16] from the union. It would appear in the case of the Mano River Union that for the time being at least, the disadvantages outweigh the advantages.

This is a rather sobering conclusion given the earlier expectations of the founding fathers discussed in the foregoing paragraphs. But that is not the only disappointment. Even at the inter-governmental level, the impact of the Union has been tenuous. On the surface, relations between member countries remain calm and cordial. This was particularly so for relations between Monrovia and Freetown while

Tolbert was alive. However, it could be argued that relations between the members were only cordial at the presidential level. Indeed, between 1973 and 1980 it was the personal friendship between Stevens and Tolbert that kept the Union superficially alive. In fact throughout these nine years, it was their personal diplomacy that received the limelight.

On the other hand, at meetings between Liberian and Sierra Leonean delegations to discuss union affairs, the atmosphere was different. Liberian and Sierra Leonean delegates regard themselves as representing Liberia's or Sierra Leone's interest or point of view and not that of the Union. Besides, there is hardly what one can call a feeling of comradeship among delegates at such meetings. The urge at such gatherings seems to be, always, to get as much as possible for either Sierra Leone or Liberia. The situation has not changed significantly in the post-Tolbert era. Indeed, it is getting worse. Commander Doe of Liberia has started evicting 'foreigners' in government employment in Liberia. About 90 per cent of all those affected are Sierra Leoneans who had lived all their lives in that country. Finally, it would seem as if the military men do not know what the Mano River Union is all about. All this does not augur well for the future. Obviously, the slow implementation of Union programmes could partly be blamed on this problem.

The suspicions and wranglings are not limited to the inter-governmental level and meetings between officials of the Union. The citizens too, have not been satisfied with their lot within the Union. Sierra Leoneans are seen as invaders and/or foreigners in Liberia and vice-versa. They are also blamed for most of what is wrong in Monrovia. For instance, they are accused of 'sucking the economic life-blood of Liberia',[17] and of responsibility for acts of armed robbery.[18] The mutual antagonism and recriminations came to the open in December 1979. A friendly football match between the national teams of Liberia and Sierra Leone ended in a free-for-all fight between players, supporters and officials of both teams.

The Union's citizens are not only antagonistic towards each other but also towards their respective leaderships. Sierra Leoneans and Liberians do not know exactly what they stand to gain from the Union. They seem to hold the view that the whole affair was a clever design by Tolbert and Stevens to 'boost their egos'. They argue that the only tangible benefit from the Union's nine-year existence is so far the Mano River Union Bridge between Monrovia and Freetown – the bridge cuts the distance between the two capitals from 1110 to 620 kilometres. But even this gain is of little utility to the majority of the citizens of both countries who are mostly illiterate.

Why has the Mano River Union had so little impact on member states and their citizens? There are two broad reasons for this; economic and political. The economic factors have already been discussed, i.e. poverty of the members, lack of local technology and so on. This section will only concentrate, therefore, on the political constraints. First, both Stevens and Tolbert seemed to have a self-interested conception of a sub-regional Union. To both presidents the Union was seen mainly as a political exercise intended to impress the rest of the continent, and the outside world as a rare case of successful cooperation between small developing African nations. According to this line of reasoning, then, the two leaders merely wanted to enhance their image and prestige internationally. They could then use their position to solicit aid from the developed western countries.[19] Second, Stevens and Tolbert saw the Union as an insurance policy against internal revolt and any threat to their personal safety. Accordingly, there was a tacit understanding that each would assist the other in the event of threats to their regimes.

Such expectations did not, however, prevent domestic upheavals in both Sierra Leone and Liberia, or for that matter, attempts on the lives of Stevens and Tolbert. There were serious riots and demonstrations in Sierra Leone in 1977 and again in 1981.[20] Similarly, there were serious riots in Liberia in April 1979 claiming the lives of several hundreds of civilians. Tolbert's regime was almost toppled by the riots. Significantly, though, neither Stevens nor Tolbert went to the other's help by way of sending troops to the other's capital. In 1979, it was Guinea which by that time had not joined the Union that sent troops to Monrovia to keep Tolbert in power.[21] However, Stevens demonstrated his solidarity with Tolbert when he teamed up with Nigeria and the Ivory Coast to mount a campaign of ostracism against the military regime of Master Sergeant Doe which toppled Tolbert's government in April 1980. The consequent strained relations between Stevens and Doe held up some of the programmes of the community for several months.[22]

The Mano River Union, then, has not provided the panacea which its founders thought it would give them. Its operations, moreover, have had very little impact on the rest of the population. The majority of citizens in member countries do not understand, nor are they aware of its existence or its functions. For the handful of enlightened citizenry, the Union is perceived as an instrument of self-aggrandisement by its founders – particularly Stevens and Tolbert (while the latter was still alive). Finally, the Union has neither prevented the overthrow of leaders of member states nor threats to the personal safety of these leaders.

The Mano River Union: External Dependence on the West

External involvement in the Union's affairs predated its formal institutionalisation in October 1973 through the Malema Declaration and subsequent protocols. The Union was itself the product of an interdisciplinary committee set up by the United Nations Development Programme (UNDP) in response to requests from the governments of Sierra Leone and Liberia for assistance 'in achieving economic cooperation with closer economic, social and cultural ties (sic).' In its final Report, the committee of experts made the following recommendations to the two countries:

 (i) the establishment of a Customs Union
 (ii) policies for cooperation in agriculture and industry
 (iii) follow-up studies and assistance needed to attain the objectives envisaged between the two states and finally
 (iv) a programme of action for 1973-1976.[23]

It was obvious even at that initial phase that both member states relied heavily on the UN as a major foreign policy objective. Such reliance was to have serious implications for the Union later. Thus further recourse to external agents – be they international institutions, governments and multinational corporations – was seen as 'normal' by the founding fathers. The result has been the increasing dependence of the members on the world capitalist system. We shall define dependence here as the increasing attachment and/or reliance by the Mano River Union members upon the developed western world. Such dependence may take a variety of forms. However, the most notable are: (i) political, (ii) economic and financial, (iii) cultural.

Such a process has already begun but it will become more pronounced as some of the so-called Union Industries take off and western multinationals become increasingly involved in the activities of the Union through such Union Industries. Alternatively, the multinationals could get involved through the so-called transfer of technology, loans and investments. Besides, particular western countries could be involved as indeed, they have already started to be, through direct grants or loans to the Union, and/or the secondment of technical advisers/experts to specific Union projects. Whatever form western involvement is going to take or has already taken, the members would at least for the foreseeable future, become incorporated into western economic and political orbits. And for the short-term future also, they would depend upon the goodwill of western countries and MNCs for the exccution of the Union's programmes, and perhaps, for the very existence of the Union itself.

A variety of reasons could be advanced in explaining this situation. First, we have the personality traits and idiosyncracies of William Tolbert and Siaka Stevens, the moving force behind the Union, as well as those of the community's first Secretary General, Cyril Bright (a Liberian). Both Tolbert and Stevens were patently conservative and pro-west. Their political, cultural and trade ties were overwhelmingly with the West. Moreover, a large proportion of aid, loans and technical assistance to both countries comes from the west. As for Liberia under Tolbert in particular, political and economic as well as cultural links were exclusively with the United States and a few other western countries. President Tolbert was a descendant of the free slaves who settled in Liberia in 1822, and like all Americo-Liberians,[24] he was extemely pro-west. Under his administration – as well as that of his predecessor William Tubman – western private and public investment was attracted into the country. The MNCs were given a free rein to exploit the country's rich mineral and natural resources; iron ore, rubber and logging. To facilitate their operations, Liberia adopted the US dollar as legal tender. That way, investors could easily export capital and profit at will. Cyril Bright, the Union's first administrative Secretary-General, was himself an Americo-Liberian, rich and conservative. As Planning and Economic Affairs Minister in Liberia, he was in complete agreement with the government over its open-door policy which allowed western MNCs into the country but discouraged links with eastern countries.

Finally, as would be expected, both Sierra Leone and Liberia practise what we can call peripheral capitalist *laissez-faire* economic systems patterned specifically on those of the United Kingdom and the United States respectively. Given these factors, then, Stevens, Tolbert and Bright perceived the involvement of the west as a *sine qua non* for the success of the Union. Bright used his position as Secretary-General of the Union to encourage private and public capital involvement in the Union's activities during his numerous trips to the USA and western Europe. His obsession with the West was so deep that he would persuade the Union to utilise western experts even when their local counterparts were available.[25]

External involvement in the activities of the Mano River Union is divisible into two broad categories: (i) bilateral, and (ii) multilateral. The two categories take various forms:

(a) direct contributions to the Union's budget for specific projects;
(b) through technical assistance, that is, the secondment of experts to the Secretariat; and

(c) through the influence of western experts on some of the Union's schemes such as the Industrial Development Unit.

Both bilateral and multilateral assistance are important for the very existence of the Union and for the execution of its projects. Under bilateral assistance the following countries are the most important donors; the Netherlands, West Germany, the United Kingdom and Austria. Among the multinational agencies, the European Economic Community (EEC) is easily the major contributor followed by UN agencies such as UNDP, UNCTAD, FAO and ILO; the Commonwealth and USAID in that order. It is significant to note that the bilateral and multilateral assistance is almost entirely from the West. The only exception is the UN. But even then, many of the UN's experts, for instance, are either westerners or western-trained. Their advice to the Union would therefore be heavily tinted with western bias. We shall in the next paragraphs examine in some detail external involvement in the Union under bilateral and multilateral assistance. Under the former, we shall deal with the records of West Germany and the Netherlands, while under multilateral assistance the activities of the EEC and the UN are examined.

(i) Bilateral Assistance

The Netherlands

The government of the Netherlands has for long been closely associated with the activities of the Union. However, it was not until 1975 that it began giving assistance to the Union on a regular basis. In that year, it provided $2 m. over a three-year period to be spent on technical experts and equipment. In the 1976/77 fiscal year, the Netherlands provided:

(i) $90 000 for soil surveys under the Union's land resources programme;
(ii) $20 000 for fellowships to Union institutions;
(iii) $56 000 for equipment for those projects to which its experts were attached; and
(iv) it donated equipment (whose amount was not specified) for use by the Interim Telecommunications and Training Programme.

Finally, the government of the Netherlands, had up to the time of writing, provided $109 450 for nineteen scholarships to train nationals of the Union in telecommunications and as forest rangers.[26]

West Germany

West Germany is an important source of bilateral aid to the Union. However, before 1978, all German assistance was channelled through the governments of Liberia and Sierra Leone. In November 1978, the Federal Republic and the Mano River Union signed an agreement aimed at institutionalising the former's aid to the Union. The agreement covered not only aid from the federal government but also assistance from private foundations as well as the German Ministry of Economic Cooperation. The first project to benefit under the new aid scheme was the feasibility study for the Freetown/Monrovia highway by a group of German experts at a cost of $800 000. This was followed by a loan of $35 m. for the construction of the road.[27]

Besides direct government assistance, the German Foundation of Duisberg-Gesechshaft (CDC) has also been helpful. The assistance has in the main been in the form of fellowships to train nationals of the Union either at home or in the Federal Republic. In 1979, for instance, the CDC awarded ten fellowships to the Union for short-term training in Germany in areas to be identified by the Union. Besides, the Foundation has on several occasions also sponsored Union personnel to seminars and symposia organised in the Federal Republic. It is clear from this brief survey of German and Netherlands aid to the Mano River that both countries are bound to be endeared to Union officials as well as to its national governments. In fact, both have spoken very highly of the help the Union is receiving from these friendly countries. In recognition of their 'invaluable' assistance, it has become a convention of the Union to pass resolutions of 'appreciation to donor governments and international organisation'[28] for their help. Such gratitude could only inspire donors to continue their assistance. However, as international relations is by and large a game of give and take, it follows that if the developed countries offer financial and technical assistance to the Union, in return Union members are expected to give a sympathetic ear to any appeals the donors might make either for political support or for access to raw materials and/or markets. This would inevitably lead to their incorporation into the West's spheres of influence.

(ii) Multilateral Assistance

The multinational agencies have been an important source of assistance (financial, economic and technical).[29] Among these agencies, the most prominent are: the European Economic Community and the United Nations. Besides contributions to the annual budgets of the Mano River Union as we would see in detail later, multilateral aid has been for specific Union projects which have already been approved by the Community. For example, the EEC has committed $1.8 m. towards the development of the Full Scale Telecommunication and Postal Training programmes of the Union,[30] $2.36 m. for the Mano River Basin development project and finally, 900 000 units of European Account for the development of an Industrial Development Unit within the Union in the 1978–9 fiscal year.[31]

Unlike the EEC, the UN's assistance has been concentrated on experts; that is, most of the help has been in the form of technical assistance. The following are some of the projects in which the UN and its agencies have featured prominently. UNIDO undertook all the prefeasibility studies for what is now called Union Industries.[32] On the other hand, UNCTAD has provided experts in the fields of trade and customs. The FAO has given steady advice on the agricultural, fisheries research and training programmes of the Union. In addition, the UN agency has been carrying out research into the feasibility of establishing a sardinella industry within the Union. Finally, the UNDP has undertaken aerial surveys of the Mano River Basin for the development of hydroelectric power. The scale of the United Nations involvement in the Union is reflected in its contribution to the Secretariat for 1974, 1975 and 1976, which is estimated at US $1.2 m. Besides, it is projected that the UN and its agencies would assist some eighteen Union projects at an estimated cost of US $20 m. in the programme cycle 1977-81.[33]

Western and external involvement in the Union's activities is undoubtedly on the increase. This opens up a lot of opportunities for western countries and MNCs to dominate the Union economically and politically in the future. At the moment, domination is not obvious to the ordinary observer because most of the Union's projects such as the Union Industries – all financed with western capital – are yet to take off. What is most obvious at the moment is that western experts attached to the Union seek to promote both the political and economic interests of their national governments and the West in general. In future, these very experts could also influence the choice of machinery and equipment for the Union Industries. Since there is a dearth of indigenous technology within the Union, it would be compelled to adopt technology recommended by the experts. The consequent incorporation of the Union and its national government would be complete if the raw materials for the industries are also imported from the West. Under such circumstances, the Union's work could be grounded by:

(i) a decision by the suppliers not to continue to supply raw materials to Union Industries, and
(ii) shortage of foreign exchange to pay for supplies.[34]

To illustrate the inbuilt danger of incorporation and its consequences, we have on Tables 8.1, 8.2 and 8.3 a breakdown of contributions to the Union's budget by western countries and multilateral agencies. The budgets are for fiscal years 1977-8, 1978-9 and 1979-80.

A number of points are obvious from a cursory look at the Union's budgets and the breakdown. The first is that the contributions from member states have increased tremendously from $1 398 240 in 1977-8 to $3 666 384 out of a budget of $4 803 554 in the 1979-80 fiscal year. This is over twice the amount for the 1977-8 fiscal year. The dramatic

Table 8.1 A Breakdown of the 1977-8 Budget Showing Contributions by Member States and External Sources

Total budget for the period 1 July 1977 to 30 June 1978 —	$4 568 901
Total contributions by Union members —	$1 398 240
Contributions from external sources —	$2 823 569

Country by Country Breakdown of External Contributions

	Project	Amount ($)
(a) The Netherlands	(i) Union CIB Project	45 500
	(ii) Middle level forestry training Project	80 000
	(iii) Interim Telecommunications training Project	40 000
	TOTAL	165 500
(b) West Germany	(i) Middle level forestry training Project	20 000
	TOTAL	20 000
(c) The European Economic Community (EEC)	(i) Union Telecommunications training Programme	288 402
	(ii) Mano River Basin Development Project	1 250 000
	(iii) Union Marine training Programme	1 101 667
	TOTAL	2 640 069
(d) Commonwealth Fund for Technical Cooperation (CFTC)	(i) Secondment of experts to Union Secretariat	85 000
	TOTAL	85 000
	Grand total of external contributions to 1977-8 Budget	2 823 569

Table 8.2 The 1978-9 Budget

Total budget	$4 979 554
Members' contributions	$3 493 779
External contributions	$1 485 775

Breakdown of External Contributions to Budget

	Project	Amount ($)
(a) The Netherlands	(i) Union CIB Project	67 750
	(ii) Union Interim Telecommunications Project	12 667
	TOTAL	80 417
(b) The EEC and the Netherlands Government	(i) Union full scale telecommunications training institute	1 015 825
	(ii) Union postal training programme	90 000
	(iii) Union Maritime programme	299 533
	TOTAL	1 405 358
	Grand total of external contributions to 1978/79 Budget	1 485 775

increase in members' contributions would give the impression of more financial sufficiency and self-reliance. This is misleading, however. Most of the contributions by members are themselves loans or grants from the developed countries in the North. As noted previously, the members are all poor and so cannot raise their contributions from domestic sources. A second point worth noting is that assistance from external sources has been concentrated on a relatively few areas or sectors. These are also sectors which would not make an immediate impact on the majority of the citizens. Agriculture has almost been totally neglected: there is not a single item that has been funded by external sources that could be classified as strictly agricultural from the Tables. The final point that emerges from the breakdown of the budgets is that they (the budgets) have remained rather 'stagnant' over the years under review. This is an indication of the pace of progress in the Union. Obviously, expansion has been slow as much of the projects remain on the drawing-board – one reason why it has made so little impact on the lives of the ordinary man in the street or village.

Table 8.3 The 1979–80 Budget

Total budget	$4 803 554
Members' contributions	$3 666 384
External contributions	$ 845 844

Breakdown of External Contributions

	Project	Amount ($)
(a) UNDP	(i) Union Secretariat	26 387
	TOTAL	26 387
(b) The EEC	(i) Union Secretariat	348 000
	(ii) Telecommunications Institute	130 000
	TOTAL	478 000
(c) The Netherlands	(i) Telecommunications Institute	256 127
	(ii) CIC Project	81 450
	TOTAL	337 577
	Grand total of external contributions	845 844

Sources: Mano River Union: Annual Report 1977–8, 1978–9 and 1979–80 (Freetown: Mano River Union Secretariat)

External Dependence on Technology

Although much of the Union's industrial programme is still to take off, there are clear indications that the Union's industries will depend on western technology. This would apply to such projects as the Mano River Basin which would eventually generate electricity for the member states. At the moment, the feasibility studies are funded by the UN and the EEC. Besides, the industrialisation of the Union would bring in its wake increased involvement and opportunities for western MNCs. This in turn would also increase the demand for, and involvement of western technology in the Union. This point is a salient point since there is an almost total absence of indigenous technology in member states. No doubt, the importation of machinery would also be followed by the importation of spares. And presumably also, there would be a need to call for experts from the West to man the machines for some time until local personnel could be trained to handle them. But even if this were to be done eventually, the dependence on the

West would still continue since spare parts could conceivably not be manufactured locally. Furthermore, technology does change involving not only a change of machines but new training for those who would handle them.

Another aspect of the dependency relates to the raw materials to be used in most Union Industries. Take for instance, the glass container industry or the synthetic textile and cotton whose raw materials would obviously have to be imported, most probably from the West. This would again increase the dependence of the members on the West for their economic activities. We have already cited the implications which such dependence has had on the beer industry in Sierra Leone. Unfortunately, so far, neither the Union nor its national governments has shown concern over such a prospect. The members also seem unconcerned about the far-reaching consequences which too much reliance on foreign experts would have on the Union's political and economic independence. This is evident from their decision to employ European experts to design and implement the Union's Industrial Development Unit (IDU). The project manager for instance, a European, was also responsible for promoting the Union's industrial strategy in Europe, and consequently, the work for the unit was done in Europe. Furthermore, it would seem that the Union had no control over the design of the strategy itself. This complete reliance on foreign expertise is rather revealing, given the broad objectives of the Union development strategy:

(i) to establish informal and formal links with all national governments/authorities concerned with industrial development in member states, in order to discuss issues on industrialisation strategies as well as the implementation of particular industries in member states;

(ii) granting technical, administrative, informative and financial know-how to individual entrepreneurs as well as to national authorities;

(iii) to establish strategies for cooperation between the member countries and other ECOWAS states.[35]

Again, it is safe to say that the experts would design a strategy which would favour their national governments in particular, and the West in general.

Union Investment Code: Difficult to Monitor

Our final area of potential incorporation in the future concerns the so-called Union investment incentive code. In a bid to attract investments into the Union the MRU has set out the following incentives:

(i) Union tariff protection when necessary for the period of the investment incentive contracts;
(ii) Unrestricted transfer of funds within and outside the Union for normal commercial purposes;
(iii) drawback duties paid in respect of goods exported from the Union;
(iv) exemption from income tax for a period to be determined by the Union investment commission;
(v) exemption of approved imports of machinery and equipment to be used in establishing the project from duty up to 90 per cent of the dutiable value of such imports;
(vi) exemption of approved imports of raw materials and semi-processed products used in the productive process of the approved investment project from import duty of up to 90 per cent to dutiable value of such imports;
(vii) any other incentive(s) negotiated with the Commission.[36]

The incentives code raises a lot of important issues with regard to the development of the Union members as well as their ability to control the activities of the MNCs in future. From the experience of Liberia with MNCs in the iron ore industry in particular, and the experiences of the Third World generally in controlling MNCs, the prospects for the Mano River Union are bleak indeed. First, as an association of small, poor and technologically backward countries, the Union would depend heavily on the MNCs for revenue in the form of royalties, taxes and duties on imports, and for its technology. However, if imports, for example, are allowed to the Union duty-free, its members would be deprived of a very valuable source of income. Besides, if investors – who are expected to be mainly MNCs – are also allowed to import many of their needs they would not be encouraged to patronise local materials even when they are available. Such a situation would also not encourage the emergence of indigenous technology as was the case in Liberia. To be sure, there would be sustained economic growth but like the Liberian experience in the 1950s and 1960s, it would be growth without development.[37] Union industries as well as those set up by MNCs would merely be enclaves in the national economy. In other words, their impact would not be felt by the majority of citizens.

Another cause for concern over the incentives relates to the provision that investors could repatriate funds within and outside the Union as long as such funds are 'for normal investment purpose'. However, the Commission which would be charged with administering these incentives did not define what 'normal investment purpose' means nor how to qualify for such purpose. In the circumstances, it would be quite easy for foreign investors – and some local ones too – to misuse the facility. Investors could earmark amounts as 'investment money' which they could then transfer to their accounts at home. It would be almost impossible for the commission to track the movement of such money or for that matter, authenticity of invoices presented to it by investors. This was the situation in Uganda before Amin expelled the Asians. What they did, then, was to get Central Bank clearance to take out money earmarked for 'normal business purposes' and buy machines/equipment which have been reconditioned at inflated prices. The machines/equipment would eventually be imported into the country but would, in most cases, never be used. However, the excess money from the transaction would have been deposited in the businessman's account abroad. It is conceivable that such a scenario would be repeated in the Mano River Union unless the investment incentives are rigorously policed and/or modified. If they are not modified there would be serious consequences for members of the Union:

(i) low revenues from taxes and royalties
(ii) the drain on scarce foreign exchange, and
(iii) their increasing dependence on the west and their MNCs for economic and political survival.

Conclusion

This chapter has tried to assess the performance as well as the objectives of the Mano River Union since its inception nine years ago. The conclusions that emerged from the analysis are:

(i) that the Union has not met the expectations of its founders in that it has not promoted the industrialisation nor the technological advancement of its members;
(ii) that its activities so far have not reached down to the ordinary man in the street or village;
(iii) that one reason for its poor performance is that, it was among other things, conceived by Stevens and Tolbert as a vehicle for their personal aggrandisement;
(iv) that in spite of its rather slow development there are clear signs that the Union will in the future enhance the dependence of its members – Sierra Leone, Liberia and Guinea – on the developed countries of the North. There are a variety of reasons for reaching such a conclusion. First, much of the Union's work has depended

upon finance and technical assistance from western countries and multilateral agencies. Second, much of the technology that would be used in the Union would eventually also come from the West. At the moment, western experts are busy preparing the way for such a situation. Finally, the poverty of the members – both in financial and human resources – has compelled them to accept aid from the West indiscriminately.

There seems to be no easy way out of the present situation. Since the members do not have the finances nor the technology to embark upon projects without external involvement, they would have to continue to rely on the developed countries even for the very existence of the Union. This development seems to negate one of the basic objectives for setting up the Union, to enable the members to be self-reliant economically and technologically. One way of reducing the influence of external factors in the Union's affairs is for the members to put in more local resources. They should also try to avoid unnecessary employment of western experts in the Union. They should encourage local experts by giving them tasks which they could handle competently. At the moment, the practice is for the Union to recruit experts from abroad even in areas where local counterparts could be obtained. Such a situation does not promote self-reliance and self-sufficiency in the economic, technological or political spheres. Until the Union is able to rely on its own resources for its activities, it will not be able to cut itself free from dependence on the west. At the same time, it could neither promote the economic development and industrialisation of its members, nor improve the social welfare of the citizens. In the long run, it would be compelled to disband and give way to the more viable ECOWAS.

Notes

1 *Address by Hon. C.A. Kamara Taylor to the Second Session of the Mano River Union, Ministerial Council* (MRU/MC/2) p. 99 Annex II (Freetown: Secretariat) 4 December 1975.

2 Siaka Stevens, quoted in *Republican Sierra Leone* (Freetown: Government Printer) n.d. p. 8.

3 For more details, see Willy Brandt: *North-South: A Programme for Survival* (Cambridge: Massachusetts, 1980) and *The World Economic Crisis: A Commonwealth Perspective* (London: Commonwealth Secretariat, 1980).

4 See for instance, the *OAU Lagos Plan of Action* (Lagos: Nigeria 1980) and *Plan of Action for the Implementation of the Monrovia Strategy for Economic Development* (Addis Ababa: ECA Secretariat, 1980).

5 For more details see Amadu Sesay: 'Societal inequality, ethnic

heterogeneity and political instability: The case of Liberia', in *Plural Societies*, Vol, II, No. 3, Autumn 1980, pp. 15–30.

6 Figures are from the *1980 World Atlas* (Washington: World Bank, 1980) p. 8. I should point out though, that growth rates alone are not necessarily indices of economic development.

7 For more details on the orthodox arguments about the utility of customs arrangements among developing countries, see Sidney Dell: *A Latin American Common Market*? (London: Oxford University Press, 1966), R.G. Lipsey: 'The theory of customs union. A general survey' in *the Economic Journal* 70, No. 279, September 1960; C.A. Cooper and B.F. Massell, 'Towards a General Theory of Customs Union for Developing Countries', *Journal of Political Economy*, Vol. LXXIII, October, 1965, No. 5; Felipe Pazos, 'Regional integration of trade among less developed countries', *World Development* 1, No. 7, July 1973, pp. 1–3; B.W.T. Mutharika: *Toward Multinational Economic Cooperation in Africa* (New York: Praeger, 1972), and finally Jacob Viner, *The Customs Union Issue* (New York: Carnegie Endowment for International Peace, 1950).

8 *Technical Cooperation Programme, FAO Agro-Industrial potential and problems of technology transfer, Mano River Union* (E/CIT/WC/IX. 5) (Accra: FAO Regional Office, 1979) p. 3, paragraph 2.1.

9 *Ibid.*, paragraph 2. 1.

10 For a more optimistic and semi-official assessment of the Mano River Union, See F.B.L. Mansaray, 'The growth of the Mano River Union' in *Regional Cooperation in Africa: Problems and Prospects* (Addis Ababa: the African Association for Public Administration, 1977) pp. 61–67.

11 See *Press Release* (Freetown: Mano River Union Secretariat [Hence MRU] no date, for more details.)

12 See *Ad hoc committee of experts from CEAO, ECOWAS, Mano River and MULPOC-ECA* (First meeting) (Freetown: Mano River Union Secretariat) 18–20 September, 1980, p. 3.

13 Although Liberia did not experience European-type colonialism, she was nonetheless colonised by the free slaves from America who settled in the country in 1822. See M.B. Akpan, 'Black imperialism: Americo-Liberian rule over the African peoples of Liberia, 1841–1964', *Canadian Journal of African Studies,* Vol. 7, No. 2, 1973.

14 *World Bank Development Report 1980* (Washington: World Bank, 1980) p. 154.

15 Between May 1981 to October 1981, intra-union trade, mainly the supply of confectionary from Freetown to Monrovia, totalled Le 147 000. This is roughly £74 000. See *West Africa* 19 October 1981, p. 2451.

16 Jacob Viner, *The Customs Union Issue*, (New York: Carnegie Endowment for International Peace, 1950) p. 26.

17 *West Africa*, December 17, 1979, pp. 2352–2353.

18 The writer was in Monrovia for three months in 1976. He witnessed some of the scenes of anti-Sierra Leonean feeling among Liberians. For instance, the inter-city bus from Freetown to Monrovia was booed on several occasions by Liberian youth who chanted 'Rogues', 'Rogues'.

19 Discussions with former Mano River Union official who wishes to remain anonymous, in Nigeria, 1982.

20 In 1977 students at Fourah Bay College, Freetown, booed Siaka Stevens during the convocation ceremony at the University. That action triggered a series of anti-government demonstrations by university, secondary school and primary school students. Their action nearly brought the government down. It did, in fact, force a general election that year. In September 1981, the Sierra Leone Labour Congress called for a general strike against the government. The call was not heeded by the entire Labour force but it shook the government of Siaka Stevens so much that a Commission of Enquiry was set up later to look into the activities of the Congress.

21 Tolbert invoked a mutual non-aggression and defence pact he had signed with President Toure in December 1978 during a state visit to Monrovia by the Guinea leader.

22 The strained relations between the two leaders led to the postponement of the implementation of the intra-union protocol which was to have come into effect on 1 July 1980. It was subsequently implemented nearly a year later, in May 1981.

23 See *Short Historical Background to the Mano River Union* (Freetown: MRU Secretariat) no date, pp. 6–7.

24 The term Americo-Liberian is used to describe the descendants of the free slaves who first settled in Liberia in 1822, to distinguish them from the indigenous Africans.

25 For instance, he was said to have hired a group of ILO officials in Freetown to carry out a study on the manpower requirements of the Union and its national governments. The ILO officials were embarrassed by the request because they knew that there were nationals available to do the job. In their Report, they mentioned that what they had done for the Union could easily have been done by local experts. Discussions with former Mano River Union official, Nigeria, 1982.

26 All the figures are taken from *Mano River Union: Annual Report,* for 1977–8, 1978–9 and 1979–80 (Freetown: MRU Secretariat) p. 12.

27 *Annual Report 1979–1980* (Freetown: Mano River Secretariat) p. 16, no date; see also: Amadu Sesay: 'The Liberian Revolution: Forward March, Stop; About-face Turn', in *Conflict Quarterly* vol. III, no. 4, Summer 1983, pp. 48–71 and M.B. Akpan, *op. cit.* (note 13 above), pp. 217–336.

28 See for instance, MRU/MC/5/Resolution LXXI (third ed.) pp. 92–3 (Freetown: MRU Secretariat) 8–11, May 1978.

29 Figures in this section are from *Mano River Union: Annual Report 1978/79* (Freetown: MRU Secretariat)

30 *Annual Report 1978–1979* (Freetown: Mano River Secretariat) p. 16.

31 *Annual Report 1977–1978* and *Annual Report 1978–1979*, p. 12 and p. 16 respectively.

32 *Annual Report, 1977–1978*, p. 12.

33 For more details see F.B.L. Mansaray, *op. cit.* (see note 11 above).

34 The author was in Freetown for five days in mid-May 1982. He discovered during that time that the price of Star Beer had more than doubled.

The reason for this, he was told later, was that there was no foreign exchange to import the hops to make other brands of beer such as Heineken. And between May and June 1982, Guinness Stout was missing in many shops in Nigeria. The reason again, is that there is no malt in the country to make Guinness. Malt is imported from the Irish Republic.

35 *E/CIT/WC/IX.8 Annex 2*, p. 3 (Freetown: MRU Secretariat) 27 October, 1980.

36 *MRU/MC/Special 1* (Freetown: MRU Secretariat) 12-15 April, 1976, pp. 58-9.

37 See R.W. Clower et al., *Growth without Development* (Evanston: Northwestern University Press, 1966) and G. Lanning with M. Mueller, *Africa Undermined* (Harmondsworth: Penguin, 1979) especially chapter on 'Liberia and the mining companies', pp. 257-76.

9 Transnational Corporations and Regional Integration

Ralph I. Onwuka

The continued expansion in the activities of transnational corporations (TNCs) in the West African subregion has been significant and controversial. This is mainly because of divergences in the interests of the two dominant parties concerned: the centre-based TNCs and their host countries in the West African periphery. If the latter intend to develop their weak and unstable economies through self-reliance, they will inevitably need capital and techology which are not easily available within the periphery. If, on the other hand, the host countries decide to welcome the TNCs which most do, then the profit-motivated interests of the foreign investors are likely to run into conflict with the development-orientated motives of their hosts. This is the dilemma confronting West African leaders.

Regional integration in West Africa can be seen, then, as a collective response to this dilemma. The development problems of the subregion include how to acquire, organise and utilise needed external resources whilst seeking to minimise external intervention in the development process. Regional integration, not in the orthodox Mitrany[1] sense, is an approach to collective development which simultaneously seeks to minimise foreign involvement.

Reasoning almost on the same lines as Aaron Segal,[2] Richard Lipsey[3] and Philip Ndegwe,[4] various United Nations (UN) agencies (particularly the Economic Commission for Africa (ECA), the European Economic Community (EEC), and the Organisation of African Unity (OAU), have variously regarded regional integration and subregional economic integration as a necessary condition for achieving self-sufficiency in food production, in generating appropriate technology and in realising industrial development. Furthermore, integration is seen as a way to control the exploration and extraction by TNCs of natural resources of a given area. Thus the general belief has spread that regional integration creates the potential for self-generating development. In a region at the periphery, like West Africa, regional integration is also expected to lessen the prevailing high level of dependence on the developed economies, especially on the market economies of the former colonial powers, and on the TNCs.

The purpose of this chapter is to assess the role of the TNCs in the West African development-orientated integration processes, and thus to confront the question of whether the TNCs are propellers of economic advancement or agents of affliction in the West African political economy. Are the TNCs, on the one hand, and the West African economic organisations (or their participating states), on the other hand, 'partners in development'? It is difficult to give a definite and clinical answer to this rather complex and intricate question. In the process of attempting to analyse the role of the TNCs in West African integration for development, I hope to advance the debate to which Samir Amin, Joseph Nye, Robert Keohane, Immanuel Wallerstein and more recently, Sanjaya Lall, Paul Streeten, Tim Shaw and a host of others, have already in various ways contributed. In treating this question, the chapter will, in a rather moderate tone, conclude prescriptively by suggesting ways of curbing, and where necessary controlling, the excesses of the TNCs in the bid to achieve more inward-looking development in the subregion. To this end, it is suggested that the Economic Community of West African States (ECOWAS) should be recognised and treated as the most powerful organ available to effect more truly regional control of the activities of the TNCs.

Development, Integration, and Transnationals in West Africa

Regional integration deals predominantly with a hierarchy of issues, interests, and institutions, and sometimes the input of transnational actors to the process is underrated. Shaw has observed in chapter 1 that *dependentistas* are critical of integration and the notion of unilineal progress, and so advocate disengagement as a prerequisite for development. What seems to be a weakness of an orthodox approach to regional integration is its neglect of 'the political economy of outcomes and distribution.'[5] We shall return to this later.

Regional integration in West Africa, as in other developing areas, is development-orientated integration in the sense that development goals constitute the central objective as well as the driving force in all joint economic activities in the region. Thus the concern of this chapter is not 'political' but 'economic' integration in the region. The latter involves 'the suppression of discrimination between economic units'.[6] Such a dynamic process 'pre-suppose(s) the unification of monetary, fiscal, social and counter-cyclical authority whose decisions are binding for member states'.[7] The level and scope of economic integration depends, therefore, on the nature of the 'restrictions' removed, so that the more restrictions that are removed between component units (states) the higher the level of economic integration. Conversely, the fewer restrictions removed the lower the level of integration.

The existing economic interactions in West Africa could be classified into three.[8] The lowest level is the cooperation level where various joint implementation programmes and policies are executed. At this level there is a cluster of such integration activities as the Cocoa Producers Alliance (CPA), African Groundnut Council (AGC), West African Rice Development Association (WARDA), Inter-African Coffee Organisation (IACO), Organisation pour la Mise en Valeur du Fleuve Sénégal (OMVA), Lake Chad Basin Organisation, and River Niger Basin. At this primary level, the organisations are principally formed in order to confront collectively common development problems such as the provision of energy, paucity of food supply and production, increasing the fertility of arid land and enhancing the navigability of rivers. Actions taken against these difficulties include the coordination of study programmes for the development and rational exploitation of basin resources or (in the cases of AGC, CPA, and WARDA) to ensure through joint action remunerative prices for the export products of the participating states.

In the second group are found a few economic organisations, some of which are now defunct, aimed at promoting intraregional trade by excluding third parties through the erection of tariff walls. The interim organisation of 1965 and the Articles of Association of 1967 were attempts which failed to materialise into a free trade area. But alive and effective are the Communaute Economiques de l'Afrique de l'Ouest (CEAO) and its monetary wing, Union Monetaire Ouest Africaine (UMOA). In article 2 of the Treaty establishing the CEAO the members agreed to instal a common external tariff with regards to both the customs and fiscal duties levied by states.

In the third group is ECOWAS, which is designed to mature into a common market by 1990. This is the highest level of integration when compared with the other two types discussed above. In this regard constant reference will be made to ECOWAS because it is the only truly regionwide economic organisation in West Africa due to its wide spread of membership in both linguistic and geographical senses.

The objectives of ECOWAS range from the liberalisation of quantitative and qualitative restrictions on trade, capital and labour to the harmonisation of agricultural, economic, industrial, and monetary policies; as well as the joint implementation of programmes to be financed from the Fund for Cooperation, Compensation and Development. From the nature and content of the objectives of the above-mentioned economic ventures in West Africa, it becomes obvious that a number of strategic factors still belie the implementation of the set intentions. These factors include finance to carry out the various development programmes, technology to manufacture, handle and transport products, and securing access to large markets for particular products, as well as the organisational setting necessary for the efficient performance of the above.

Before Independence

Those corporations with subsidiaries in the West African periphery, with headquarters in one or two of the centres of the world system, and engaging in transnational interactions of various types – for example in information, labour, capital, management and marketing – are for the purposes of this chapter regarded as TNCs. The early colonial powers in the region (Britain, France, Portugal and Spain) dominated the business activities in their respective areas of governance. So that, in the former British West Africa, for example, other than the Royal Niger Company, such Manchester-based companies as John Walkden and Liverpool-centred John Holt dominated business activities particularly in distribution and industry.[9] Aside from distribution and trade, there was a marked interest in mining and through such large concerns as the Ashanti Goldfields Corporations (1897), the Sierra Leone Consolidated African Selection Trust (1932; later the Sierra Leone Selection Trust, 1935), and Amalgamated Tin Mines of Nigeria Limited (1939). Monopoly super-profits were guaranteed for the imperial centres at the expense of the colonies.[10]

In French West Africa a similar but more centralised pattern of domination over the colonies prevailed. Mining, manufacturing and distribution activities were dominated by either the government aid agencies, such as Fonds d'Aide et de Co-opération (FAC) and Caisse Centrale de la Coopération Economique (CCCE), or by other Paris-based corporations that benefited directly from these aid agencies. Liberia, though not officially colonised, has had a business life equally dominated by an American-based firm, the Firestone Rubber Company, which has run the country's rubber plantations and various manufacturing and distribution enterprises. Thus the period before the independence of most West African states in the 1960s was the high watermark in the era of bilateral and very unequal centre-periphery connections.

After Independence

From the 1960s onwards, non-colonial OECD countries, notably Japan, emerged as serious competitors to the established imperial centres of Paris, London and Lisbon. Between 1960 and 1971 Japanese overseas direct investment in Africa increased fifteen times, from $45 m.[11] It is notable that Japan, as a resource-deficient country, concentrated larger percentages of its direct investment in Africa in extractive industry than did other centre states. And by 1970 the value of the foreign subsidiaries and branches of the United States-based corporations was more that $65 billion.[12] Petroleum, copper, iron, bauxite, phosphate, and gold operations have been the major targets of transnational activity in Nigeria, Ivory Coast, Liberia, Sierra Leone, Ghana to mention a few (see Table 9.1). In the early years of independence, the monopoly of the TNCs in extractive

Table 9.1 Some Transnational Corporations in West Africa

Host Country	Enterprises wholly or partly owned or controlled by TNCs	Nature of Enterprises
Nigeria	Coutinho, Caroy & Co., ITT, Julius Berger, Solen-Boneh, Dumez, UAC (Nigeria)	*manufacturing* (construction, telecommunication, distribution)
Senegal	Taiba	*extractive* (phosphates)
Ivory Coast	Energie electrique de Côte d'Ivoire	*extractive*
Ghana	Lonrono, CAST, Union Carbide, Aluminium Company of America (ALCOA), The Volta Aluminium Company (VALCO)	*extractive* (gold, bauxite, diamonds, aluminium, manganese)

Table 9.1 Cont'd.

Host Country	Enterprises wholly or partly owned or controlled by TNCs	Nature of Enterprises
Sierra Leone	Sierra Leone Petroleum Refining Co., National Diamond Mining Co., Sierra Leone Rutile, Sierra Leone Ore and Metal Co. NATCO-member of T. Choitram Group of Companies, Sierra Leone Oxygen Factory, Aureol Tobacco Company, Feetown Cold Storage	*refining* extractive (petroleum, diamonds, iron ore) *manufacturing*
Liberia	The Liberian American Swedish Minerals Company (LAMCO), The Deutsche Liberian Mining Company (DELIMCO), Liberian Iron and Steel Corporation (LIMSCO), Liberia Mining Company, National Iron Ore Company	*extractive* (iron ore)
Mauritania	Compagnie Miniera du fe Mauritanie (Iferma) controlled by the Bureau francais de recherches géologiques et minière (Bram) and Societé Minière de Mauritania (Somina)	*extractive* (iron and copper)
Guinea	Compagnie des bauxite de Guinea, des mines de fer de Guinea	*extractive* (bauxite and iron ore)
Nigeria	Shell/BP, Esso, Mobil, Agip, Safnap, Minatone	*extractive* (petroleum and uranium)

Sources: L. Rood, 'Nationalisation and Indigenisation in Africa', *Journal of Modern African Studies; African Contemporary Record, 1975/76* and *1977/78; African Research Bulletin*, 1971; *West Africa*, 31 March 1980.

businesses was first threatened and then broken by most participating governments. Mining of non-renewable resources became a sensitive issue in the exercise of sovereignty of the new nations; hence the patriotic wave of nationalisation or indigenisation policies in the region.[13] In services or distributive areas – particularly in petroleum distribution, banking and insurance – foreign participation is conceded only where foreign technical input is imperative. This is the case in petroleum distribution in Nigeria and Sierra Leone where continued reliance on foreign expertise has made a mockery of the apparent government take-over of the dominant shares in the respective mining industries. In terms of the manufacturing sector, the TNCs usually establish subsidiaries in the sub-region which are operated within a wider global framework in a vertical monopoly position. Thus products manufactured elsewhere are found readily in many West African markets. This is the case with a number of household goods (e.g. Omo washing powder, Blue Band margarine, Astral soap, Gibbs toothpaste) distributed in the subregion by numerous subsidiaries of Unilever.

In post-colonial West Africa it could be said that the activities of the TNCs have intensified, instead of diminishing, as their direct investment met in most cases with investment conditions which they perceive as favourable. This positive attitude can be attributed to two major features. First, members of the ruling class have happily become 'agents' or 'carriers' for the TNCs in the area. Wallerstein[14] has argued, supported by Cooperstock, that the central prevailing contradiction is 'between the interests organised and located in the core countries and their local allies on the one hand, and the majority of the population on the other'. Cooperstock[15] rightly observed, in support of such established views, that 'the subordination of African states to the requirements of the world economy represents the familar pattern of the 'development of underdevelopment'. These 'agents' of 'underdevelopment' have been vexatiously referred to by Shehu Umar Abdullahi in a recent lecture, as those who

> do everything within their ability to justify even the unjustifiable as long as it can help the western world. They are mentally sick and intellectually dwarf. They employ their intellect to defend whatever they know can help their western material masters even when that can clearly wreck or weaken the economy of their fatherland.[16]

The second factor is not unconnected with the first: namely, TNCs have a relative monopoly of supply of both capital and technology. Thus, with an efficient network of marketing and organisational facilities, they acquire the capacity to spread a capitalist mode of production in the subregion, usually on their own terms. And because their activities are profit-based they tend to concentrate more in areas of high returns than those more functional for development. Thus in 1971 there were more transnational activities in Liberia than in Mali. Table 9.2 shows that direct investment in West Africa, as a percentage of Gross National Product, is highest in the former and lowest in the latter. Also in 1972, direct investment in Nigeria, which is the fourth on the ranking scale, totalled $2.1 billion. The largest single piece of this was held by Shell-BP whose investment in the country at the time amounted to 7 per cent of all foreign investments in Africa.

Transnationals also dominate all stages of scientific and technological processes. They invest extensively in research and development (R & D) and own most of the patents granted and registered in periphery countries. The dominance relationship between the TNCs and West Africa is reinforced by the superior management, distributive network, and bargaining power of the former over the latter. The TNCs have gained an efficient organisational network

Table 9.2 Stock of Foreign Direct Investments as Percentage of GNP in West African States (1969 & 1971)

Country	Year 1967 %	Year 1971 %	Rank
Liberia	125	100	1
Mauritania	65	73	2
Guinea	30	39	3
Nigeria	21	22	4
Togo	21	21	5
Senegal	19	17	6
Ivory Coast	19	17	7
Ghana	15	15	8
Sierra Leone	18	13	9
Benin	10	8	10
Gambia	10	6	11
Niger	8	6	12
Upper Volta	6	5	13
Mali	2	2	14

Compiled from Carl Widstrand (ed.), *Multinational Firms in Africa* (Stockholm: Almqvist & Wiksell, 1975) 84.

through experience and research and a high entrepreneurial ability through their international operations. These attributes are very significant compared with developing countries' standards. The resulting asymmetrical relationship between the parties – the sellers and buyers of technology – is perpetuated further by the buyers' inability to 'clarify supply and demand conditions in the international flow of advanced knowledge or to articulate their requirements adequately',[17] an issue well treated by Leff in his study on technology transfer and US foreign policy, in *ORBIS*, 1979.

In West Africa, many of the transnational interactions are with states themselves rather than with particular organisations. This is because until the recent past when ECOWAS was formed, there was no truly West African economic community capable of providing the *point d'appui* for the needed action and discourse on the TNCs. Thus one could safely say that regional integration in West Africa has not matured into a condition comparable to that in Central America or Europe where collective measures are readily applied towards foreign corporations. The prevailing low level of integration in West Africa has made bargaining with TNCs state-centric to date. Because of this characteristic of regional integration in West Africa much of the discourse in this chapter will be based on state-TNC relationships. But where and when necessary, references will be made to the CEAO or ECOWAS or to other economic organisations in the development integration process.

Growth: Rationale for Co-existing with TNCs

Some renowned and consistent nationalists have acknowledged that they are helpless to operate an open economic policy towards the TNCs. This is because, it is argued, they are eager to develop their economies, and so a measure of dependence on the transnationals for capital and technology is almost inevitable. President Nkrumah of Ghana, despite his socialist leanings, rationalised his dealings with western capitalism thus:

> It was considered in the circumstances of the time that the undertaking of joint ventures with already operating capitalist concerns was better than the alternative of economic blockade by the West and the consequent lack of development until the assistance of the socialist states could be procured and becomes operational.[18]

To Nkrumah, therefore, intercourse with the western-based TNCs was temporary and functional. In his book, *Neo-Colonialism*,[19] Nkrumah further explained how development-orientated and independent actions are constrained and indeed determined by international finance. For instance, his desire to develop the Volta River multipurpose scheme which was regarded as essential to the overall industrialisation of Ghana, forced Nkrumah into accepting the technological and financial services of the United States-based consortium, the Volta Aluminium Comany (VALCO). Nkrumah and Ghana are not alone in this reluctant admission of the inevitability of international technology and finance in national or regional growth processes. Each West African government has tended to welcome foreign investments (both direct and portfolio), based on the argument that it was in a hurry to develop. Having argued that capital and technology are the major determining factors in coexisting with the TNCs, it is necessary to explore how these resources relate to the economic growth of the subregion.

Dependence on International Finance and Technology: Who Gains?

It would seem that development integration will be slowed down without international capital and technology. This is sometimes true. For example both the expertise and the capital needed to produce a detailed map of Lake Chad and its perimeter were supplied by Britain in 1972. And it was France that has supplied much of the financial, technological and administrative backbone needed by OMVS, and when French assistance was incapable of satisfying all OMVS needs, advances were made to Abu Dhabi, Saudi Arabia, and other countries. This was the case, for instance, in the $1 billion needed for the construction of two dams.[20] In similar manner, the World Bank has supported the activities of the inter-governmental cement industry, Cimens de l'Afrique l'Ouest (CIMAO). Air Afrique was established in 1961 by eleven OCAM States in partnership with a French consortium (SODETAF),[21] one of the TNCs that has undertaken joint ventures with mainly Francophone West African economic organisations. It would seem that at the intergovernmental level, TNC involvement in the provision of capital and technology is less significant than their involvement at national level. Examples abound in TNC involvement in national growth as opposed to regional development.

We have argued that most leaders in West Africa regard the role of international finance and technology (supplied by TNCs, governments or international financial institutions) as a necessary condition for national economic growth. This is particularly so when the foreign corporations supply the initial capital outlay for the operations of various development ventures. The TNCs also contribute, as in the case of Nigeria for example, in providing or aiding in the supply of additional revenue from profit-sharing, taxation and royalties, and customs, excise and sales duties. With respect to those TNCs – and they are plentiful – involved in mining operations, Greg Lanning and Marti Mueller have rightly observed that 'taxes are the main linkage between the mines and host economy.'[22] For the 1979–80 financial year, for instance, Nigeria realised a sum of over ₦12 billion from customs and excise, petroleum profit tax, mining royalties and company earnings tax. Of course, revenue from petroleum profit tax yielded the dominant share of over half of the grand total as shown in Table 9.3.

It is noteworthy that the realised petroleum profit tax jumped to a higher total than either the revised or approved estimates, an indication that with an increase in petroleum-mining activities and

Table 9.3 Nigeria's Revenue (Estimated and Collected) from Direct Taxes, and Customs and Estimates 1979–80

Revised Estimates	Approved Estimates	Collected Revenue
Customs and Excise ₦1 429 798 323	1 240 639 190	1 208 004 000
Direct Taxes		
Petroleum Profit Tax 6 098 029 044	4 784 500 000	6 687 350 000
Mining, Rent and Royalty 2 217 175 000	1 552 545 000	2 122 180 000
Earnings and Sales 27 897 370	27 897 370	1 737 888 000
Company Tax 525 182 000	525 182 000	540 002 000
		₦12 115 424 000

Source: *Business Times* (Lagos, 22 April 1980), p. 1.

indeed price, the profits of the producing companies rose by an even greater percentage, a possible indication that the corporations benefited more than the host country. Thus an *ex post facto* argument could be raised: that Nigeria could have benefited more without (rather than with) international finance and technology. Perhaps the inceptive outlays could be delayed if not halted but in the process the host country may be forced to generate locally embodied technology adapted to the extractive circumstances of the area. In the end, an external dependence relationship with the TNCs would have been replaced by one of interdependence, so that the terms for TNC participation would be determined by internal not external factors.

Terms of Agreement between TNCs and Host West African Countries

Whatever a West African host country realises from direct taxes and customs and excise depends on the prevailing tax regime and ongoing agreements between the host country and the TNCs concerned. Sometimes the host country has had reasons to seek revision of the ongoing agreement. In French West Africa, the French metropolitan agencies FAC and CCCE were useful in transferring capital from France to West Africa through the TNCs. By 1970 eight large French TNCs had procured 50 per cent of the CCCE's development fund. In course of time this triangular relationship met with the disapproval of such countries as Benin, Guinea and Mauritania.[23]

This system of tripartite deals complicated the relationship between the host country and the TNCs. In addition, it introduced political consideration into the operation of the system. Understandably, Niger[24] preferred a direct partnership with such TNCs as Esso and Texaco for oil exploration and with SOMAIR, a French-German-Italian consortium, for uranium prospecting. Senegal, a democratic socialist state, would like indigenes to take a more active role in the private sector which is strongly tied to French multinational concerns operating basically in the French industrial zone in Dakar. Senegal has a 50–50 deal in most of its ventures with TNCs (e.g. MIFERSO); Guinea has a more radical relationship with the TNCs within its borders. It has 51 per cent in the Boke mining project vested in the Compagnie des bauxite de Guinea. The Mauritania People's Party (PPM) has a 'Party Charter' which defines the government's policy towards TNCs. This charter, *inter alia*, provides for the nationalisation of key sectors in the economy. And in keeping with the PPM doctrine, SOMINA[25], a largely British-owned company, was nationalised in 1975.

Nigeria has developed more stringent rules guiding foreign participation in businesses than either Liberia or Nkrumah's Ghana. Under the 1977 Nigerian Enterprises Promotion Decree, oil milling, mining and quarrying fall under enterprises in Schedule 2 in respect of which Nigerians must have at least 60 per cent equity interest.[26] Such a decree should, allowing for the international financial practices of foreign investors, reduce the 'take home' or the net transfers of these TNCs operating in the mining sector.

Sometimes the superior bargaining power of the participating TNC or the eagerness of the host country to harness international finance can result in unequal contracts. The Ghana-VALCO agreement seems to be of this type. The agreement made provisions that compelled the Ghanaian government to institute fiscal provisions which allowed VALCO a long-term tax relief which in effect allowed the company 'to operate outside the general legislation of the country'[27] for the euphemistic reason of attracting foreign investment. The London-based weekly, *West Africa,* has revealed in detail that

> Tax relief under the Pioneer Industries and Companies Act permitted VALCO to avoid tax for up to ten years either to recover an amount equivalent to the paid-up shares capital ($12 m) or an amount equal to half of the total capital cost of the smelter. Schedule C, dealing with tax stabilisation, was even more generous. When income tax did become payable, it was to be calculated at the rate applicable in 1961 and it was to be fixed at this rate for the duration of the contract. The rate was to be 40 per cent on retailed profits and 2.5 per cent on retailed profits transferred out of Ghana.[28]

The position in Liberia was similar to that in Ghana. In addition to a generous tax regime, the agreements establishing the principal mining concessions in Liberia ranged between 30 and 80-year term periods. LAMCO, a joint venture between the Liberian, American and Swedish Mineral Company and Bethlehem Steel Corporation was to pay 50 cents per ton royalty in 1963-4 and thereafter 50 per cent of the net profit.[29]

The Ghanaian and Liberian concessionary agreements are good examples of unequal contracts which were detrimental to the development effort of the countries concerned. It would seem that though these two agreements had almost identical effects, they were prompted by different motives. On the one hand, Nkrumah was perhaps influenced by a genuine desire to industrialise Ghana and in the process was hoodwinked by subtle bargaining techniques of the foreign corporations involved. On the other hand, the two recent

Liberian regimes of Tubman and Tolbert were functioning essentially as the *comprador* agents of the American-based company. In effect the Liberian leaders functioned as allies of the TNCs in 'undeveloping' the country.

Profit is the *sine qua non* of continued operations by the TNCs in the world system, including the West Africa sub-culture. Thus where the host government, as in the case of Nigeria, adopts strict rules guiding the operation of TNCs, the transnational concerned might intensify any irregular financial policies in order to reduce risks and uncertainty. Based on a global business strategy the foreign company readily manipulates

> international differences in tax and tariff rates, multiple exchange rates, quantitative restrictions on profits remission, existence of local shareholders, exchange rate instability and the overstating of apparent costs as a means to obtain higher protection against imports.[30]

Where in spite of these financial business practices the corporation is confronted with the possibility of nationalisation, the TNC concerned might decide to go into liquidation or at least curtail operations. The Sierra Leone Development Corporation (DELCO), then a subsidiary of William Baird of Scotland, which began mining iron ore in the country as far back as in 1933, was liquidated in 1975. Also under the intense pressure of the threat of being nationalised as in the Sierra Leonean case, bauxite mining companies in Guinea were forced to cut down operations. Generally, a foreign corporation desiring to commence, expand or liquidate operations in any part of the region usually considers the prevailing investment conditions before making any decision; these include political stability, currency stability, and government policies towards investment and trade. The utility of international finance and technology, particularly in the short-run, is indisputable, but in a development-orientated integration process they are like a two-edged sword, serving two parties in opposite directions. It is possible that the side serving the central interests of the TNCs is sharper and more purposeful than that serving the region and here lies the contradictory or problematic impact of the role of TNCs.

Impact on Employment and Welfare

We have established that international finance and technology usually serve multiple interests; thus the contradiction in the role of the TNCs in the region. Their impact on employment and welfare in the host region is equally contradictory, because of the diverse goals pursued by the parties involved: the TNC, its subsidiaries, and the host country. The TNC determines the mode of production, which determines the technological and capital input and consequently the number of nationals to be employed. Depending on the orientation and intention of the host government, it will hope for a reduction in unemployment and in welfare problems with the operations of TNCs within its borders. But invariably such transnational activities are not directed towards solving these domestic ailments, although it is possible that they could be minimised (and sometimes complicated) as a consequence of the extractive or industrial activities of the foreign companies.

With regard to mining, it has been forcefully argued that:

> The promised direct benefits of mining to employment are reduced by the trend to massive open-cast mines, with their smaller unit production costs and increased capital intensity. The investment of two or three hundred million dollars will establish a mine employing only a few hundred workers.[31]

Thus the mining company referred to above chose to strike a favourable balance between capital and labour in order to lower costs, not to improve the lot of the indigenes of, in this case, Liberia. Employment possibilities are further reduced by the fact that the TNCs need for their global operations a highly specialised cadre of managerial and technical staff not readily secured locally. Generally recruited around the operating areas are poorly-paid unskilled workers needed for construction and allied unskilled processes. Their services are cheap and their employment temporary.

So, in terms of offering either qualitative or quantitative employment to the host country, the effect of the TNC's presence is questionable. Qualitative employment effects of transnational operations are beginning to be positive in those countries (for example, Ghana and Nigeria) where the governments and the foreign companies, under the pressure of the former and the expense of possibly both, have embarked on joint or private technical programmes for the nationals of the host country. Such an understanding could institutionalise dependence on the TNC concerned if the accord does not result in more self-reliant production. Although, as we have argued, the TNCs are not basically concerned with the welfare and employment problems of their host West African countries, nevertheless export-orientated production could still lead to infrastructural development around the industrial or mining zones.

This is particularly so in areas such as petroleum-mining in Nigeria, copper operations in Mauritania, or iron-ore and bauxite-mining in Liberia and Ghana respectively. It is possible for the local communities to benefit (though this seems to be a somewhat marginal spillover) from such facilities as good road and railway system, and electricity, port and water facilities, which otherwise would not have been readily available. Thus Ghana's Volta Scheme, despite its neo-colonial contents, had led to increased fishing and agricultural activities and thus to valuable food protein. However, national policies could negatively affect the net employment results, as in Ivory Coast where the country's 'dual nationality'[32] policy, which accords citizenship rights to Voltaic migrant labour numbering over half the total labour force, has aided in reducing the employment and welfare advantages of transnational activities. In the commercial section in 1979 there were 455 Ivorian directors as against 1572 non-African directors and 2 non-Ivorian African directors.[33] Thus in the Ivorian case, it could be confidently said that TNC operations have had a negative impact on the employment position of the country.

Despite fringe benefits arising from most operations of TNCs, it is possible for these companies to constitute a threat to the lives of the local inhabitants in special or general circumstances. For instance, the oil spillage in the delta region of Nigeria which occurred in early 1980 threatened the lives and livelihood of over half a million people. Equally threatened were people's cultural and pastoral traditions when the mining companies deprive villagers of their land, on which their livelihood wholly depends. In most cases no resettlement exercises could adequately repay the loss.

Other than having destablising effects on the social and cultural order, the TNCs have aided in maintaining and intensifying the unequal distribution of income in each West African state. Before the dramatic execution of President Tolbert,[34] Liberia had remained a classic case of a few families[35] dominating the economic and political life of the country at the expense of the majority of the population. At the locus of economic and political power in almost all West African states are a few people who maintain a symbiotic relationship with the TNCs. These *compradors* sustain and nourish the dominant position of the TNCs *vis-à-vis* the host country. It could also be argued that though TNCs contribute to the provision of the international finance and technology needed in most 'plant' projects, these are sometimes isolated and uncoordinated in both time and space with the general development programmes of the nation or region.

As already indicated, TNCs are mainly interested in maximising returns and minimising costs rather than in the development of the host country *per se*. In addition, a West African integration process that does not duly recognise the impacts (both negative and positive) of the activities of TNCs is bound to be frustrated by the TNCs' extraneous actions. Thus to make self-generated development possible ECOWAS, as the rallying point, should attempt to establish and effect regional policies for the control of TNC activities. In particular it should regulate the generation and utilisation of technology and adopt other necessary steps that would create propitious conditions for more autonomous development.

Regional Policies on TNCs and Technology

There is a need, then, to establish in West Africa more equitable societies where there is no undue concentration of a country's wealth in the hands of a few. Clarence Zuvekas[36] has suggested a number of consistent income redistribution measures which developing states might take. These include fiscal policies, increases in the level of education, agrarian reforms, and industrial development and population policies. Sometimes these policies have proved difficult to pursue due to their related social and political effects. For example, the 1977 Nigerian Land Decree, a positive redistribution policy, was still attracting criticism three years after its promulgation. Changes such as those suggested above would require fundamental and courageous shifts in leadership behaviour and content at the national level. Towards this end, and indeed in the absence of any such changes, ECOWAS could act as the nerve-centre for encouragement and possible action.

ECOWAS itself should be directly concerned with the control of TNC operations and in the adoption of integrated common investment policies in the region. The founding fathers in the Lagos Treaty made inadequate provisions for an evolving Community economic policy. Chapter VII of the ECOWAS Treaty expects a common transport and communication policy to evolve gradually. Article 48 specifically envisages 'consultation' and 'cooperation' in energy and mineral resources while Article 59 permits (economic) relations betweeen members states and third parties, if such links do not 'derogate from the provisions of the Treaty'. It seems that it was not the intention of the founding fathers of the Community to evolve an integrated common economic policy other than to suggest *ad hoc* provisions that would enhance infrastructural links and encourage the coordination of policies on energy and mineral resources.

ECOWAS could learn from the Andean Pact[37] about establishing integrated common investment policies. For the multilateral control of foreign investments in the Andean Community, a common code – Decision 24 – was ratified in June 1971. Article 18 of this Decision regulates that

> any contract regarding importation of technology or regarding use of patents and trademarks shall be reviewed and submitted to the approval of the pertinent agency of the respective member country, which shall evaluate the effective contribution of the imported technology by means of an appraisal of its possible profits, the price of the goods embodying technology or other specific means of measuring the effect of the imported technology.[38]

In addition, licensing agreements for the exploitation of foreign trade marks in the Andean Group cannot contain restrictive[39] clauses (e.g. prohibition or limitation to export or sell products manufactured under certain trademarks or their products in given countries). Importantly, it is a breach of Decision 24 to grant foreign investors more favourable treatment than that granted to national investors. A policy such as that of the Andean Pact would minimise undue competition among the West African countries for foreign investments. Another goal of Community policy towards the TNCs should be not only to avoid inappropriate technology, but also to ensure that the appropriate forms are marketed under acceptable conditions. Such conditions, given an appropriate bargaining situation, should minimise the much-talked-about 'exploitation' of the host country by the TNCs.

Collateral to the above step to curb the excesses of the TNCs is the need for an ECOWAS technology policy to ensure the generation and assimilation of technology resources within the region. Although considerable emphasis has been placed on technology planning at both national and regional levels, very few African countries have integrated technology policies in practice. Rather, most have science and technology policies as integral parts of their respective development plans, whilst their technical and manpower development programmes are defused into several related ministries. Except for Ghana and Nigeria in 1980, there has been no frontal programme in the region to generate technology internally. The Andean Pact is instructive with regard to adopting an integrated regional plan for technology generation. The group's Decision 24 stipulates measures aimed at subregional technology development under conditions of high unemployment. In addition, according to this landmark decision, any imported or locally-generated technology should be evaluated in terms of its effect not only on employment but also on technical development, on specific development plans, on the balance of payments and on the environment.

Problems of Policy Implementation

A major problem to be envisaged in the implementation of any agreed common investment and technology policies in the West African region is that of building the necessary technical resources, and training engineers, architects, accountants, and others who would have to conduct negotiations with foreign as well as Community corporations. Without this cadre of technical experts a second problem – of having a clear grasp of regional technological problems with regard to specific programmes or projects – would persist for a long time. Because of the proven paucity of technical staff required in regional technology building, the initial problem of trying to attract Community-trained personnel for this purpose could generate controversy and continued debate. Member states are bound to weigh their national needs against those of the Community as a whole. Other than this, problems rooted in the distribution of costs and benefits are bound to arise in the implementation of any Community economic policies. Evidence has shown so far that much of the internal bickering with ECOWAS, particularly in its inceptive years, was centred on which state gets or loses what,[40] particularly in the areas of Community finance, staffing and sectoral programmes.

Another problem likely to surface from Community efforts to control and direct the use of international finance and technology is the danger to overbureaucratisation evident in the functioning of the Andean Pact. Overbureaucratisation arises from the multiple layers of decision-making which are unavoidable in cases where the Community has to interact with both the TNCs and with such international institutions as the ECA, IBRO, and IMF, as well as with the member states. This problem also results from the fact that 'most of the bureaucratic apparatus lacks understanding of the content and scope of the decisions'[41] of the Community as is the case in the Andean Pact. However, the merits of instituting regional technology and investment policies outweigh the demerits of such action.

In conclusion, some observations need to be made. First, regional integration in West Africa is still at a primitive stage. Until 1975, there was not a truly regional common market and now ECOWAS is in a vulnerable state, dependent on prevailing circumstances in the region. The result is that many transnational interactions are in fact state-centric. Second, as the result of an absence of strong multilateral economic activities in the sub-region, there exist multifarious rules and regulations guiding international investments. Third, it is obvious that the TNCs, aided by resident *compradors* have in most cases continued to exploit the economic deficiencies of the host countries. The TNCs have used various oligopolistic advantages (e.g. possession of international finance and technology) in exerting in West Africa a dominance relationship with the host countries. Finally, fourth, strong centralising and coordinating action by ECOWAS is imperative: (i) to minimise the effects of the prevailing high dependence on international capital and technology and consequently, (ii) to counteract the negative impact of TNCs on the development of the regional economy to date.

Notes

1   Cf. David Mitrany, *The Functional Theory of Politics* (London Martin Roberts, 1975).

2   Aaron Segal, 'The Integration of Developing Countries: some thoughts on East Africa and Central America' *Journal of Common Market Studies*, 5(4), 1967, pp. 252–282.

3   Richard G. Lipsey, 'The Theory of Customs Union: a general survey' in Melvyn B. Krauss (ed.), *The Economics of Integration* (London: George Allen and Unwin, 1973), p. 57.

4   Philip Ndegwa, *The Common Market and Development in East Africa* (Kampala: East African Publishing House, 1968.

5   Timothy M. Shaw, 'Dependence to (Inter) Dependence: review of debate on the (new) international economic order,' *Alternatives*, 4(4), March 1979, p. 562.

6   B. Balassa, *The Theory of Economic Integration* (London: George Allen and Unwin, 1973).

7   *Ibid*.

8   See details in Ralph I. Onwuka, *Development and Integration in West Africa: The Case of ECOWAS* (Ile-Ife: University of Ife Press, 1982)

9   Anthony G. Hopkins, *An Economic History of West Africa* (London: Longman, 1975), p. 210.

10   *Ibid*.

11   Patrick F. Wilmot, 'Multinational Corporations in Africa' *New Nigerian*, Tuesday 18 April 1978, p. 5.

12   P.B. Evans, 'National Autonomy and Economic Development' in Robert Keohane and Joseph S. Nye (eds) *Transnational Relations and World Politics* (Cambridge: Harvard University Press, 1973), p. 325.

13   See the penetrating study by L. Rood, 'Nationalisation and Indigenisation in Africa,' *Journal of Modern African Studies*, 14(3), 1976.

14   Immanuel Wallerstein, 'Class and Class-conflict in Contemporary Africa' *Canadian Journal of African Studies*, 7(3), 1973, p. 380.

15 Henry Cooperstock 'Some Methodological and Substantive Issues in the Study of Social Stratification in Tropical Africa' in Timothy M. Shaw and Kenneth A. Heard (eds), *The Politics of Africa: dependence and development* (London: Longman & Dalhousie University Press, 1979), p. 24.

16 Shehu U. Abdullahi, 'The Role of the Nigerian Intellectuals in Nation-building,' *New Nigerian*, Tuesday, 18 April 1978, p. 5.

17 N. Leff, 'Technology Transfer and U.S. Foreign Policy: The developing countries' *Orbis*, 23(1), Spring 1979, p. 146.

18 Quoted in *West Africa*, 3271, 31 March 1980, p. 571.

19 Kwame Nkrumah, *Neocolonialism: the last stage of imperialism* (New York: International, 1966).

20 *West Africa*, 3284, 30 June 1980, p. 1173.

21 Each member state contributed 6 per cent of the share capital with the balance held by SODETRAF, *Africa* (London) 52, December 1975, 117.

22 Greg Lanning and Marti Mueller, *Africa Undermined* (Harmondsworth: Penguin, 1979), p. 21.

23 A. Oke, 'The Nation-State and Multinational Corporations: the West African experience', unpublished MA thesis, Department of International Relations, University of Ife, 1979.

24 *African Contemporary Record*, Volume 8, 1975/76 B778.

25 *Ibid*. B762.

26 *Nigerian Enterprise Promotion Decree (1977): Promotion of Nigerian Enterprises* (Lagos: Nigerian Enterprises Promotion Board, July 1977), p. 10.

27 *West Africa*, 3271, 31 March 1980, p. 573.

28 *Ibid*.

29 Lanning and Mueller, *op. cit.*, p. 262 (see note 22 above).

30 Sanjaya Lall and Paul Streeten, *Foreign Investment: Transnationals and Developing Countries* (London: Macmillan, 1978), p. 59.

31 Lanning and Mueller, *op. cit.*

32 Alex Rondos, 'Ivory Coast: the French factor' *West Africa*, 3224, 30 April, 1979, p. 743.

33 *West Africa*, 3222, 16 April 1979, p. 657.

34 On 12 April 1980, President Tolbert was killed in a *coup d'état* which installed Master Sergeant Samuel K. Doe as the Head of State and Chairman of the People's Redemption Council (PRC). See *West Africa*, 3274, 21 April 1980, p. 689.

35 See the analysis in J.G. Liebenow, *Liberia: the evolution of privilege* (Ithaca: Cornell University Press, 1969).

36 Clarence Zuvekas, *Economic Development* (London: Macmillan, 1979), pp. 287–290.

37 The Cartegena Agreement was signed on 26 May 1969 by Bolivia, Chile, Columbia, Ecuador and Peru. On 13 February 1973 Venezuela acceded to the Treaty. The 'Commission', 'Junta' and 'Board' are respectively the plenipotentiary, the decision-making and the technical institutions of the Pact. See Junta del Acuerdo de Cartegena, *Technology Policy and Economic Development* (Ottawa: International Development Research Centre, 1976), p. 7.

38 *Ibid.*, p. 37.
39 Article 25, Decision 24.
40 See Ralph I. Onwuka, 'The ECOWAS Treaty: inching towards implementation', *World Today* (London) 36(2), February 1980, pp. 52–64.
41 Rafael Vargas-Hidalgo, 'The Crisis of the Andean Pact: lessons for integration among developing countries', *Journal of Common Market Studies*, 8(3), March 1979, p. 220.

Part Three

Regionalism in Eastern and Southern Africa: Trials and Failures

10 The End of the East African Community: What are the Lessons for Regional Integration Schemes?

Arthur Hazlewood

Introduction

The East African Community was established in 1967 by the Treaty for East African Cooperation between Kenya, Tanzania and Uganda. The Community of the three partner states formally came into existence on 1 December of that year.[1] No such precise date can be set for the Community's demise, but the middle of 1977, when the partner states failed to approve the 1977–8 budget for the Community comes closest to it. Effectively the Community came to an end earlier that year, soon after the completion by an outside authority of a review of the Treaty and the submission of recommendations, when Kenya set up her own airline and Tanzania closed her border with Kenya. The Community died, therefore, well before its tenth birthday could be celebrated.

This chapter begins by explaining the background of the Treaty for East African Cooperation. It then outlines some main features of the Treaty and analyses the issues which arose between the partner states during the lifetime of the Community. It concludes by posing questions which, it is suggested, it must be possible to answer to the satisfaction of participants if an integration scheme is to succeed.

When the Treaty was signed, after negotiations between the three countries in the Philip Commission, it was widely regarded as an instrument for achieving economic development and progress through cooperation. The Community soon attracted applications for membership or association from neighbouring countries, though not all were serious, and the partner states carried on rather desultory negotiations with the applications for several years. It seemed at one time possible that a zone of cooperation in Eastern Africa could come into existence around the nucleus of the community states, achieving something like the Economic Community of Eastern Africa which the United Nations had earlier been trying to bring into existence.

The United Nations, particularly through its various regional Commissions, has for many years been prominent in propagating the view that regional integration and cooperation is an important device for fostering development, especially industrial development, in the countries of the Third World. There have been many attempts at economic integration in different parts of the Third World, but nowhere has there been even a proposal for a scheme covering so wide a range of activities within so highly organised a system, as that of the East African Community. Yet within a decade the scheme had collapsed, leaving the wreckage of the arrangements in such an atmosphere of hostility and recrimination that two years later the borders beteween Kenya and Tanzania remain closed.[2]

Integration Before the Treaty

It is, in fact, possible to interpret the establishment of the Community not as a stride forward in cooperation but as a stage in a process of disintegration. Although it would be difficult to understand this view from a simple reading of the Treaty, it is comprehensible when the Treaty is seen in its historical context. There had, indeed, been even closer integration of the economies of the three countries before any of them achieved independence. In barest outline, the integration arrangements had comprised a customs union with a common external tariff and free trade between the countries, common customs and income tax administrations, common transport and communications services (railways, harbours, posts, telecommunications, airways), a common university, common research services, and a common currency. By the time the Treaty was signed, however, the common currency had been abandoned, after the failure to find an acceptable system of East Africa-wide central banking, and the operation of the customs union was being seriously inhibited by quantitative restrictions.

The integration arrangements, which had their origins in the early years of the century, could not have been expected to continue unchanged from their colonial past into the era of independence. Most dissatisfaction was with the distribution of the benefits of integration.

Change was essential once integration became voluntary and not enforced by the colonial power, because it was firmly believed in Tanzania and Uganda that the arrangements worked overwhelmingly to the benefit of Kenya as the most industrially developed country of the three, and as the headquarters of the various common services were established in Kenya, the employment and income-creating benefits of the services were believed also to accrue mainly there. The extent to which these beliefs were justified is not entirely uncontroversial, but it was the strength of the beliefs that counted.

The independence settlement, which established an East African Common Services Organisation to replace the High Commission of colonial days, provided for a redistribution of revenue in favour of Tanzania and Uganda, but this proved an inadequate measure, and restrictions began to be imposed on trade between the countries. Discussions about the establishment of an East African Federation came to nothing and an *ad hoc* agreement on industrial location, known as the Kampala Agreement, was not implemented. Relations between the countries were rapidly deteriorating when the Commission, composed of ministers and an outside chairman, which negotiated the Treaty, was appointed.

The Treaty

The Treaty was intended to put cooperation between the partner states on a firm footing of mutual advantage, and not simply to paper over the cracks in the old structure of colonial relationships. It set up a formal structure for administering Community institutions and provided measures to achieve an acceptable distribution of the benefits of cooperation between the states. The main features were: the introduction of a device known as the transfer tax to give limited protection for industries in the less-developed states against competition from those in the more-developed; the establishment of an East African Development Bank (EADB) which was to allocate its investments disproportionately in favour of Tanzania and Uganda; the relocation of the headquarters of some of the common services, including the community secretariat, so that they were not concentrated in Kenya. The Treaty made no more than formal reference to agriculture.

During the life of the Treaty separate universities were established in the three partner states and the assessment and collection of income tax ceased to be a common service, but a new institution, the East African Management Training Centre, was added, and survives.[3] Formally the main structure, including the common external tariff, stood until the final collapse, but the common market became increasingly a dead letter and some of the common services effectively disintegrated. The East African Development Bank survived the final collapse but in a largely moribund condition.

Issues Between the Partner States

It would be convenient if the failure of the Treaty to achieve its intentions could be attributed to some single cause. In reality there were so many interacting influences and issues, some deriving from the Treaty and some not, that no simple lesson can be easily drawn from the experience of the EAC. Nor is it sensible to allocate the 'blame' for the break-up. One way to classify the issues that arose between the partner states, and which affected the course of cooperation, is into those which were (a) dealt with in the Treaty, even if inadequately; (b) those not dealt with in the Treaty, but which could have been, by amendment or extension of the Treaty; (c) those of a kind not amenable to settlement by Treaty. This is not an entirely satisfactory classification of the issues, and some can be seen to fall under either (a) or (b), but it is a helpful way to approach an examination of them.

The most important matter with which the Treaty attempted to deal was the distribution of the benefits of cooperation. The integration of states which are at different levels of development tends to concentrate further development in those already most-developed, and to result in an unequal distribution of the benefits of cooperation. For an integration scheme to be born and to survive, every member must be satisfied and must remain satisfied with the distribution of the benefits. Measures to achieve an acceptable distribution, which would not be achieved in an unregulated common market, are therefore an essential feature of an integration scheme. The Treaty dealt with this matter partly in a chapter entitled 'Measures to Promote Balanced Industrial Development', which provided for the transfer tax and the EADB. It is evident that the mechanisms of the Treaty were inadequate, given the context within which they operated, to persuade the partner states that continued cooperation was worthwhile. But it is not self-evident that the mechanisms of the Treaty were inherently inadequate, let alone inappropriate, for their purpose.

Transfer Tax

The transfer tax is sometimes seen as a device for encouraging the duplication of industries within East Africa, whereas the rationale of the common market was to avoid such duplication and to enable industries to enjoy economies of scale resulting from access to the whole East African market. But this criticism seems to derive from a misunderstanding, even though in practice it may be true that uneconomic duplication took place – the multiplication of steel-mills has been given as an example. The rationale of the transfer tax system was that it would allow Tanzania and Uganda temporarily to protect from Kenyan competition industries which could operate efficiently on a scale provided by their national markets. For these industries, the encouragement of duplication was the whole purpose of the transfer tax, not an unwelcome and unintended side-effect. There were other, large scale, industries the location of which would not, according to this rationalisation of the system, be affected by transfer taxes, because only a single plant would be economic for the whole of East Africa. Herein, however, lies the weakness of the rationalisation: the distinction between the two types of industry is nothing like so clear-cut as the rationalisation presumes, and if sufficient incentives are provided, industries with important economies of scale could be duplicated to serve national markets at high cost. Such inefficient duplication cannot be blamed on the transfer tax. As formal fiscal incentives differed little between the partner states it is probable that practices incompatible with the Treaty, including discriminatory purchasing by state trading corporations (see below) and quantitative restrictions on imports, were the major causes of inefficient duplication of industries, and that the transfer tax was never really given a fair trial.

East African Development Bank

The effectiveness of the East African Development Bank as an equalising device may be questioned because of the limited scale of its activities. By the end of 1975 its investments in total were little more than twice the original contributions of the partner states. On average the annual commitment of funds by the Bank accounted for no more than 4 per cent of industrial investment in the partner states. It may be that a much larger scale of operations was expected by the less-developed partner states when they agreed to the constitution of the Bank. But the Bank did rapidly achieve the prescribed distribution of its investments between the partner states (until its activities in Uganda were disrupted by political developments) and it is possible that if the Community as a whole had proved a success, outside finance would have become available to enable the scale of Bank operations to increase substantially. However, the most important role of the Bank could be seen as to act as a catalyst for complementary industrial development rather than to undertake a major part of industrial investment itself. And in that respect there is certainly a reason to question its effectiveness. The projects in which the Bank invested (textiles, sugar, paper, tyres, cement, for example) do not appear particularly relevant to the aim of making the economies of the partner states more complementary. It would have been difficult for the Bank alone to pursue this aim. It could have done so if agreements had existed between the partner states on a pattern of industrial specialisation into which the Bank's investments would fit. But regional planning, which is discussed later, did not get very far during the life of the Community.

Common Services

A further mechanism in the Treaty for distributing the gains from cooperation more equally was the relocation of the headquarters of the common services, which was combined with some decentralisation of the operations. Perhaps too much was expected from these changes, because the greater part of the local expenditures made by the services, and of the employment provided by them, continued to benefit Kenya. The main activities of the services continued to be in Kenya, in consequence of her higher level of development, as well as of geographical factors, and a change in the distribution could only occur in the longer run with relatively greater economic growth in Tanzania and Uganda.

Community Government

The Treaty established a complicated institutional structure to administer and control the community. In addition to a secretariat there were a number of Councils, at which discussions took place between representatives of the partner states, and an East African Minister and Assistant Minister for each partner state. Ultimate control rested with the Authority composed of the three Presidents. Although in the end the structure proved powerless to ensure the survival of the Community, its effectiveness should not be judged by the experience of the period following the coup which took place in Uganda in January 1971. It can be objected that the system relied too much on harmonious relations between the Presidents, and that control of the Community collapsed when relations became bad, and the source of initiative for the continuation and development of cooperation died. It is also true that even during the first few years the existence of the Authority seemed to deprive lower levels in the administration of the Community of initiative and of willingness to seek solutions to issues between the partner states by compromise. The structure of control encouraged the pursuit of national interests and discouraged compromise, because there was always the Authority to reach an agreement in the end. And in the first three years of the Community's existence it did reach agreement, and although the history of the Community even before the Uganda coup can be read as a lurch from crisis to crisis, the Authority was adept at resolving crises.

There is something to be said for the view that a system which encouraged compromise at a lower level – ministerial rather than presidential, and among officials – would have made the relations between the partner states less crisis-prone, and the Community machinery of cooperation would have run more smoothly. There is also something to be said for the view that the Secretary-General and the secretariat had too limited powers with all decisions requiring the specific agreement of the partner states. However, it is certain that at the time the Treaty was signed, the partner states would have been unwilling to allow any delegation of powers to the secretariat of the Community. The importance of sovereignty in the first flush of independence would have prevented any delegation of powers, and this gives credence to the view that arrangements which require a surrender of sovereignty if they are to work efficiently – even if it goes no further than a commitment to consultation before decisions are taken – are exceptionally difficult for new nations.

Unanimous or majority rule is a related issue. The partner states did not, and certainly would not have agreed to action by majority decision. In a community of three members majority rule is in any case difficult because of the risk that one country may find itself repeatedly in a minority of one. But even in a large community it is almost inconceivable that majority rule would have been acceptable, and unanimity would have been even more difficult to achieve in a larger grouping.

The issue of the enlargement of the Community may, in fact, be taken as the first of the issues which the Treaty could have dealt with in principle, but did not. The Treaty allowed negotiations for the accession of new members, but it did not provide for it. The Treaty could certainly have been adapted for a larger Community, but it is probably true that only Zambia was ever a serious applicant, so a solution to the issue of unanimity or majority rule could hardly have been found in that direction.

Transport Issues

A number of issues concerning transport, and the related issue of tourism, cause tensions between the partner states. The Kenya tourist industry benefited from access to the game parks of northern

Tanzania. They were generally included in a circuit for Nairobi-based tourists, using Kenya vehicles. Although payments were made for the use of Tanzania's hotels and game parks, and for other goods and services, nonetheless it was strongly contended by Tanzania that she received only minor benefits from the traffic. Geographical convenience made northern Tanzania a natural part of a Nairobi-based tour, and at the time it would have been implausible to expect a cross-border tour to be based anywhere else. Arusha could have been an alternative base, but not until there had been a very substantial expansion in the infrastructure for tourism, and a change in Tanzania's somewhat ambivalent attitude towards the industry. Tourism is an industry where a redistribution of the benefits rather than a relocation of activities was the way to maximise total benefits and improve their distribution. A greater share for Tanzania would have required an agreement permitting discriminatory charges and other measures, and such arrangements could have been brought under the Treaty. The closure of the border, and the disappearance of cross-border tourism with the collapse of the Community, must have reduced the total benefits of tourism. Although it has stimulated Tanzania's interest in tourism, and she may be gaining more from tourism than in the past, the gains could have been greater still from cross-border tourism with an equitable distribution of the benefits.

A substantial road traffic developed between Kenya and Zambia crossing Tanzania. The benefits of the trade accrued to Kenya whereas it imposed costs on Tanzania from the use of Tanzanian roads by heavy vehicles. Tension arose between Kenya and Tanzania over this issue. Competition between road and rail was also a cause of tension. It was thought by some that the growth of road transport in Kenya was to the benefit fo private business in Kenya at the expense of the jointly-owned public railway. In fact, the issue was a good deal more complicated than that, competition between road and rail being a matter of long standing in East Africa. Large investments in road vehicles for the carriage of petroleum products had been made by private interests in Kenya, but as it happens these investments had been made at a time when large investments in railway rolling stock would also have been needed if the railway was to handle the traffic. In any case, the opening of a publicly-owned pipeline from the coast to Nairobi to carry petroleum products, displacing both road and rail, suggests that a juxtaposition of private and public transport interests was too simple an interpretation of the issue. Nevertheless, the simple interpretation had some effect in souring relations between Kenya and Tanzania, and Tanzania eventually closed the border to Kenya's heavy vehicles, even before the general border closure.

The omission from the Treaty of detailed provisions for road transport followed naturally from the fact that it did not exist as a common service. The issues arising could nevertheless have been dealt with under the Treaty. The costs imposed by the use of Tanzanian roads by heavy vehicles from Kenya could have been dealt with by the levying of appropriately heavy charges, so long as the charges did not formally discriminate in favour of Tanzanian vehicles. The issues of road - rail competiton were discussed in the Communications Council, one of the Community institutions established by the Treaty, but much more needed to be done to produce and implement the plan for the coordinated development of surface transport throughout East Africa. Without it, transport issues were a disruptive influence on the Community.

State Trading

Transport coordination was an old issue left unsettled by the Treaty in which the absence of a settlement led to strains between the partner states. A new issue of the same kind was that of state trading, which came into prominence soon after the Treaty was signed. The Treaty was implicitly written for a common market of market economies, in which marketing decisions were based on prices. The transfer taxes were designed to protect national industries while preserving a preference for the goods of other partner states over goods from outside East Africa.

The whole system was based on the assumption that the transfer tax and the external tariff would establish certain price relationships, and that purchasing decisions would be based on those prices. The assumption became rapidly out of date with the growth of state trading in the partner states. State trading corporations, with a monopoly of purchasing for distribution, could be directed and might be expected even without direction to discriminate in favour of domestic suppliers, and there was evidence that this was occurring. Rules were drawn up in the regulation of state trading, though they would have been difficult but not impossible to enforce. It must be said, however, that state trading could have been turned into an integrating rather than a disintegrating force if it had been able to operate within a system of, and an instrument for the implementation of, interstate planning.

Planning

It might be argued that the importance of interstate planning in an integration scheme of developing countries is enhanced by the extent to which industrial development is undertaken with foreign capital, and in particular by transnational corporations. In a largely *laissez-faire* context, including a scheme in which the market is rigged by a device such as the transfer tax, even if fiscal incentives are harmonised, the members will be competing for the favour of foreign firms, and consequently their bargaining power will be drastically reduced.

There will be duplication of investments which will dissipate the gains, and the gains in any case will go mainly to foreign enterprise. This possibility provides a further argument for interstate planning to reinforce cooperation, but its relevance to East Africa is a good deal diminished by the apparently unwelcoming face presented at times by Tanzania to foreign enterprise. However, the development of manufacturing in Kenya by transnationals led some to the view that by importing from Kenya, Tanzania was allowing herself to be exploited by these concerns.

It would be too easy in fact, to blame the absence of planning for the failure to solve these problems and, indeed, the whole issue of the distribution of the benefits of cooperation. Planning is one of the matters which fall partly under (a) and partly under (b) in the classification proposed earlier (page 175). It had a place in the Treaty where provision was made for an Economic Consultative and Planning Council, and a committee of officials, the East African Committee of Planners, was set up. Of course, the Treaty could have given a central role to planning, and established a planning instead of a pricing mechanism to deal with the distribution of industry. But it is certain, particularly as it was so soon after the failure of the Kampala Agreement on the allocation of industries, that a planning system would not have been accepted. There would have been no treaty signed if that had been its central feature. Despite discussions within the Community institutions planning proposals never came anywhere near to implementation. If planning, particularly of the development of industry, is a *sine qua non* of successful regional integration, as some authorities believe, the failure to undertake such planning was obviously a major cause of the collapse of the Community. But it may be that successful regional planning requires such a high degree of harmony between the member states that, if the conditions for success exist, many of the problems planning is required to solve would not have arisen.

Balance of Payments Problems

Another issue which falls partly under (a) and partly under (b) of the classification, in that it was neither ignored in the Treaty nor given sufficient importance, concerns the balance of payments and foreign exchange problems of the partner states. The issue was to become more serious and express itself in ways which it may be guessed were not fully foreseen at the time the Treaty was drawn up.

The settlement of net indebtedness arising from interstate transactions had in effect to be in foreign exchange. There was a provision for the extension of credit by a state in surplus in interstate trade to one in deficit, but the maximum credit was relatively small, and the scheme was in fact never brought into use, though there may have been informal interstate lending. The provisions of the Treaty were to the advantage of Kenya, which relied on a surplus in interstate trade to balance a significant part of her deficit in external trade. It is unlikely that Kenya would have accepted a scheme which provided for balance to be inconvertible and which did not allow her to earn foreign exchange from interstate trade, given that she had accepted discrimination against herself in the form of the transfer tax and the investment allocations of the EADB, and given the lower free market rates of Tanzania and Uganda shillings. But the resulting large foreign exchange costs of inter-state settlements had very serious consequences.

Foreign exchange scarcity, though it was already a problem, suddenly became of major importance with the rise in oil prices, and to save foreign exchange became a major preoccupation of governments. It would have been consistent with a commitment to East African cooperation if interstate transactions had been immune from restrictions. But that was not to be, and in the application of restrictions to imports there was no discrimination in favour of imports other partner states.

A perhaps unforeseen effect of foreign exchange scarcity, which played an important part in the collapse of the Community institutions and in souring the atmosphere in the last years of their existence, was the imposition of restrictions on the transfer of funds from the regions to the headquarters of the common services. It is unnecessary to rehearse the sorry tale of squabbles and recriminations, and the charges and counter-charges of responsibility for the failure to transfer funds. The blame cannot be entirely attributed to the desire to save foreign exchange, for if the affairs of the common services had been in good order it would have been more difficult for payments to be stopped on exchange control grounds. But the fact is that the common services, already in a state of disarray, were fundamentally disrupted by the drying-up of the flow of funds to headquarters, where lay the responsibility for large expenditures, including the purchase of equipment and loan charges. This disruption in the financial operation of the services led directly to their effective dissolution as common institutions and to the collapse of a major part of the structure of the Community.

Amin

The founders of the Community could not have been expected to legislate against the appearance of General Amin; his seizure of power is one of the matters which was not amenable to settlement in advance by Treaty. Nevertheless, the crucial position of the Authority, to which reference has already been made, raises again the question of whether a different structure of control would have been less sensitive to such events. The Authority did not meet after Amin came to power in Uganda, although after initial disruption the essential business was conducted by obtaining the agreement of the members individually. But the atmosphere was not conducive to smooth operation of the Community, let alone to that progressive extension of cooperation which some have seen as necessary for success. Uganda ceased to be an effective participant in Community discussions and the balance of the Community's tripartite structure disappeared.

Ideology

Nor is it easy to see that the Treaty could have done anything about the growing ideological division between 'capitalist' Kenya and 'socialist' Tanzania, if these shorthand terms may be allowed to represent the positions of the two governments. When there were all the other disruptive influences at work, the different ideologies of the governments of Kenya and Tanzania certainly made cooperation increasingly difficult, particularly as they were used from time to time as pegs on which to hang mutual political abuse. However, too much can perhaps be made of this cause of dissension as the reason for the inevitable collapse of the Community. After all, procedures for dealing with the problems created by the establishment of state monopoly trading corporations had been devised by the Community Secretariat, though they had not been implemented. Certainly, determined proselytisation of one side by the other could make cooperation impossible. But it would be a conclusion of despair that mutually beneficial economic cooperation requires a close similarity of social and political outlook. And it must be emphasised that the fundamental assumption on which the Treaty was based was that integration was a 'positive-sum game' from which all could benefit, particularly in the longer run when the volume of mutually beneficial intra-Community trade had expanded. In the words of the Treaty:

> It shall be the aim of the Community to strengthen and regulate the industrial, commercial and other relations of the Partner States to the end that there shall be accelerated, harmonious and balanced development and sustained expansion of economic activities the benefits whereof shall be equitably shared.

And here, perhaps, we come to the heart of the matter. As time went on the partner states increasingly behaved as if they believed it was in fact a 'zero-sum game', or even a 'negative-sum game'.

Changing Perceptions

There was, it must be admitted, some justification for such a belief, to an extent because of the way the partner states had behaved. The benefits from the common market began to disappear with the duplication of industries. The benefits of the common services were dissipated in inefficiencies and financial difficulties. With increased road competition on the Mombasa-Nairobi rail route, and with extra rail traffic in Tanzania arising from the construction of the Tanzania-Zambia railway (itself established as a separate entity from East African Railways) the pattern of cross-subsidisation within the railway system shifted, and Tanzania appeared to be benefiting less than before from the joint system. The establishment of TAZARA (the Tanzania-Zambia Railway) outside the Community was a sign of less than wholehearted commitment in Tanzania, and the increase in imports from China under the agreement for financing the local costs of the railway, Tanzania having failed to obtain support from Western donors or international institutions, had an adverse effect on interstate trade.

But even more important than the objective situation was the perception of the Partner States about the costs and benefits of the system. If the perception of the partners is that there are gains for all, then the bargaining is about how much much better-off each shall be, and only if one partner is pushed to the limit will it be worth its while to withdraw. Even where it is such a positive-sum game, however, the perceptions of the partners may be inconsistent. One partner may think it is not receiving enough of the benefit, at a time when another partner thinks it has itself been pushed to near the limit. There is reason to think that the perceptions of Tanzania and Kenya, respectively, were something like this when the Treaty was signed. It is doubtful if Kenya would have accepted a more unfavourable bargain. It would be a mistake to think that at the signing of the Treaty the Kenya ministers and officials were chortling at the thought that they had made a very advantageous deal. Yet Tanzania may have felt that the Treaty gave her little more than the minimum she was prepared to accept, and developments in the succeeding years may have made her even less satisfied.

Although the definition and the measurement of the 'gap' between the levels of development in Kenya and Tanzania are fraught with difficulties, which are enhanced by the different ends of 'capitalist' and 'socialist' societies, the gap evidently did not narrow and probably increased in the perceptions of both Tanzania and Kenya, despite the growth of industry in Tanzania. Given that the growth of the Kenya economy was to a significant extent the consequence of the welcome it gave to foreign investors, a route to development of which Tanzania to say the least was wary, the equalising mechanisms of the Treaty were attempting to swim against a strongly flowing stream. That inequality was perceived to remain or increase led to a loss of interest in cooperation, because of *hubris* in Kenya, where the ill effects of a loss of exports to Tanzania and Zambia may have been greatly underestimated, being concealed by the boom in the price of coffee, and because of despair in Tanzania at cooperation with Kenya as a route to development. All in all, there was a change in the perceived benefits of continued cooperation and in the perceived costs of dissolution. Perceived as a zero- or negative-sum game the Community had no future, even though the perceptions may have been erroneous.

Other Influences

Interest in East African cooperation was crumbling also for other reasons. Reference has already been made to the coup in Uganda as disrupting relations between Tanzania and Uganda. In addition, the focus of political interest in Tanzania moved towards the south. The future of Zimbabwe, and Tanzania's position as a 'front line state' attracted political attention at the highest levels, and, it may be suspected, diminished the concern with the strengthening of East African relations. If this is so, it would be one reason why the crisis-solving function of the Authority ceased to be effective.

Discussion has been in terms of the interests and benefits of the partner states, but the states are not monolithic and within them there are different interests which would be affected differently by the success or by the failure of cooperation between the states. A full understanding of the brief history of the Community is impossible without an understanding of how that history was both affected by and affected these various interests; it is very difficult to research, and is largely unresearched. And much the same must be said about the influence of external interests – foreign governments, transnational corporations and international institutions.

Questions

It has already been remarked that there was no single cause of the death of the East African Community, but rather a multiplicity of ailments, each of which by itself could have been survived, but which together were too much for the weakened body to bear. Nor can it be said that the Community was killed: rather it faded and died from a lack of interest in keeping it alive, though not without a nudge or two along the road to the grave, and not without some squabbles between the heirs to the estate. In short, the political will was lacking in the partner states to keep the Community in being.

Spilt milk is, notoriously, not worth crying over. However, it may be worthwhile to examine the reasons for the spillage, particularly if to do so will help to prevent a similar waste in the future. It is perhaps surprising that the death of the Community has not killed the apparent interest in regional integration schemes among developing countries, in Africa and elsewhere. There are still schemes in various stages of development in different parts of the world. The members of new schemes elsewhere would not have the history of disagreement which in East Africa began with the unregulated common market of colonial times. A well-designed new scheme which fully met each member's perception of the costs and benefits, if such a scheme could be designed, would not have the tensions created by years of controversy. On the other hand, most groupings lack what might be expected to be the valuable lubricants for smoothly-working cooperation of common languages, as with English and Swahili in East Africa, and the common educational background provided by Makerere for some politicians and for many of the generation of civil servants who took over the administration of all three East African countries at independence. ECOWAS (the Economic Community of West African States) and the proposed preferential trading area for which sixteen Eastern and Southern African countries signed a treaty of intent in March 1978, and which was seen as a first step in a process of regional integration, are two schemes that might benefit from the lessons of the East African Community.

It is not easy to summarise the lessons for the planners of other schemes. Perhaps the best approach is to list some of the questions about the requirements for successful regional integration that are suggested by a study of the Community's history.

1 Is it necessary only that all members of the scheme should benefit, or must they benefit equally, or must the poorer or less-developed members gain most, or must the gap between the members in their wealth and level of development actually narrow over time? The last is a very strong requirement, because it is perfectly possible for the gap to widen; even though the integration arrangements themselves have a strong equalising element.
2 Is there a limit to the difference in levels of development and 'economic size' of members of a grouping beyond which integration cannot work? Are giants and pygmies incompatible cohabitants?
3 Are members willing to take a longer-term view, and see the benefits from cooperation grow with the growth of trade between them, or do their assessments inevitably have a short horizon within which transactions between them, and hence the benefits of cooperation, are likely to be small?
4 If there are gains from the scheme for the members as a whole and for every member individually, can it be ensured that they all perceive the benefit, and do not have incompatible perceptions of the distribution of the benefits?
5 Are the members prepared to agree on a common system of fiscal incentives to encourage an acceptable distribution of investment between them and to prevent the competitive offering of concessions to investors?
6 Is it possible for the operation of the scheme to be insulated from the effects of foreign exchange scarcity in the member countries?
7 Is a substantial degree of regional planning over such matters as the location of new industries and the pattern of industrial specialisation essential to achieve an acceptable distribution of the benefits of integration?
8 If so, are the member countries prepared to accept the constraints imposed on them by such planning?
9 How does such planning cope with strong preferences by potential investors about the location of production?
10 Is a complex or 'package' scheme, embracing different fields of cooperation, as in East Africa, where some parts of the scheme may be of particular benefit to some member(s), and other parts

to others, most likely to lead to all members perceiving that there are benefits from membership?

11 Would a less comprehensive scheme, in which areas of cooperation with the greatest potential for conflict were excluded, be more viable?

12 Would 'functionally specific' arrangements of limited scope be the best bet?

13 Would provisions in the Treaty for a common agricultural policy have been a cohesive influence in the Community? Is it important to include agriculture in integration arrangements for countries where it is the major economic activity?

14 Is a broadly similar ideology in the member countries essential for success?

15 Is continuing political harmony between the states essential and must it go beyond the minimum of good will without which cooperation would be impossible?

16 Must the members be willing to surrender sovereignty to the extent of allowing decisions to be reached by majority vote?

17 Must the members be prepared to delegate substantial powers to the bureaucracy of the scheme?

18 Can a scheme be protected from the effect of a wavering commitment to integration at the highest levels in one or more of the partner states?

19 Is the absence of political rewards at the regional level likely to reduce the political will and interest in integration below the minimum necessary for success?

20 What is the balance of influence within each country and what interests will be harmed or benefited by the progress of integration?

21 What external influences are at work, and which favour and which oppose integration?

22 Are the expected gains from industrialisation to serve a protected regional market great enough to make it worthwhile surmounting the difficulties, given the possibilities for manufacturing for extra-regional export, including export to developed countries through the medium of multinational corporations? The expectation will differ from country to country according to the size of its domestic markets. A firmly affirmative answer from every member would probably be necessary if a grouping were to have strong prospect of success.

The answers to at least some of these questions might seem obvious, but the implications of such answers have not always been taken into account in regional integration proposals. And unless the founders of regional integration schemes in developing countries are satisfied with their answers to all these questions their efforts may be described, in Dr Johnson's words on the second marriage of a man whose first had been unhappy, as the triumph of hope over experience.

Notes

1 This chapter was written when I was a Senior Research Officer at the Institute of Economics and Statistics, before my election as Warden of Queen Elizabeth House and Director of the Oxford University institute of Commonwealth Studies. I have had the benefit of discussions on the subject of the article with, or comments on a first draft from the following: Tim Curtin, Amon Nsekela, Robert Ouko, Peter Robson and William Tordoff. I am also indebted to the participants in a panel disussion at the Convention of the International Studies Association held in Toronto in March 1979, and in particular to the contributors of papers: Richard Fredland, Domenico Mazzeo, Christian Potholm and John Ravenhill. None of those named can of course in any way be held responsible for the views I have expressed. A study of economic integration in East Africa up to the early months of 1975 is contained my *Economic Integration: The East African Experience* (London: Heinemann, 1975).

2 Some easing of attitudes seemed to be in prospect following a meeting in Arusha between Presidents Moi and Nyerere in March 1979, when there was agreement on the use of each other's air space which allowed Kenya Airways to overfly Tanzania en route to Zambia but no other relaxation of the border closure followed. The fighting between Tanzania and the Amin regime in Uganda in 1978 and 1979, which led to the defeat of Amin, is a separate matter as Uganda had ceased effectively to be a member of the Community some years before its final collapse, though Ugandans (often in effect refugees from the Amin regime) continued to be employed in Community institutions. Uganda had an interest in maintaining a voice in the operation of Community services, particularly the railway link to the coast, but in general Ugandan officials at Community meetings were given no consistent policy to pursue and were unable to make decisions even on minor matters without reference to Kampala.

3 An Eastern Africa National Shipping Line was also established, but this organisation was outside the formal structure of the Community and includes Zambia as an owner along with three Community countries. It survives, together with the Interstate Standing Committee on Shipping.

11 The Southern African Development Coordination Conference: Politics of Dependence

Layi Abegunrin

Introduction

Southern Africa has become a battleground between two constellations of states which are ideologically and fundamentally opposed – South Africa's 'constellation' of Prime Minister P.W. Botha, and the Lusaka constellation of nine Southern African states: Angola, Botswana, Lesotho, Malawi, Mozambique, Swaziland, Tanzania, Zambia and Zimbabwe.[1] The conflict between the two constellations therefore basically concerns South Africa's future and its domestic racial policies in whatever modified forms they may take. Thus the declared aim of the present 'Southern Nine' was to form an alliance which would pursue an economic strategy that would reduce their economic dependence on South Africa. Significantly, the nine states and the South African occupied territory of Namibia unanimously adopted a programme of action to stimulate interstate trade with the ultimate economic isolation of South Africa as the final objective.[2] This chapter is an attempt to trace the evolution of what is now known as the Southern African Development Coordination Conference (SADCC), and to examine and analyse the aims, problems and prospects of this new regional economic grouping and to give some suggestions regarding its prospects in the 1980s.

The two constellations (Pretoria's domestic constellation of Prime Minister Botha launched on 22 July 1980, and the Lusaka constellation of nine Southern African states launched on 1 April 1980) have as their major objectives close regional economic cooperation in Southern Africa, but politically, the two are poles apart. Botha's axis is essentially a strategy to use South Africa's economic power and wealth to manipulate its black members, and to exert subtle pressure to ensure that they (the nine black-ruled states of Southern Africa) cohere with the white minority regime in South Africa. This constellation's ambition is a vital part of the total strategy of survival of the Botha government, which especially involves the economy as an instrument of maintaining ultimate political power and control based on the maintenance of the basic structures of apartheid, hence its opposition to the SADCC's policies. SADCC's main objective, on the other hand, is to end white minority political and economic hegemony in Southern Africa. In addition, it is designed to minimise areas of potential conflict among its members. To that end, members are encouraged to contribute effectively to the SADCC programmes. Moreover, there is a division of labour to prevent duplication or overload of responsibilities.[3] Each state would have some clear role and it is hoped that this will in the long run cement closer political and economic relationships among SADCC's members.

The Evolution of SADCC

The launching of the Lusaka constellation before the Pretoria constellation was a major political setback for South Africa because in terms of the original grandiose plans, South Africa was convinced that its constellation would include at least many of its neighbouring states in Southern Africa.[4] The Lusaka meeting brought together representatives from nine black-ruled Southern Africa countries now known as the 'Southern Nine'. This economic cooperation has proved to be of an historic significance in the struggle to overthrow the apartheid regime of the Republic of South Africa. 'The Six Frontline States – Angola, Botswana, Mozambique, Tanzania, Zambia and Zimbabwe – were joined by Lesotho and Swaziland which were relying heavily on the South African economy, and Malawi, the only African country to have diplomatic relations with Pretoria'.[5] It was also significant that Sam Nujoma, President of the South West Africa People's Organisation (SWAPO) was present at the Lusaka Conference as an observer representing Namibia. On the other hand when the Pretoria constellation was launched four months after the launching of the Lusaka constellation, it was something of a non-event in the sense that the launching took place between Prime Minister Botha and the Presidents of the three so-called 'independent' Bantustans: Transkei, Bophuthatswana and Venda. The three homelands – including Ceskei – are islands within the territory of apartheid South Africa and have been refused recognition by the world community.

The idea of regional economic cooperation – that is, the pooling of economic resources on a regional basis – in Southern Africa dates back to 3 July 1974, when President Kaunda of Zambia, proposed the 'establishment of a transcontinental belt of independent and economically powerful nations from Dar-es-Salaam and Maputo on the Indian Ocean to Luanda on the Atlantic.[6] Thus, since 1974, a series of economic discussions and meetings have taken place between the foreign and economic ministers as well as heads of government and state of the Frontline States. One such meeting was the May 1979 Gaberone conference between the foreign ministers of the five Frontline States. The series of economic conferences and discussions culminated in what is now known as Southern African Development Coordination Conference (SADCC) held in Arusha, Tanzania 3–4 July 1979. The Arusha meeting was followed by the 1 April 1980 Lusaka economic summit which was attended by the nine Heads of government of state of the SADCC countries. The Lusaka Economic Summit produced the historic declaration: 'Southern Africa Toward Economic Liberation'.[7] Gaberone, the capital of Botswana, was chosen as the permanent headquarters of the Southern African Development Coordination Conference, with a staff of eight, and a Zimbabwean, Arthur Blumeris, the former Zimbabwean Ambassador to Belgium, was appointed in July 1982, as the first Executive Secretary and head of the SADCC Secretariat.[8]

Objectives

The Lusaka economic declaration is a remarkable policy statement reflecting the ever-evolving African strategy of achieving total liberation of Southern Africa, building upon the Lusaka Manifesto of 1969 and the 1975 Dar-es-Salaam Declaration. The 1 April 1980 Lusaka declaration clearly reflected the growing concern of black Southern Africa over the continuing economic domination of white-ruled South Africa. The Declaration is also a recognition of the need for devising a collective economic strategy to lessen the economic dependence of the SADCC states on Pretoria. To this end, the Lusaka Declaration noted that 'future development must aim at the reduction of economic dependence not only on the Republic of South Africa, but also on any single external state or group of states'.[9] And according to the late President Seretse Khama of Botswana, the first Chairman of the SADCC, the ultimate objective

> is to achieve economic liberation and to reduce our economic dependence on the Republic of South Africa ... through regional and coordinated efforts. It is not our objective to plot against anybody or any country but, on the contrary to lay the foundation for the development of a new economic order in Southern Africa

and forge a united community wherein will lie our strength of survival in the future. I am convinced that with the collective will and determination with which we have struggled for political freedom we can succeed in our struggle for economic liberation.[10]

The SADCC countries view their Programme of Action as part of the liberation struggle in Southern Africa which, with the independence of Zimbabwe, will shift its focus to Namibia and later on to South Africa itself.

The primacy given to regional economic cooperation and economic liberation by the Nine states is supported by the rest of Africa and it reflects the shift towards preoccupation with economic survival on a continental scale. As if to emphasise this point, the Lusaka summit was attended by both the OAU Secretary-General, Edem Kodjo, and the Economic Commissioner for Africa's (ECA) Executive Secretary, Adebayo Adedeji. The Southern African Development Coordination Conference fits neatly within the OAU policy of encouraging regional economic groupings as the basis for an eventual all-African economic community and continental unity. President Kaunda of Zambia put the SADCC in a proper historical and continental perspective when he said:

> the journey to SADCC started many years ago. The founding fathers of the OAU expressed our aspirations when they adopted the Charter of the Organization ... The SADCC is an expression of Africa's deliberate and planned effort in forging links which not only have political objectives but also economic and social meaning .... African unity must be given economic substance out of which the social-cultural fabric will grow so strong that our continent will no longer be vulnerable.[11]

Reduction of dependence on South Africa is central to the achievement of economic development, and to the advancement of the dignity and the basic human needs of the people of Southern Africa. South Africa's apartheid system denies its citizens their dignity, and both its military and economic power are increasingly being used systematically to destabilise its black neighbours. But as long as SADCC member states do not have an integrated transport and communication system distinct from that of South Africa, nor self-sufficiency in food, it will be difficult for them to prevent such destabilisation from crippling their national development efforts.

Another aspect of the SADCC programme is a regionally coordinated industrialisation and energy project. Angola has the responsibility for regional energy conservation while Tanzania is responsible for the harmonisation of a regional industrialisation programme.[12] Angola's oil reserves are sufficient to meet a substantial portion of the needs of the SADCC countries. The SADCC's aim is to reduce the region's economic dependence on South Africa and other external economic powers. Angola's oilfields are exploited mainly by an American Company – Gulf Oil – and their product is exported to the West. The energy plan is to harness and harmonise collectively, the energy resources of the SADCC states. Under a joint energy programme, Mozambique will supply electricity from the Cabora Bassa Dam[13] to countries like Lesotho, and Swaziland. This will reduce their dependence on electricity supply from the South African Electricity Supply Commission (ESCOM).

The programmes of the SADCC also embrace regional agricultural development for self-sufficiency in food. Food security, which is at the top of the OAU *Lagos Plan of Action*, is also at the top of SADCC priorities. Regional responsibility for food and agricultural development has devolved on Botswana, Zambia and Zimbabwe. In their desire to break away from economic dependence on South Africa, the SADCC states have identified food production as one of the most important areas. Crash plans are being drawn up to make these SADCC countries much more self-sufficient as far as food production is concerned, and Zimbabwe and Zambia have been assigned a special role in this connection.[14] Within the context of broader agricultural development, SADCC envisages the establishment of a regional agricultural research centre whose functions are yet to be spelt out.

The SADCC plan on regional agricultural development also includes the control of foot-and-mouth disease. Botswana has approached the 'Commission of the European Communities to undertake a feasibility and design study for a system of coordinated control of foot-and-mouth disease in cattle on a region-wide basis.[15] SADCC programmes also include a 'review of existing training facilities in the region'. Swaziland is expected to make recommendations for their better usage. The exploration by Zambia of the prospects for establishing a Southern African Development Fund is the last item on the agenda of the SADCC countries.

Two billion dollars are needed for the execution of the 97 capital projects already identified. Forty per cent of the total development budget will go to Mozambique for development of Beira and Maputo harbours, and the upgrading and improvement of the railway links between Mozambique and Zimbabwe. This is 'vital for the success of the medium and long term strategy to re-unite the goods to and from the SADCC countries, at present mostly going through South African harbours'.[16] Beira and Maputo ports, it is hoped, will be able to handle the export and import trade of the SADCC states. Pretoria will then no longer be able to cause an artificial shortage of goods through the delay of the SADCC states' imports at her ports.

The priorities of the Southern Africa Transport and Communications also include the development of a functional network of roads among the SADCC countries.[17] The inter-regional development of a network of roads among the SADCC states is a prerequisite for effective movement of capital goods and peoples among the cooperating states. The effective movement of capital, goods and peoples is an important variable in forging regional economic cooperation. In early 1982, Mozambique and Zimbabwe agreed after months of negotiations, on the terms for reopening the 180-mile pipeline intended to carry all of landlocked Zimbabwe's gasoline and diesel fuel inland from the Mozambican port of Beira. The pipeline was last used shortly before the white-minority government in Salisbury – now Harare – under Ian Smith, unilaterally declared independence in November 1965. The agreement was signed in Maputo, Mozambique on 7 March 1982 by Mozambican finance minister Rui Baltazer and the Zimbabwean minister for energy, Simba Makoni.[18] The line can handle about one million tons of liquid fuel a year, more than enough to meet Zimbabwe's annual requirements of 600 000 tons. Its recommissioning will mark an important step in Zimbabwe's drive to re-route its import-export trade away from South Africa, and also to relieve congestion on its railway system, which has been bringing in some of the imported fuel through Maputo.

The Parameters of SADCC Dependence on South Africa

For the black-ruled states in Southern Africa, their vulnerability to economic sanctions by Pretoria – a consequence of their chronic economic dependence on the racist economy – raises the issue of their freedom in determining their foreign policy options *vis-à-vis* apartheid South Africa. This is because, with the possible exception of Tanzania and Angola, the SADCC states are economically dependent on Pretoria. Most of the SADCC countries have migrant labour relationships with Pretoria (this is shown on Table 11.1). In 1976, Lesotho had 160 630 migrant workers in South Africa while Mozambique, Zimbabwe and Malawi respectively had 40 000 and 18 000 migrant workers in the Republic in 1977. The incomes of the migrant workers constitute significant proportions of the foreign

Table 11.1 Black Foreign Workers in South Africa 1965–77

Countries	1965	1970	1971	1972	1975	1977
Lesotho	117 000	147 400	165 000	131 749	80 526	160 630 (1976)
Mozambique	161 000	144 900	132 000	121 708	127 000	40 000
Malawi	80 000	107 180	100 000	131 291	11 000	18 000
Botswana	59 000	47 360	51 000	31 960	34 020	NA
Swaziland	39 000	24 260	12 000	10 108	17 000	NA
Zimbabwe (Rhodesia)	27 000	11 640	NA	6200	16 000	30 000
Angola	11 000	3400	NA	4466	2862	NA
Zambia	16 000	NA	NA	638	NA	NA

NA = Figures not available
Sources: G.M. Carter and P. O'Meara (eds) *Southern Africa: The Continuing Crisis* (Bloomington: Indiana University Press, 1979), p. 306.

exchange of the SADCC states. Thus for Lesotho in 1975, remittances from migrant workers totalled $250 million, a figure more than double the gross domestic product of the country. As reported by Weisfelder,

> the repatriation of goods and cash by migrant workers plays a major role in offsetting Lesotho's enormous trade deficit, where imports are eight times greater than exports.[19]

Migrant workers are also important to Mozambique. In 1975 alone, the foreign exchange remittances of Mozambican migrant workers in South Africa totalled $175 million – about one-third of the total foreign currency earnings of Mozambique in that year.[20]

The regional dependence of SADCC states on Pretoria is also reflected in the transport and communications sector where the regional dominance of South Africa is acutely felt. Thus, landlocked Botswana depends on South Africa's railways for access to the sea. Similarly, 90% of Zimbabwe's railways depend heavily on South African Railways for coaches, maintenance and expertise. Zimbabwe is therefore highly susceptible to the rail sanctions of Pretoria, as we saw in October 1981 when South Africa suddenly withdrew twenty locomotives on loan to the country. However, there have been plans since early 1982, by the Mugabe government, to reduce its dependence on the apartheid regime of South Africa for transport.[21]

Like Zimbabwe, Zambia also utilises the South African Railways for the transportation of her copper to the ports of Durban, East London and Port Elizabeth along the coast of the Indian Ocean. South African ports like the South African railway system 'remain vital for the trade of all the SADCC countries apart from Angola and Tanzania ....'[22] In fact, the export and import trade of most of the SADCC states are interwoven with that of Pretoria. For instance, 18% of Mozambique's imports, 29% of Malawi's, about 66% of Botswana's and over 90% of Swaziland's and Lesotho's imports originate in South Africa.[23] The imports of the SADCC countries from Pretoria include, fuel, maize, canned food, beverages, fertiliser and iron and steel. These are survival products. Their exports to South Africa include sugar, rice, citrus frutis, cotton, cattles, hides and skins, copper, nickel and sulphur.

In the process of implementing their programmes, SADCC states have faced several obstacles. First, their continued dependence on South Africa economically imposes serious constraints on their ability to execute any self-reliant policies. SADCC's 'struggle for economic liberation is being bitterly contested as has been the struggle for political liberation.'[24] The SADCC countries continue to face stiff challenges from Pretoria which is increasingly using its economic power to frustrate their programme in the subregion. On 6 September 1981, Pretoria caused an artificial fuel shortage in Zimbabwe by delaying four months' supply in transit. Consequently, the country was left with only forty days supply of diesel fuel. Furthermore, the operations of the Zimbabwe Air Charter Companies were almost grounded, while harvesting was temporarily disrupted.[25]

The chronic dependence of the SADCC states continues to affect their support for the liberation struggle in Southern Africa. Botswana, Mozambique and Zimbabwe are likely to follow a policy of peaceful co-existence with Pretoria for the foreseeable future. Already, Botswana, Lesotho, Mozambique, Swaziland and Zimbabwe have refrained from providing bases to the guerrilla movements of South Africa – the ANC and PAC.

One serious politico-military problem which SADCC states will continue to face in the near future is South Africa's two-pronged policy of military incursions into their territories and its support for insurgency movements and sabotage in the black-ruled states in Southern Africa. For many years now, the racist South African authorities have embarked upon an undeclared war against the SADCC states generally and Angola, Lesotho, Malawi, Mozambique and Zimbabwe in particular. In Mozambique, the Pretoria regime's main weapon has been the reactionary Mozambique National Resistance (MNR) while in Angola the National Union for the Total

Independence of Angola (UNITA), led by Joans Savimbi, continues to receive financial and material assistance from the racist Republic.[26]

South Africa's economic and military threats against SADCC and support for the MNR and UNITA have two interrelated motives: first, to destabilise Mozambique and Angola and second, to sabotage SADCC's efforts at promoting cooperation and liberation in the subcontinent. Thus, South Africa's military and financial assistance to the MNR and UNITA rebel groups cannot be separated from Pretoria's increasing economic and military pressures against Mozambique and Zimbabwe, its daily military raids into Angola, its assassination activities in Lesotho and its political pressure to induce Swaziland with the Ingwavuna piece of land in return for the former's support for an independent Kangwane Bantustan.[27] Viewed from this regional perspective, then, MNR activity in Mozambique and that of UNITA in Angola, are a valuable political weapon in the hands of Pretoria to keep the Southern African subregion divided and in continual turmoil.

One other major problem facing the SADCC is the issue of the ability of Zimbabwe and Zambia to play their assigned roles in food security and agricultural development. The problem concerns the sensitive issue of relations between black political power and residual white economic dominance in agriculture in the two states. Two-thirds of the maize produced in Zambia is grown on large commercial farms, mainly white-owned. In addition, white farmers own half of the nation's cattle. White food producers equally dominate Zimbabwe's agriculture. What is not generally understood is that there is a coordinated strategy by South Africa and the white farmers in Zambia and Zimbabwe to control food supplies to the two countries. Thus, the importation of maize by Zambia and Zimbabwe from South Africa has less to do with any absolute shortage than a decision by white farmers in the two states to establish a dependency relationship with South Africa for food.[28] The problem therefore, is how to overcome white-farmer dominance in Zambia and Zimbabwe. The white farmer is therefore an important cog in the wheel of accelerated self-reliant food and agricultural production in the SADCC states.

The SADCC also faces the problem of lack of capital and funds for the execution of its capital projects, especially the development of communications, ports and rail lines. So far, the international community has made financial pledges of $650 million over a period of five years as part of the $2 billion needed for ten years to carry out the SADCC priority programme.[29] The biggest financial pledge, $380 million, came from the African Development Bank (ADB). The pledge was for the period 1980 to 1985. The European Economic Community promised $100 million, Italy pledged $50 million, Holland $16 million and the United States $25 million. Whether the financial pledges by international donors will be honoured is another issue entirely. For instance, it is doubtful whether the USA under the Reagan Administration will honour its financial pledge to the SADCC. The Reagan Administration is vehemently opposed to the presence of Cuban troops in Angola and Mozambique. It is possible that the USA under Reagan would tie her honoring a huge financial transfusion to SADCC to the withdrawal of Cuban troops from Angola. Such a condition would be unacceptable to Angola.

Despite pledges of about $650 million made at the Maputo Conference of November 1980, only $180 million has so far been actually raised to meet the estimated cost of about $2 billion required to implement 106 regionally integrated and country projects. Though the cost of the projects presented to international and bilateral financing agencies at the Maputo conference has been scaled down from the original estimate of about $2 billion to $1920 million, actual aid disbursements so far available are sufficient to meet only the cost of a small number of the projects.[30] Thus capital remains a major obstacle to execute the SADCC programmes.

Prospects for a Self-reliant Development

The strategies of the SADCC states represent a blueprint for regional self-sufficiency in industrialisation, energy (fuel, coal and hydro-electricity), communications, transportation and agriculture. In pursuit of regional self-sufficiency, SADCC has mapped out programmes that revolve around the execution of 106 capital projects. Particular emphasis is given to overcoming the bottlenecks in the transport/communications sector, where the regional dominance of Pretoria is pervasive. Seretse Khama, who until his death was the Chairman of SADCC, recognised the importance of breaking the dominant position of Pretoria in transport and communications; he pointed out that 'we consider that the first and most crucial step to undertake is to strengthen and coordinate transport and communications systems in our region. For this purpose, it is proposed to establish as a matter of urgency, a Southern African Transport and Communications Commission (SATCC) to be based in Maputo, Mozambique'.[31] The Commission will coordinate the use of existing facilities and the planning and financing of additional regional facilities. The dominance of South Africa is reinforced by the strategic locations of its transport system. Without the establishment of an adequate regional transport and communications system therefore, other areas of cooperation will become impracticable. In addition to their individual pledges totalling $36 million, the Nordic countries have pledged to finance the Transport, Harbour and Communications Commission Secretariat for SADCC, to be built in Maputo.[32]

From Table 11.2, it is obvious that the intra-regional trade between the SADCC states is very low compared with their trade with South Africa. Clearly, there are many obstacles (as already enumerated) confronting the new regional economic community. It is an undertaking that in a very fundamental sense, represents another phase in their continuing struggle for real independence from white economic domination. In that regard, substantial gains have been made since the Lusaka Economic Summit in 1980. Work is already being effected on railway rehabilitation in Malawi and Angola, on telecommunications links between Botswana, Zambia and Zimbabwe and on a new airport in Lesotho.[33] These constitute physical evidence that SADCC is making some progress. Moreover, it should be emphasised that the very fact that the SADCC has now been institutionalised is in itself a major political advance in terms of the evolution of a Southern Africa liberation strategy.

To the 'Southern Nine', then, the 1980s will be a decade of consolidation of the new multilateral economic grouping. Samora Machel of Mozambique said 'the new phase is fundamentally one of economic cooperation.'[34] The late Khama of Botswana similarly claimed, 'we believe that the time has now come to demonstrate our solidarity in the struggle for economic liberation'[35] through regional economic cooperation. The statements of the two presidents demonstrate the general determination of all the leaders concerned to prosecute the objective of SADCC. The achievement of self-determination in Zimbabwe and the impending independence of Namibia will give the SADCC states a much-needed respite to pursue regional economic relations and reconstruction. Robert Mugabe has already acknowledged the central role Zimbabwe will play in the cooperation effort:

> I think Zimbabwe will be the pivot in the economic arrangement [that is, the SADCC] because in all of the free countries of Southern Africa and even Central Africa, we probably have the most highly developed economy and infrastructure .... In terms of our industrial performance, we are second to none and hence it is necessary that we play quite a leading part in the economic constellation of Southern African States.[36]

Table 11.2 Southern Africa: Intra-Regional Trade

Southern Africa: Merchandise Imports and Exports 1972 in Thousands of Dollars

Exports / Imports	South Africa	Zimbabwe	Malawi	Zambia	Angola	Mozambique	Botswana	Lesotho	Swaziland	Namibia	Total
South Africa	x	83 851.6	1524.6	45 236.8	3014.2	26 600	6531	21 294	22 078	176 400	385 530.6
Zimbabwe	30 737	x	20 242.6	114 051	631.4	3269	5549.6	9.8	134.4	168	174 792.8
Malawi	2185.4	4566.8	x	1281	NA	347.2	8.4	NA	12.4	1.4	8402.8
Zambia	28 368.2	15 110.2	1360.8	x	19.6	86.8	142.8	NA	5.6	47.6	45 141.6
Angola	1831.2	156.8	9.8	326.6	x	2991.8	NA	NA	NA	NA	5352.2
Mozambique	9916.2	3855.6	644	72.8	3451	x	NA	NA	210	NA	18 149.6
Botswana	5696.6	921.2	NA	435.4	NA	NA	x	NA	NA	NA	7053.2
Lesotho	6916	4.2	NA	NA	NA	NA	NA	x	NA	NA	6920.2
Swaziland	13 662.6	182	NA	133	NA	103.6	NA	NA	x	NA	14 081.2
Namibia	105 676.2	158.8	NA	60.2	NA	NA	NA	NA	NA	x	105 893.2
TOTAL	204 989.4	108 805.2	23 779.8	161 632.8	7116.2	33 298.4	12 231.8	21 303.8	11 440.8	176 617	3 510 141.6

NA = Figures not available

Source: This is an abridged version of Table 2 in Christian Potholm and Richard Dale (eds) *Southern Africa in Perspective: Essays in Regional Politics* (New York: The Free Press 1972), p. 288.

The second key state upon whom the success of the SADCC depends is Mozambique, where the ports of Beira and Maputo are expected to be the answer in breaking the bottlenecks in transport and communications.

The SADCC represents, in the final analysis, a move towards a regional economic community among the majority-ruled states in Southern Africa. A viable and prosperous regional economic community in Southern Africa would put tremendous pressure on South Africa both economically and politically. Pretoria would lose most, if not all, of its traditional markets in the Southern Africa subregion as well as cheap labour for its mines. A viable regional economic community will also frustrate Pretoria's intention to 'parley its active trade policy into political acceptance or foreign policy clientage' in Southern Africa.

The SADCC as a regional economic institution is being complemented by a Preferential Trade Area (PTA) for Central, Eastern and Southern Africa. The states of the SADCC are signatories to a draft treaty of Preferential Trade Area of the Economic Commission for Africa.[37] The Preferential Trade Area is a significant step towards a common market in the subregion with a population of 125 million people. Although the draft treaty emphasises a preferential trade area, its provisions go beyond cooperation in trade matters alone. The twelve protocols of the draft treaty call for regional cooperation in industrial, agricultural, transport and communications. The treaty also has provisions to facilitate re-exporting within the region, to remove tariff and non-tariff trade barriers to ease transit trade. Furthermore, the treaty aims at establishing clearing and payment arrangements among member states. Given the political will of the SADCC states and continued international cooperation, a viable regional economic community will certainly emerge in majority-ruled Southern Africa in the 1980s.

In conclusion, we envisage a scenario of formalised military relations between the SADCC states – this move has been made by the Frontline States which constituted two-thirds of the SADCC states.[38] The present pattern of *ad hoc* military cooperation between the SADCC states will become more formalised through a defence treaty. Inevitably, the SADCC states would need a formal military alliance to deter the increasingly destructive aggression of the apartheid regime in South Africa. The 1980s will be a period of challenge and promise for the SADCC states, who will continue to be crucial 'influence vectors' and actors involved not only in economic matters but also in the processes of liberation and change in Southern Africa.

Notes

1   For details see Olayiwola Abegunrin, 'The Southern Nine' *Current Bibliography on African Affairs*, Vol. 14, No. 4, (1981–2).
2   'Economic Front Against South Africa', *West Africa*, No. 3272 (7 April 1980), p. 604.
3   See Richard F. Weisfelder, 'SADCC: A New Factor in the Liberation Process', in Thomas M. Callaghy, (ed.) *South Africa in Southern Africa* (New York: Praeger, 1983).
4   'Southern Africa: Union of the Southern Nine', *Africa*, (London), No. 105, May 1980, p. 45.
5   'The Collapse of Botha's Constellation Strategy', *Africa*, No. 111, November 1980, p. 48.
6   *An address by President Kaunda of Zambia to the Lusaka Economic Summit of Southern African Development Coordination Conference* (SADCC) (Lusaka), 1 April 1980, pp. 3–4.
7   *West Africa*. 7 April 1980, p. 604.
8   'Black Southern Africa: Realistic route to Self-reliance', *The Times* (London), 9 August 1982), p. 5.
9   *SADEX*, Vol. 2, No. 3 (May/June, 1982), p. 3.
10   See 'In Memoriam: Opening Statement of the Southern African Development Coordination Summit, Lusaka, 1 April 1980, by the Chairman, His Excellency Sir Seretse Khama, President of Botswana, *SADEX*, Vol. 2, No. 3, (Washington, DC: African Bibliographic Center), May–June, 1980, p. 20.
11   *An address by President Kaunda of Zambia*, p. 4.
12   For details on the energy programme of the SADCC states, see *SADEX*, Vol. 2, No. 5, pp. 4–5.
13   The Cabora Bassa Dam is the fourth largest hydroelectric scheme in the world.
14   O. Abegunrin, 'The Southern Nine', p. 5.
15   *SADEX*, Vol. 2, No. 5, p. 2.
16   *Africa*, No. 113, January 1981, p. 25.
17   'Southern Nine: A two billion dollar question', *Africa*, No. 111, November 1980, p. 43.
18   'Zimbabwe, Mozambique agreed on Pipeline' *Daily Sketch* (Ibadan), 9 March 1982, p. 12.
19   Richard Weisfelder, 'Lesotho: Changing Patterns of Dependence', in G.M. Carter and P. O'Meara (eds), *Southern Africa: The Continuing Crisis* (Bloomington: Indiana University Press, 1979), p. 257.
20   Tony Hodges, 'Mozambique; The Politics of Liberation', in Carter and O'Meara, *op. cit.*, p. 81 (see note 19 above).
21   For the percentage of the import trade of Zimbabwe that goes through South African Railways, see *African Business*, No. 41 (New York), January 1982, p. 13.
22   *Ibid*. p. 13.
23   Kenneth W. Grundy, 'Economic Patterns in the New Southern African

Balance', in Carter and O'Meara, *op. cit.*, p. 295 (see note 19 above).
24   See, *Statement by His Excellency late President Khama of Botswana*, *op. cit.*, p. 20 (see note 10 above).
25   'Mozambique: Threat to SADCC Strategy', *Africa Now* (London), December 1981, pp. 19-20.
26   For details see Allen and Barbara Isaacman, 'South Africa's Hidden War', *Africa Report* (New York), Vol. 27, No. 6, November-December 1982, pp. 4-9.
27   'Swaziland: A risky deal', *Africa Now*, August 1982, p. 21.
28   See *SADEX*, Vol. 2, No. 3, p. 6.
29   'Southern Nine: Money Matters', *Africa*, No. 113, January 1981, p. 25.
30   'SADCC Plans are Hit: Cash Snarl is Blamed', *New African* (London), January 1982, p. 29.
31   *SADEX*, Vol. 2, No. 3, p. 19.
32   *Africa*, No. 105, May 1980, p. 45.
33   See, *New African* January 1982, pp. 29-30.
34   *SADEX*, Vol. 2, No. 3, p. 1.
35   *Ibid.*, p. 18.
36   *Ibid.*, p. 12.
37   'Lusaka Summit to approve PTA Plan', *Africa*, No. 124, December 1981, pp. 92-3. Member States for PTA include the SADCC States, the Comoro Islands, Djibouti, Ethiopia, Kenya, Malagasy, Mauritius, Seychelles and Somalia.
38   On 11 April 1976, it was announced that following a joint defence and security meeting in Maputo, the governments of Zambia, Mozambique and Tanzania agreed to set up a joint institute for the training of their defence and police forces. The success of this joint defence and security agreement could lead to military cooperation of the entire SADCC states. See Tony Hodges, 'Mozambique: The Politics of Liberation', in Carter and O'Meara, *op. cit.*, p. 78 (see note 19 above).

12 The Future of Regionalism in Africa

John Ravenhill

Is there a future for regionalism in Africa? Sceptics appear to have good grounds for posing this question for in the last two decades the African continent has hosted a number of spectacular failures (among the most notable being the East African Community, the West African Customs Union (UDAO), and the Central African Federation); other regional organisations which existed only on paper, e.g. the Ghana-Guinea-Mali Union, or which have assumed a decidedly moribund appearance, e.g. the African and Mauritian Common Organisation (OCAM); and only a handful of arrangements which might legitimately claim to have achieved a moderate degree of success, e.g. the West African Economic Community (CEAO), and the Organisation for the Development of the Senegal River (OMVS). In aggregate, the balance sheet on regional cooperation is far from encouraging, and as a distinguished student of integration commented, the problems of state and nation-building in Africa are of such a magnitude as to make regional collective action 'seem beside the point'.[1] Yet interest in regionalism in Africa is far from dead; in recent years, two new major groupings have emerged – the Economic Community of West African States (ECOWAS), and the Southern African Development Coordination Conference (SADCC).

Regionalism retains a strong emotive/symbolic appeal for African leaders (it is surely no accident that the political grouping of African states is the only continental/regional organisation whose title includes the word 'unity'). To this must be added two factors which have revitalised the interest in regionalism since the early 1970s. The first of these was the success of OPEC which, however much this has ultimately rebounded to the disadvantage of most African states, nevertheless provided a compelling case for collective 'Southern' action in pursuit of counter-dependency ambitions. Secondly, if the growth of international economic interdependence in the 1960s and 1970s suggested that regional integration was an obsolescent strategy, then the subsequent failure of global North-South negotiations, and the disappointing results of closer linkages with groups of industrialised states (one dramatic instance being the Lome Convention), has caused LDCs in general, and African countries in particular, to rediscover regionalism as a potential strategy for reducing external vulnerabilities. As the signatories of the OAU's *Lagos Plan* noted:

> The effect of unfulfilled promises of global development strategies has been more sharply felt in Africa than in the other continents of the world .... Africa is unable to point to any significant growth rate, or satisfactory index of general well-being, in the past 20 years. Faced with this situation, and determined to undertake measures for the basic restructuring of our continent, we resolved to adopt a far-reaching regional approach based primarily on collective self-reliance.[2]

It remains the case that the regional level is the locus of African states' principal foreign policy concerns.[3] The economic, military, and political weaknesses of most African countries render them particularly vulnerable to intervention by dominant regional powers e.g. Libya and South Africa or extra-continental actors.

If African leaders, in their pursuit of regionalist aspirations, are not to fall victims to Santayana's famous dictum, then they must internalise and apply the lessons to be learned from the lack of success of previous integration efforts not only among African countries, but also in other Third World regions. The implications of these past failures are presented in the first part of this chapter; the second analyses the extent to which these have been absorbed in the designs of ECOWAS and the SADCC.

Two Decades of Regionalism in Africa

Most African countries came to independence at a time when enthusiasm for regional integration reached its peak. Rapid economic growth in Europe, attributed in large part to the success of the European Economic Community, and the arguments for regionalism among LDCs put forward by the Economic Commission for Latin America under Raoul Prebisch, reinforced the Pan-African sentiments of African leaders. This was the era of naive wishful thinking on regionalism: integration was viewed as a collective good – a goal to be pursued for its own sake. Concurrently regionalism was often treated as if it would be a *deus ex machina* bringing immediate solutions to Africa's many developmental needs. Given these exaggerated expectations it was scarcely surprising that enthusiasm for the concept, and for the paper schemes that were created, quickly collapsed when confronted with the reality of Africa's political economy. In retrospect, what potential realistically existed for the union of such non-contiguous states as Ghana and Guinea?

Africa, in fact, is uniquely ill-suited for regional integration; at least, for the form most typically adopted by developing countries: the integration of markets.[4] The world's least developed and most politically unstable continent possesses few of the features identified by theorists as propitious for integration. Trade between African countries linked in regional schemes has been lower (with the partial exception of the East African Community) than between member states of other integration systems – not only significantly below the intra-bloc trade of the EEC but also that of other Third World regions. African economies, far from complementing each other, compete in the world market as exporters of primary products. But, more important, African economies are simply irrelevant to the needs of their neighbours – a problem compounded by the lack of physical infrastructure, which hampers communications. Add to this a variety of languages, currency areas, continuing close ties to ex-metropoles, and a critical shortage of skilled personnel, and one arrives at a very dismal scenario indeed. This is not to say that integration is precluded in Africa: rather, these factors inevitably make integration more difficult. The key problems facing African leaders are those of deciding what forms of regional cooperation are most likely to succeed and of how to design arrangements for mutual benefit.

Generally it has been the case that the more grandiose the design of the regional scheme, the greater the likelihood of its failure.[5] This was particularly true of political unions but free trade areas, customs unions, and common markets have been equally vulnerable. Integration schemes based on the liberalisation of trade were particularly popular in the decade of independence. In part this was a colonial legacy: the former metropoles had created federations and common markets for reasons of administrative convenience and/or to favour white settler populations. The European experience of market integration, buttressed by the arguments of orthodox theorists of integration such as Viner, Meade and Lipsey, appeared to justify further experimentation along these lines. But it soon became obvious that orthodox integration theory was entirely inappropriate for regions where the problems were non-orthodox, i.e. where the principal need was not for the consolidation and rationalisation of existing production according to comparative advantage, but to promote development by employing previously non-utilised factors of production.

It was not so much a question of the principal method advocated by orthodox theorists (market integration) being wrong in principle but that the unintended consequences of its application gave rise to major problems which fostered regional disintegration. Some initial gains in trade occurred but these were modest and based on only a limited number of products since no significant developments in production structure were realised.[6] More important, the experience of all Third World integrative schemes has been that trade liberalisation, undertaken without corrective measures, has accentuated intra-regional inequalities as new production activities locate primarily around regional growth poles. This problem is sometimes referred to as the 'Matthew' effect.[7] Inevitably a situation is produced which neo-functionalist theorists have labelled 'premature politicisation': the development of damaging political disputes within regional groupings before significant gains from regional cooperation are realised. Attempts to correct the imbalance of benefits have tended to reduce intra-regional trade: either governments acted unilaterally in imposing non-tariff barriers to protect domestic industry as regional tariffs were removed, and/or the corrective measures developed at the regional level, e.g. the transfer tax system of the East African Community, and the 'single tax' system of the Customs and Economic Union of Central Africa (UDEAC), acted perversely to protect inefficient domestic firms and to encourage intra-regional import substitution.[8]

Besides the issue of inter-country distribution of gains, market integration also creates problems for the participating states with regard to the sharing of gains with multi-national corporations (MNCs). A merging of markets enhances the bargaining power of MNCs which are contemplating establishment within the region since, in the absence of a regional agreement on the conditions to be offered to foreign investment, they will be able to supply the regional market from the state which offers them the most favourable terms. Studies have also shown that MNCs established within a region tend to oppose rationalisation of production structures where they have estabished parallel investments in each of the national markets, preferring instead to integrate vertically with the parent corporation and reap monopoly profits in each of the protected national markets. Accordingly, they have been enthusiastic proponents of measures such as the 'single tax' system which protects inefficient production in segmented markets, and have lobbied effectively for high external tariffs and other barriers to discourage the entry of competitors.[9]

Various measures which have been adopted in an attempt to

ameliorate the distribution problem have seldom been effective. By far the most popular type of technique is fiscal compensation but, as Vaitsos notes, although this is claimed by orthodox theorists to be the most efficient redistributional mechanism, it 'has proven in various cases to be of the least appropriate and politically most unacceptable instruments'.[10] This is largely because it fails to address the most fundamental issue in the distribution crisis: the location of industrial production within the region with its spillover effects on employment, technological transfer and learning-by-doing. Another frequently-deployed mechanism – the creation of regional development banks, often charged with the mandate of favouring the less-developed states in a region – has had a similar lack of success largely because the banks have been unable to attract a sufficient volume of extra-regional capital to make a significant contribution to productive activities.

These observations suggest a stark conclusion: regional schemes in Africa based on the integration of markets have very little prospect of success owing to the distributional crises that are generated. Such crises cannot be solved through market machanisms, e.g. fiscal compensation alone. Rather, the problem of ensuring an equitable distribution of regional productive activities can be solved only through sectoral planning, and the allocation of industries by agreement among the participating states. Yet this solution is unpalatable for most African countries in that it necessitates a surrender of some critical policy-making autonomy. Successful regional planning would require not only a harmonisation of policies *vis-à-vis* foreign investors, but of fiscal and monetary policies. This form of policy integration may well conflict with other objectives of national policy; since the benefits to be derived from integration are at best extremely uncertain and likely to affect only marginally a country's development prospects, it is scarcely surprising that governments have rejected the planned integration that would be necessary to bring an acceptable distribution of benefits from free trade.[11]

Here we appear to have arrived at a dead end, or at least a vicious circle: regionalism in Africa based on the liberalisation of trade will give rise to an unacceptable imbalance of gains; the measures necessary to correct this problem will not be taken since they impose unacceptable constraints on the latitude of decision-makers. Is regionalism, then, doomed to failure? Fortunately the answer is negative or, more accurately, conditional: if the liberalisation of trade is the principal basis for integrative activities then the probable outcome will be failure. Yet while market integration has been the most popular basis for regional integration in Africa, as in other Third World areas, it is by no means the only possible approach. Other methods offer a greater probability of success.

An Alternative Basis for Regionalism in Africa

A realistic approach to regionalism in Africa must start with the recognition that integration is an instrument for the realisation of desired ends: integration itself is not necessarily good nor evil; no *a priori* case can be made for any regional scheme.[12] This appeared to be acknowledged by African leaders in their actions, if not their rhetoric, in the two post-independence decades. Similarly, there is no point in refusing to acknowledge the structural diversity of African states and their ideological diversity. None of these factors precludes the realisation of gains from regional cooperation but they do suggest that these will not automatically be realised through the operation of market forces, and that certain types of integration should be discounted on both economic and political grounds.

A consideration of these factors should produce a more realistic assessment of the type of gains that can be expected from regional cooperation. In Africa, the low levels of development and the limited possibilities for profitable intra-regional exchange simply do not provide the basis for integration at the present time. Regional cooperation must start from the premise that the requisites for integration do not presently exist but must be created. This is in contrast to the dominant approach of the first two decades where there appeared to be a belief that integration could be legislated from above, *ex nihilo*. There is little purpose in liberalising trade when the parties have nothing to exchange; regional cooperation *inter alia* must create the basis for trade.

The approach advocated is based on incrementalism. It asserts that mutual gains will not arise automatically from market integration, and that the disputes that these grandiose schemes generate are likely to be counter-productive to cooperation in Africa (would relations between Kenya and Tanzania be so bitter had it not been for the East African Community?). If integration is not to be guided by market forces, considerable effort will have to be devoted to identifying possible areas for profitable mutual cooperation. Accordingly, unlike many of the previous integrative efforts, the foundation on which cooperation will be built must be planning, rather than *laissez-faire* forces.

Prospects for success will be improved if efforts are concentrated on projects where cooperation is perceived as being essential to the realisation of gains, and the actual benefits from the projects might reasonably be expected to be realised in the short term. A number of areas with the potential for mutually profitable cooperation can be identified:

(a) Joint ventures for the production of certain goods or services. This might include sectoral planning in order for intra-industry specialisation to occur. In this manner, all participants acquire some expertise in the sector concerned, and a package deal is constructed with sufficient payoffs to interest all participants. This might, but need not necessarily, include joint ownership of the projects. One example of cooperation along these lines is the West African clinker project.

(b) Joint action to promote the development of common resources. Here one of the best examples is joint development of river basin resources. Hydro-electric power represents one of the most efficient solutions to Africa's energy problems, but its high initial capital costs in combination with the problem of interfering with other countries' access to a common resource make exploitation of its potential difficult for an African country acting alone. Cooperation for this purpose has already been successfully pursued by the Organisation for the Development of the Senegal River (OMVS).

(c) Promotion of intra-regional trade. Here the emphasis would be on utilising existing regional production in an effort to match regional surpluses and deficits. Unlike the market approach to integration, the participating countries make no commitment to a permanent reduction of trade barriers; their obligations are limited to the quantities agreed in interstate negotiations. Ideally, payments for such trade would be made in local currencies in order that scarce foreign exchange might be conserved.[13] Tanzania and Mozambique have conducted a not inconsiderable volume of trade on this basis.

(d) Joint action to improve bargaining positions *vis-à-vis* extra-regional economic actors. This might take the form of coordination of marketing of certain primary products (the success of which will depend in part on the market share of the regional partners). The potential for cooperation in other areas exists, e.g. in negotiating conditions for foreign investment in a region, but the restraints that the necessary measures would place on decision-making autonomy are unlikely to be acceptable to most states at the present time.

(e) Cooperation to mobilise financial assistance from foreign sources. This is particularly attractive at a time when the international aid community continues to favour regional projects, e.g. 15 per cent of the funds available for programming under the second Lome Convention are reserved for regional ventures. Again, the OMVS provides the example of a success story: it has gained Western and Arab funding for 90 per cent of the costs of two dams for an ambitious hydro-electric power and irrigation project.

Implicit in these proposals is considerable flexibility in the definition of the 'region'. This is necessary because not all programmes are of equal relevance to all states within a geographical area.[14] Not only do interests differ but differential commitments to regional goals can be anticipated. Considerable scope exists for bilateral or trilateral cooperation which is largely beyond the corncern of neighbouring states. A rigid framework, as was the case with the Treaty For East African Cooperation, makes it impossible for countries to participate selectively in those activities which are of most interest to them.

Flexibility of institutions and instruments of regional cooperation is desirable also in that this recognises that actors' interests do not remain constant. In part this is related to change in the extra-regional economic environment, which is likely to remain more important than intra-regional economic activities for most African states for the foreseeable future. It also anticipates that there will be a continuing rapid turnover of governments in many African states, possibly accompanied by dramatic shifts in policy. Since such transformations have often precipitated the collapse of regional institutions in the past, it is desirable that the framework of cooperation be insulated as much as possible from the consequences of sudden withdrawal by a member state. Flexible arrangements improve the prospects for projects to be continued with a minimum of damage. As a background paper prepared for the SADCC notes:

> Flexibility does not imply absence of institutions: it creates a need for bodies able to build, modify, and phase out arrangements. What it does imply is avoiding massive, interlocked institutional structures in which the institutional frame (not the content of the programme) becomes the justification of continued cooperation and through which problems of cooperation in one field are magnified into a general crisis of regionalism.[15]

Flexible, functionally-specific organisations have the advantage of impinging little on the sovereignty of participating states: decision-making power remains concentrated at the national level.

An incremental approach to regionalism in Africa based on the identification and implementation of limited functional projects is by no means a guarantee of success. Given the costs involved, a major infrastructural project, for instance, might consume a significant portion of a country's capital investment for that year – functional cooperation among poor states is inevitably highly politicised. But the incremental approach advocated does appear to avoid many of the problems that have beset the more grandiose schemes based on an integration of markets. The extent to which the lessons of earlier regional failures have been absorbed in current attempts at cooperation in Africa is examined in the second part of this chapter.

ECOWAS

The Economic Community of West African States, founded in May 1975, is the most ambitious sub-continental integration scheme attempted in Africa. Linking sixteen countries, ECOWAS is the first major regional scheme to bridge the Anglophone-Francophone divide which bedevilled previous cooperative movements in West Africa.[16] Yet despite its relatively recent date of establishment, ECOWAS, in its reliance on *laissez-faire* principles of integration, appears to be a throwback to the ideas of the 1960s. At a time when regional schemes in other areas of the Third World, e.g. the Caribbean Community (CARICOM), and the Association of South-East Asian Nations (ASEAN), have moved towards more intensive integration on a less extensive scale and, in particular, increasingly have adopted a *dirigiste* approach to sectoral planning, ECOWAS has staked its future on the ultimate construction of a common market.

In attempting to give free reign to market forces, including the free movement of factors of production, the drafters of the ECOWAS Treaty apparently have failed to heed the lessons of the previous two decades of experience of Third World integrative systems, and have missed some of the more exciting possibilities for cooperation in West Africa. That ECOWAS should revert to the ideas predominant at the time of independence is understandable in that its own origins date from this period. ECOWAS is the realisation of a long-frustrated drive for a West African Economic Community which can be traced back to proposals made by the Economic Commission for Africa in 1963 for coordinated industrial development in the region. From 1965 to 1968 negotiations were held with the aim of establishing a West African Regional Group whose ultimate goal would be the creation of a regional common market. The Nigerian civil war effectively terminated this stage of the integrative movement. But following the war's conclusion, Nigeria once again took up the regionalist cause and aided by the breaking-down of Anglophone-Francophone barriers in the successful negotiation of the Lome Convention, successfully prompted its neighbours into agreement on the regional scheme.[17]

The drafters of the ECOWAS Treaty did avoid one mistake of earlier integrative movements in that allowance is made for a gradual phasing-in of the trade provisions (the common market is not scheduled to be fully implemented until fifteen years after the coming into force of the Treaty). From the perspective of institutional survival, this approach has certain advantages: ECOWAS has already prolonged its existence for seven years without the member states having to make difficult choices which impose significant costs on their economies. Whether this has fostered loyalties to the Community remains to be seen since the true test of the commitment of the members has yet to be faced. But the failure of participating countries to pay their contributions to the ECOWAS budget (close to twelve million dollars was outstanding from ten of the sixteen members at the end of 1981), and the delays in implementing the first stage of the customs union – a freezing of tariffs – might be perceived as indicators that there is no great faith in the future of the scheme.

One advantage which orthodox theorists of economic integration see in common markets is that the commitment to liberalise trade inevitably spills over to necessitate harmonisation of policies in other fields. Where large volumes of trade are involved, and therefore significant gains expected, as was the case with the EEC, participating countries may be willing to tolerate the erosion of their decision-making autonomy. In Third World integrative schemes, the reluctance of governments to relinquish any of their sovereignty is compounded by the lack of perception of significant gains from trade liberalisation. The ECOWAS Treaty spells out the spillover logic in that it requires eventual harmonisation of agricultural, industrial and monetary policies. If the aims of the Treaty are to be realised, the participating states will eventually have to agree on common pricing for agricultural products (to prevent growers in one country from selling to governments in another), common rules of origin for manufactured products, and the convertibility of currencies (there being presently ten different currency areas within ECOWAS). The issue to be faced by national policy-makers is whether the gains from the liberalisation of intra-regional trade (which, for 1973, was estimated to be only 2.1% of the total external trade of ECOWAS members),[18] are likely to compensate for the inevitable erosion of their autonomy in policy-making, and interference with the pursuit of other national objectives.

Policy harmonisation will disrupt existing regional cooperative arrangements. One of the most significant of these is the West African Monetary Union, the governing body of the Central Bank of West African States, which issues the CFA Franc. It is difficult to imagine that continuing participation in the franc zone as presently constituted would be compatible with obligations for monetary harmonisation under the ECOWAS Treaty. The six members of the UMDA would be required to give up an arrangement which, although having experienced some difficulties in the last few years, has been widely regarded as a stabilising factor in the economies of these states.[19] France also is unlikely to display any enthusiasm for the termination of these arrangements, given the advantages that they offer to French investors, trading companies, and expatriates. ECOWAS will also come into conflict with CEAO, an organisation widely perceived at the time of its establishment as a Francophone counter to Nigerian hegemonial designs within the region. Although created only two years prior to ECOWAS, CEAO has progressed more rapidly towards the realisation of similar goals. While the two organisations are not inherently incompatible, in that CEAO might eventually be subsumed under ECOWAS, their concurrent existence pits them as rivals in the quest for foreign assistance, staffing, etc. (see chapter 5). Implementation of the ECOWAS Treaty will require Francophone countries to give up functioning regional arrangements for an alternative whose benefits are uncertain.[20]

The thrust of this argument is not to dispute the desirability of regional cooperation in West Africa but to question whether the means selected by ECOWAS for its realisation are the most efficient. By aspiring to create a common market, ECOWAS has chosen the maximum constraints on the autonomy of the member states. The gains which might conceivably be realised from the liberalisation of trade are modest in comparison with the costs imposed. And ECOWAS, perversely, appears to be creating unnecessary difficulties for itself in its choice of initial projects. The first protocol to be implemented – on the free movement of people – while ultimately required in order to complete a common market, is one which is guaranteed to arouse considerable opposition given the social tensions that have arisen between migrants and host populations in West Africa in the past. Rather than beginning with a project which will bring immediate and recognisable gains, the planners have chosen a controversial project with little immediate payoff. Similarly, the leaders of the Community have unnecessarily complicated their task by adopting the politically sensitive protocol on Defence. Why this should be part of the baggage of an economic organisation which has no commitment towards political integration is unclear, except as a means of appeasing the long-standing ambitions of certain heads of state.[21]

On the matter of probably unequal distribution of the gains from regional cooperation, the drafters of the Treaty again appear to have learned little from the past. The only mechanism in the Treaty which addresses this issue is Article 50, which provides for the creation of an ECOWAS Fund. According to the Treaty's fourth protocol, the purposes of the Fund will be to provide compensation and other forms of assistance to member states which have suffered losses as a result of the application of the provisions of the Treaty, or as a result of the location of Community enterprises; to provide grants for financing national or community research and development activities including feasibility studies and development projects; to promote development projects in the less-developed member states; to guarantee foreign investments made in member states; and to facilitate the mobilisation of internal and external financial resources. While this mandate is a broad one, and might justify a wide range of activities, particularly in the name of promoting development, it appears that the Fund will not go beyond the traditional fiscal compensatory devices which have proved so inadequate in other Third World schemes. Certainly it appears to offer no solution to the vexatious problem of imbalance in the location of production activities. Cynics might be excused for noting that it has been Nigeria, the most potent industrial force in the region, which has been the most enthusiastic proponent of the scheme.

If ECOWAS has yet to come to terms with the intra-regional distributional problem, the same can be said for the problem of the sharing of gains with foreign investors. Although the trade liberalisation programme requires that 51% of the shares of industries be in indigenous hands by the date that the common market is inaugurated, this is but one of the less important issues in negotiations with foreign investment on the conditions of its entry. A more complete harmonisation of policies would probably be unacceptable to those states more closely integrated into the international division of labour. This problem is symptomatic of the difficulties that the scheme will face: decision-making on the basis of the lowest common denominator is likely to prevail in a situation where few of the parties are convinced that the benefits of collective action will compensate for the loss in decision-making autonomy required to realise these benefits, and where decisions require the unanimous consent of the parties. Again, the design of the scheme unnecessarily complicates matters. ECOWAS provides a rigid framework in which all members are required to accept all aspects of the Treaty. Yet some of these may have little relevance to a number of the parties (there would appear to be little gain from a common market linking Niger and Guinea Bissau, for instance). A lack of flexibility in the Treaty and the institutions reduces the likelihood that it will be possible to insulate the cooperative arrangements from damaging inter-state disputes (a problem experienced already with the exclusion of Master Sergeant Samuel Doe from the fifth ECOWAS summit conference).

Rather ironically, the most successful project undertaken by ECOWAS to date – the telecommunications project – illustrates the potential of regional cooperation on functional issues, independent of more grandiose designs for market integration. Prospects for the success of the Community will be greater if more energy is devoted to this type of cooperation rather than to chasing inappropriate and largely illusory goals.

The Southern African Development Coordination Conference

In contrast to the framers of the ECOWAS Treaty, the leaders of the SADCC consciously eschewed those forms of regional cooperation which were so markedly unsuccessful in the first two decades of Africa's independence. In part, this can be attributed to a learning process by key leaders who had been involved in two of the more spectacular failures among African regional schemes: the East African Community, and the Central African Federation. As the late Sir Seretse Khama noted at the first SADCC summit:

> The basis of our cooperation, built on concrete projects and on specific programmes rather than on grandiose schemes and massive bureaucratic institutions, must be the assured mutual advantage of all participating states.[22]

The SADCC grew out of a political grouping, the Frontline States, whose objective was to bring about independence under majority rule for Rhodesia and Namibia.[23] As the liberation of Zimbabwe increasingly appeared imminent, the attention of the Frontline States turned towards the development of a strategy for attaining their objectives in the two remaining territories under white domination – Namibia and South Africa. Acknowledging that the struggle for majority rule in the latter would entail a long-term commitment, the leaders sought to institutionalise the informal cooperation which had been achieved within the Frontline Group. Explicit recognition was given to the importance of economic factors and, in particular, to removing the constraints that economic dependence on South Africa placed on the autonomy of decision-makers. As the late Botswana President stated: 'economic dependence has in many ways made our political independence somewhat meaningless'.[24] A vivid illustration of this occurred in 1978 when Zambia felt obliged to re-open its border with Rhodesia in order to relieve its transport difficulties. Damage to regional infrastructure which occurred during the struggles for Zimbabwean and Namibian independence had increased the dependence of the Frontline States on South African transport facilities.

Since two of the countries – Botswana and Zambia – along with Zimbabwe are landlocked, a resolution of their transport problems inevitably requires cooperation with their neighbours. A regional approach was attractive also in that it appeared to offer an effective alternative to South Africa's proposals for a 'constellation of states'. Economic independence might best be attained through the development of the sub-continent as an integrated region 'rather than a cluster of impoverished chauvinistic entities' (in the words of Sir Seretse Khama). There was recognition from the beginning, however, that the diversity of countries within the region precluded a regional scheme based on the integration of markets. An independent Zimbabwe would dominate the region's economy: its GNP would be 50% above that of the second largest economy, Zambia, and its unusually diversified production structure would serve as a focal point of industrial development within a regional free trade area. (The evolution of SADCC is discussed in chapter 11).

SADCC was not to be a rigid institution. The final declaration issued by the Arusha conference stated that:

> We, the majority-ruled states of Southern Africa, do not envisage this regional economic coordination as exclusive. The initiative towards economic liberation has flowed from our experience of joint action for political liberation. We envisage regional coordination as open to all genuinely independent Southern African states.[25]

Accordingly, an invitation was extended to Lesotho, Malawi, and Swaziland to join the grouping, and an announcement was made that Namibia and Zimbabwe would also be welcome once they had attained 'genuine independence'. The rapid unfolding of events in Zimbabwe which led to its independence in the following April greatly improved the SADCC's prospects for success.

At the first summit conference of the group, each participating state was given responsibility for drawing up plans for cooperation in one or more of the principal areas identified at the Arusha conference. Rather than creating an elaborate regional superstructure, cooperation would be designed and implemented by national governments: the purpose of the grouping is exactly what its name suggests – a means of coordinating the activities of the national governments in the region. At the second SADCC summit in July 1981, agreement was reached on an institutional framework which includes summit meetings, a council of ministers, a standing committee of officials, functional commissions, and a secretariat. Bureaucratisation at the regional level would be kept to a minimum: the summit communiqué observed that

> These institutions will provide SADCC with an effective and flexible mechanism for regional consultation and decision-making. SADCC has eschewed the creation of a large and unwieldy bureaucracy in favour of a system which places responsibility for implementation of its programme on the Governments of the Member States.

The functional commissions were to be located in the member state assigned major responsibility for that area of cooperation; each state therefore would gain a share in the revenues spent in support of regional activities. There would be no single SADCC headquarters. A Secretariat, consisting of four professionals and four support staff, was scheduled to begin activities as soon as possible. This was to be established in Gaberone, and initially funded by the Swedish government. Its small size was to limit the costs imposed on the national governments – both financial and in terms of encroachment on the autonomy of national decision-making. An approach to cooperation based on specific projects minimises the problem of imbalances in the distribution of gains from regional cooperation – countries within the SADCC are not obliged to undertake all projects; they are free to choose those which they perceive as offering concrete benefits while not impinging on other national development goals.

SADCC's decision to focus regional cooperation on specific projects appeared to pay early dividends. By the time of the second summit, 22 of the 97 original transport and communications projects were being implemented; a further 29 had been prepared and submitted to international financing agencies. Upgrading and rehabilitation of existing transport links was laying the foundations for increased trade between the member states. But this was occurring not through a grand design, such as a common market, but by taking advantage of regional complementarities – an approach which had already led to an encouraging volume of exchange between Mozambique and Tanzania. In their design for the SADCC, the leaders of the Frontline States appear to have avoided some of the most obvious factors which contributed to the failure of regional cooperation in Africa in the past. A process of learning has occurred. This, of course, is no guarantee of the scheme's success. A variety of significant problems remain for the Conference to overcome. In its efforts to reduce its dependence on South Africa, for example, the Conference has placed great emphasis on infrastructural projects, most of which can only be realised with the help of exchanging one dependency for another, but if aid is not forthcoming in significant quantities then there is the possibility that momentum will be lost.[26] Here there is something of a vicious circle: some Western donors have stated that they are not convinced of the need for new infrastructure in the absence of present trade to justify these links; but without the necessary infrastructure it is unlikely that commerce will ever develop.

SADCC remains extremely vulnerable to South African action which can disrupt the cooperative endeavour through the exercise of its considerable positive and negative power. The Republic has already demonstrated that it has the capability and willingness to launch military strikes deep inside its northern neighbours; it is also supporting anti-government guerrillas in Mozambique which have cut communications and power links in the south of that country. South Africa can also offer a carrot by exploiting the extreme dependence of Botswana, Lesotho, and Swaziland on its infrastructure and labour market. Improvements in the Southern African Customs Union, and plans for new transport links might tempt the three 'hostage states' into closer links with the Republic, and divert them from the dependency-reduction goals of the SADCC.

Conclusion

ECOWAS and the SADCC offer alternative paths to the realisation of African aspirations for regional cooperation. ECOWAS is in the tradition of the grand design for regionalism, common in the early post-independence period and still advocated by the OAU (e.g. the *Lagos Plan of Action* commits member states to work for an African Common Market by the year 2000), and the Economic Commission for Africa. Too often, this approach has been marked by wishful thinking, with little attention being paid to the manner in which the aspirations might be realised. Regionalism will find few adherents in

Africa unless it provides demonstrable benefits to the participants, and the plans for cooperative action provide good reason to believe that such benefits can be realised. African countries have become increasingly sceptical of the grand designs put forward by the continental organisations: the most recent ECA Treaty, for a Preferential Trade Area for East and Southern Africa, was signed by only nine of the eighteen states in the region.

Little thought appears to have been given by the continental organisations to whether a preferential trade area is necessary or sufficient or even desirable in realising regional cooperation in Africa. There has been little learning from the dismal experience of two decades of such schemes on the continent. A similar statement can be made regarding the ECOWAS Treaty. In this instance, it would be a pleasure to have a critic ridicule this argument in fifteen years' time by pointing to a successful West African Common Market. I fear that this will not be the case. ECOWAS has yet to go beyond an elaborate statement of intent; when implementation and thus hard choices are required of the member states, then the fragility of commitment to the scheme will be exposed.

The principal problem with cooperative schemes based on the integration of markets is that they impose considerable constraints on the latitude of national decision-making without providing the means by which sufficient gains to warrant this sacrifice might be realised. Trade liberalisation schemes generate internal contradictions which tend to disjoin such programmes in the absence of planning on a regional scale to distribute the benefits from cooperation more equitably. Inequalities generated by the operation of market forces can be solved only through *dirigiste* actions, but these require further inroads into the decision-making autonomy of the member states. Although African countries may have found a new enthusiasm for regional self-reliance, the case for harmonisation of policies is for most states insufficiently compelling to justify the necessary erosion of their sovereignty.

SADCC offers an alternative approach to regionalism, one which is better grounded in the realities of the African situation and which draws on the past experience of failed regional schemes. It has chosen to identify concrete projects where gains from cooperation may be realised in the immediate future, projects which can lay the foundations for further cooperation once the basis for trade has been established. In its flexible institutions, with their minimal demands on national decision-making autonomy, the SADCC appears to point to the only feasible route for regional cooperation in a continent which is likely to be increasingly characterised by a growth in inter-country inequalities, and political instability.[27] There are problems with this incrementalist and functionalist approach: regional cooperation based on a number of bilateral agreements may miss opportunities for wider participation and thus be sub-optimal in terms of the realisation of potential gains. A further weakness of a project-based approach is that it lacks the automatic spillover effects associated with market integration; there is a danger that cooperation will become encapsulated in a limited number of projects unless efforts are continuously made to identify new prospects for cooperative action. Here the role of the regional secretariat will be vital. If it is to have a staff of only four professionals, as in the SADCC case, considerable support will be required from the national bureaucracies. Certainly, the approach adopted by the SADCC is no guarantee of success for any regionalist scheme in Africa, given the formidable economic and political constraints under which they must operate. But it does appear to offer greater potential than the wishful thinking and grandiose schemes proposed by Africa's continental organisations.

Notes

1 Ernst B. Haas, *The Obsolescence of Regional Integration Theory* (Berkeley: Institute of International Studies, University of California, Berkeley, Research Series No. 25, 1975), p. 17.

2 Organisation of African Unity, *Lagos Plan of Action for the Economic Development of Africa 1980-2000* (Geneva: International Institute for Labour Studies, 1981), p. 5.

3 Timothy M. Shaw, 'Regional Cooperation and Conflict in Africa' *International Journal* 30, 4 (Autumn 1975), p. 671.

4 John Ravenhill, 'Regional Integration and Development in Africa: Lessons from the East African Community', *Journal of Commonwealth and Comparative Politics* XVII, 3 (November 1979) pp. 227–46.

5 Cf. John P. Renninger, *Multinational Cooperation for Development in West Africa* (New York: Pergamon Press for UNITAR, 1979), p. 25.

6 On the East African Community see Arthur Hazlewood, *Economic Integration: The East African Experience* (London: Heinemann, 1975). See also Chapter 9. It was reported that trade between the member states of the Mano River Union following the elimination of tariff barriers consisted mainly of confectionery! *West Africa* (19 October 1981, p. 2451); see also Chapter 8.

7 'For whosoever hath, to him shall be given, and he shall have more abundance: but whosoever hath not, from him shall be taken away even that he hath.' (Matthew 13:12) See Robert K. Merton, 'The Matthew Effect in Science', *Science 159* (January 1968) pp. 56–63; and Robert W. Jackman, 'Dependence on Foreign Investment and Economic Growth in the Third

World' *World Politics* XXXIV, 2 (January 1982), pp. 175-96.

8   The UDEAC experience is examined in Steven Langdon and Lynn K. Mytelka, 'Africa in the Changing World Economy' in Colin Legum, I. William Zartman, Steven Langdon and Lynn K. Mytelka, *Africa in the 1980s* (New York: McGraw-Hill, 1979), pp. 179-88.

9   Constantine V. Vaitsos, 'Crisis in Regional Economic Cooperation (Integration) among Developing Countries: A Survey', *World Development* 6 (June 1978), pp. 729-736; and Langdon and Mytelka, *op. cit.*, (see note 8 above).

10   Vaitsos, *op. cit.*, (see note 9 above).

11   Hazlewood notes, for example, that an extension of planning activities in the East African Community would have been totally unacceptable to the Kenyan government; see chapter 9. The experience of the Andean Pact suggests that regional industrial planning is no panacea for the distributional problems encountered by cooperative efforts among LDCs.

12   Peter Robson, *The Economics of International Integration* (London: George Allen & Unwin, 1980) p. 147; cf. Vaitsos *op. cit.*

13   The possession of a neighbouring state's currency would be expected to encourage purchases from that state. Limitations placed on the utilisation of local currencies to finance payments deficits within the East African Community made such imbalances particularly burdensome for Tanzania and Uganda; efforts to conserve foreign exchange by delaying transfers of revenues to the headquarters of Community corporations were a precipitating factor in the Community's collapse. John Ravenhill, 'The Theory and Practice of Regional Integration in East Africa' in Christian P. Potholm and Richard A. Fredland (eds), *Integration and Disintegration in East Africa* (Lanham, Maryland: University Press of America, 1980), pp. 49-50.

14   There is no such thing as a 'natural' region: they are the artificial constructs of participating countries and external agencies. On the general problem of defining regions see Richard Falk and Saul Mendlovitz (eds) *Regional Politics and World Order* (San Francisco: W.H. Freeman, 1974).

15   Southern African Development Coordination Conference, 'First Steps Toward Economic Integration: Interests, Instrumentalities' (Arusha: mimeo, 1979) p. 36.

16   See appendix for Members of ECOWAS.

17   On the origins of ECOWAS see Isebill V. Gruhn, 'The Lome Convention: Inching towards interdependence', *International Organisation* 30, 2 (Spring 1976), pp. 242-62; Aguibou Y. Yansane, 'The State of Economic Integration in North West Africa South of the Sahara: The Emergence of the Economic Community of West African States (ECOWAS)', *African Studies Review* XX, 2 (September 1977), pp. 63-88; and Olatunde J.B. Ojo, 'Nigeria and the formation of ECOWAS', *International Organisation* 34, 4 (Autumn, 1980), pp. 571-604.

18   Cited in R.I. Onwuka, 'The ECOWAS Treaty: inching towards implementation', *The World Today* 36, 2 (February 1980), p. 53.

19   Andrew Liddell, 'Financial Cooperation in Africa – French Style', *The Banker* 129, No. 643 (September 1979), pp. 105-111.

20 On the potential incompatibilities between ECOWAS and other West African regional organisations see Ralph Ihheanyi Onwuka, 'Independence within ECOWAS', *West Africa* (10, 17 October 1977) pp. 2078–9 and 2126–7.

21 It is interesting to note that the OMVS, whose objectives are limited to the pursuit of economic and technical projects has been markedly more successful than its predecessor – the Organisation of Senegal River States (OERS) – which pursued cultural and political goals in addition to economic cooperation.

22 Quoted in *Africa Research Bulletin* (Economic, Financial, Technical Series) (June 15–July 14, 1979), p. 5155.

23 For further details on the origins of the SADCC and its strategy see Michael Clough and John Ravenhill, 'Regionalism in Southern Africa: the SADCC', in Michael Clough (ed.) *Political Change in Southern Africa* (Berkeley: Institute of International Studies, University of California, 1982), chapter 6.

24 *Africa Research Bulletin* (June 15–July 14, 1979), p. 5155.

25 SADCC, 'Southern Africa: Toward Economic Liberation', Declaration by the Frontline States (Arusha, 3 July 1979), p. 6.

26 The initial proposals of the SADCC called for a total of $2 billion in assistance but donor-pledges realised at the first SADCC donor conference in Maputo in November 1980 amounted to only $650 million. The majority of this total was not additional funding, but a re-designation of funds previously committed to the region by the principal donors.

27 See, for instance, Colin Legum, 'Communal Confict and International Intervention in Africa', in Legum *et. al., Africa in the 1980s: a Continent in Crisis* (New York: McGraw Hill, 1979), pp. 23–66.

13 The Southern African Customs Union: Politics of Dependence

Robert D.A. Henderson

The United Nations Conference on 'Regionalism and the New International Economic Order' (8–9 May 1980) recommended that 'developing countries should urgently and seriously study the feasibility of implementing the "Regional and Inter-Regional Strategy for Collective Self-Reliance", not as a substitute for, but as a positive, necessary complement to the global negotiations on the new international development strategy and the establishment of the new international economic order (NIEO).'[1] It was also agreed that regionalism was necessary with 'its roots in the soil of real economic, social and financial cooperation' and proposed such cooperation among developing countries 'on the subregional, regional and inter-regional levels in a number of areas.'[2] In the light of these statements, can the Southern African Customs Union (SACU), composed of Botswana, Lesotho, Swaziland,[3] and South Africa, be seen as an example of an effective, functional regional organisation which could contribute to a Third World unity and thus, be a useful component in North-South negotiations to bring about NIEO?

Can SACU more accurately (for the purposes of analysis and prediction) be seen in terms of possible roles it could play as a regional organisation in international relations? Charles Pentland has argued that international organisations can play three different, though not mutually exclusive, roles in international relations. These include being used by a state(s) as an instrument of national foreign policy in accordance with the traditional state-centric view; to serve as an institutional manifestation to modify states' behaviour (perhaps interdependently); and to achieve a measure of institutional autonomy operating as an actor in its own right.[4] In addition to considering SACU as a viable regional economic organisation within the Third World and whether it can be better seen in terms of specific roles with their implications, this chapter will outline SACU's prospects for the future both regionally and inter-regionally.

But what is SACU? Basically, it is an international governmental organisation (INGO) comprising four member-states. Its organisational objective or purpose is the pursuit of common economic aims (as opposed to other possibilities such as joint military security or being multi-purpose) within a regional geographical scope (as opposed to a global scope) for its interactions.[5] Furthermore, as a customs union (i.e. free interchange of goods and uniform customs tariffs), it has a higher level of economic integration among its member states than either a preferential trade area (PTA) or a free trade area (FTA), though such integration is less than that of a common market. The remainder of this chapter is divided into five sections. The first outlines the historical background of SACU from 1889 to the present. The next three sections attempt to utilise Pentland's three roles for international organisations to analyse how SACU interacts both among its member-states and within Africa. And finally, mention will be made of SACU's future prospects in the short-, medium-. and long-term.

Historical Background[6]

In 1889, the Cape Colony and the Orange Free State Republic established a general customs union based on free trade between parties to the agreement, a common external tariff, and equitable division of the total amount of the duties collected.[7] By 1910, the customs union included almost all of the colonies and states of Southern Africa; the original members being joined by Transvaal, Natal, Southern Rhodesia, North-Western Rhodesia, and the British Protectorates of Basutoland, Bechuanaland and Swaziland. (Basutoland and Bechuanaland had joined in 1891, followed by Swaziland in 1903.)

However, as a result of the May 1910 agreement to form the Union of South Africa out of the Cape Colony, Natal, the Orange Free State and Transvaal, it was decided to scrap the old customs union. Under a new agreement concluded in September of the same year, the new customs union would only be composed of the Union of South Africa and the three British protectorates. The basic features of the new customs union were: (1) maintenance of a common external customs tariff unless altered by the legislation enacted by South Africa or the three territories, (2) conformity of the territories to the relevant tariff laws of South Africa, (3) free interchange for the manufactured products of South Africa and the territories, and (4) payment by South Africa to the territories of a share of the total pool of customs revenue in proportion to the level of their trade between the years

1906-1908. The distribution of customs and excise revenue was determined as follows:

Table 13.1 1910 Customs Union Revenue-sharing

Country	Percentage share
Union of South Africa	98.68903
Basutoland (Lesotho)	0.88575
	(total share of BLS countries = 1.31097%)
Bechuanaland (Botswana)	0.27622
Swaziland	0.14900
	100.0%

While the customs union reduced the overall costs of administration (especially for the territories) as well as decreasing the profitability of smuggling between the members, it did include a number of disadvantages to the three territories. First, unlike the CEAO and ECOWAS analysed in chapter 5 by S.K.B. Asante, South Africa exercised effective control over customs and excise rates and policy, which were a major source of government revenue to the future BLS countries (Botswana, Lesotho and Swaziland), as well as a key instrument of economic policy. Second, there was no direct relationship between economic growth in the BLS countries and the growth of customs revenue (both of which were dependent upon South Africa's dominating volume of trade and level of customs duties). And third, while the agreement opened up the markets of the BLS countries to South African products, the agreement in principle provided for the 'free interchange' of manufactured goods. In practice, this was interpreted as 'free of duty', permitting South Africa to impose quotas on those BLS goods which could compete with its own large-scale, technically advanced industries; thus few manufacturing industries catering primarily for the South African market have developed within the BLS countries (i.e. no Hong Kongs mass-producing for export into South Africa).[8]

In 1967, the BLS countries compiled their grievances with the 1910 agreement into a memorandum for renegotiating the customs union. Among the grievances for which solutions were being sought were the 1910 revenue-sharing formula, the attraction of industry to the most developed sector (i.e. South Africa) of the customs area (referred to as

the 'polarisation' effect), quantitative restrictions upon imports into the South African market, the price-raising effect of South African-determined tariffs, loss of fiscal decision-making, etc. On December 11 1969, the four parties to the negotiations signed a new agreement. According to their joint communiqué,[9] the agreement included provision for:
  (i) duty-free interchange without quantitative control of domestic products;
  (ii) free interchange of duty-paid goods imported from outside the common customs area;
  (iii) levying of uniform customs, excise and sales duties;
  (iv) consultation on the imposition and amendment of customs duties;
  (v) imposition of additional duties for prospective purposes by Botswana, Lesotho and Swaziland;
  (vi) maintenance or increase of external tariffs necessary for the protection of specified industries in Botswana, Lesotho and Swaziland;
  (vii) regulating the marketing of agricultural products;
  (viii) a revised method of calculating the division of customs, excise and sales duty revenue;
  (ix) establishment of machinery for intergovernmental consultation through a Customs Union Commission; and
  (x) other related matters.

The 1910 agreement was to be terminated when the new agreement came into operation on 1 March 1970, but the arrangements for the division of revenue was to be effective as from 1 April 1969.

The new agreement's preamble set out the underlying basis for the new economic relationship between South Africa and the newly-independent BLS countries: (1) to ensure the continued economic development of the customs area as a whole, (2) to ensure in particular, that these arrangements encouraged the development of the less advanced members (i.e. the BLS countries) of the customs union and the diversification of their economies, and (3) to afford to all parties equitable benefits arising from trade among themselves and with other countries.[10] According to one observer, the most significant aspect of the new agreement was 'the implicit acceptance by South Africa of the principle of compensation for polarisation of development, price-raising effects and the loss of fiscal discretion'.[11]

Under the new revenue-sharing formula,[12] a 'multiplier' or 'enhancement factor' of 1.42 was introduced as a quantifiable method for providing the compensation which the BLS countries needed, despite the fact that this was less than the original BLS proposed factor. This meant that each of the BLS countries would receive 42 per cent more from the Consolidated Revenue Fund (which included the collected customs, excise and sales duties from all four member-states) than they individually paid into the fund. Under the old 1910 revenue-sharing formula, the BLS countries would have received R4 755 600 for 1968; the newly negotiated formula resulted in a total payment from the common fund of an unprecedented R17 007 200 (according to the Estimates of Additional Expenditure tabled in the South African House of Assembly[13]). This treble gain in customs union revenue provided the BLS countries with badly needed government revenue for recurrent expenditure as well as development capital.

In 1976, a further amendment to the new agreement was made. Since South Africa accounted for more than 90 per cent of the customs area's imports and dutiable production, the total revenue collected was a determinant of the South African economy. Generally, the BLS countries received 20 per cent of the value of their imports as revenue. But the fluctuations in the duties collected by South Africa alone have tended to result in parallel fluctuations in the revenue shares of the BLS countries, disrupting their ability to reasonably estimate available revenue for government expenditure and capital investment planning. The 'stabilisation' amendment substituted a percentage related to the actual calculated share (not less than 17 per cent and not more than 23 per cent) when the share differed from 20 per cent. This was intended to stabilise projected revenue shares from one year to another, but James Cobbe has argued that the 1976 amendment has made the original 1.42 enhancement factor 'largely obsolete and irrelevant' to the 1969 revenue-sharing formula and has in fact now resulted in the compensation element in the formula being an unknown factor.[14]

Instrument of National Foreign Policy

Pentland argues that 'the national policymaker weighs the costs and benefits (insofar as they can be estimated) of participating in an international organisation or attempting to mobilise it for specific purposes.'[15] If this is so, then what are the costs and benefits to South Africa for participating in SACU? Or for the BLS countries for that matter? Second, can an individual member-state mobilise SACU to act as an instrument of its national foreign policy?

In relation to South Africa, it does appear to possess the capability to mobilise SACU to achieve its own foreign policy objectives. According to K.J. Holsti, 'needs that cannot be filled within national frontiers help create dependencies on other states' and 'possession of these (economic) resources can be transformed easily into political influence'.[16] So what are the needs of BLS countries that can be filled by South Africa's membership in SACU and in what ways can SACU be utilised to achieve that country's national foreign policy objectives? In order to answer these two questions, it is necessary to consider what South Africa's foreign policy objectives are, and whether they can be achieved by economic instruments of foreign policy.

Like all sovereign states, the Republic of South Africa is committed to defending its territorial integrity and to maintaining its political and socio-economic system. Under its *apartheid* system (i.e. an official ideology of white political dominance over the other three racial groups), the white-minority government is committed to retaining complete control over South Africa's domestic (as well as foreign) policies. This ideology (with its implementation) has placed South Africa in a position of increasing confrontation with the black-majority-ruled states within the region, as these states have gradually achieved independence since the mid-1960s. During the 1960s and early 1970s, South Africa sought to protect itself from the threat of guerrilla warfare by liberation movements (e.g. the African National Congress and the Pan-African Congress) by creating economic dependencies out of the surrounding countries. These 'relations of dependence' were achieved by such institutionalised means as the SACU agreement (i.e. the BLS countries) and by more informal economic instruments as control of the rail transit facilities through South Africa, South African commercial dominance of the industrial and commodities markets of the surrounding countries, provision of wage-earning employment (i.e. South African mines and factories) for foreign Africans, etc. Even the Portuguese colonies of Angola and Mozambique and the then white-minority-ruled Rhodesia were brought within South Africa's sphere of economic dominance, thus affording the racist regime influence over a surrounding buffer of dependent, if not friendly, African states. With the independence of Angola and Mozambique in 1975 and Zimbabwe in 1980, South Africa's dominant influence over the surrounding dependencies has been reduced to the BLS countries and Namibia (which is likely to achieve a negotiated independence from South Africa in the near future). But it must still be noted that South Africa retains, to various degrees, a number of the above-mentioned levers of economic pressure on the surrounding countries.

Throughout the early 1960s and the 1970s, the economies of the BLS countries have remained dependent upon South Africa. The major instrument for maintaining this dominant role in their economies has been the SACU agreement. In order to establish this point, it is necessary to point out the ways in which the BLS economies are controlled through SACU and the earlier 1910 customs agreement. First, the national shares from the common revenue pool constitute a substantial portion of the BLS governments' annual revenue; see Table 13.2. Between 1974 and 1977, the national share for Botswana

Table 13.2   Customs Share Government Revenue of BLS Countries

	Customs and Excise Revenue from Consolidated Fund (Rand millions)	% of Government Revenue
Botswana		
1974	30	47.6%
1975	25	31.6%
1976	15	21.7%
1977	38	NA
1978*	38	38%
Lesotho		
1974	17	59.5%
1975	15	57.1%
1976	15	51.5%
1977	33	68.8%
1978/79*	56.1	72%
Swaziland		
1974	19	41.8%
1975	18	25.9%
1976	13	24.1%
1977	39	48.1%
1978/79 (est.)*	54	62%

Sources: Standard Bank Economic Research Department (Johannesburg), typed briefing, 15 October, 1981; and *R.J. Davies, *Trade Sanctions and Regional Impact in Southern Africa* (London: Africa Bureau, 1981), p. 32.

Note: In 1978, Transkei, Bophuthatswana and Vanda began to receive a revenue share out of South Africa's share of the Consolidated Fund and were included in the figures for 'transfers and payments to neighbouring countries' published in the South African Reserve Bank *Quarterly Bulletin* (Pretoria).

(as an average percentage) was 33 per cent, Lesotho was 60 per cent and Swaziland was 25 per cent. Thus the SACU common pool of customs, excise, sales and additional duties constitutes an essential revenue source for the BLS countries. But by what institutionalised procedure are the duties collected into the common pool and later redistributed back among the member-states? All the duties collected by the BLS countries (plus those collected by South Africa) are required under the SACU agreement to be paid into the common pool (i.e. the Consolidated Revenue Fund) at the end of each quarter of the financial year, with the common pool being administered by the South African government. The technical subcommittee of the SACU Commission determines the sharing-out of the pool's revenue which can not be done until two years hence due to the South African declared time which is required to compile and calculate each member-state's accrued share. In the example of Lesotho,[17] the revenue collected by the Lesotho Department of Customs and Excise during the first quarter of the 1980–81 financial year must be paid into the common revenue pool at the end of that quarter, but the calculated revenue share for Lesotho for that quarter would only be paid two years later at the end of the first quarter of the 1982–83 financial year. Thus these customs duties become 'money on deposit' which can not be withdrawn for two years and even then, it is interest-free.

For the BLS countries, this delayed payment has become one of the major issues for renegotiating the SACU agreement. In 1981, the BLS countries sought to renegotiate Article 14 ('The pool of customs excise, sales and additional duties') to shorten the time period between collection of duties and repayment as well as to argue for an increase in their proportion of the pool's revenue. The proposal to shorten the time period for calculating the share was turned down by the South African authorities. On the issue of increasing the BLS proportion of the common pool, the South African members of the technical subcommittee appeared to have agreed in principle to the BLS proposal for amending Article 14, but in February 1982 the South African government refused to accept the subcommittee's recommendations. Rather, it took the view that the SACU agreement must be renegotiated as a whole or not at all, i.e. no amendment of individual articles.

It is widely understood that South Africa would like its 'independent' homeland governments of Transkei, Bophuthatswana and Venda (TBV, and now including Ciskai) to be included in the existing SACU agreement[18] or into a renegotiated one. After its 'independence' from South Africa in September 1976, it was reported that Transkei was not represented at the subsequent annual SACU

Commission meeting nor did it have any customs agreements with any country except South Africa.[19] The BLS countries have consistently refused any request or demand for the inclusion of the TBV homelands into the SACU agreement. Thus at present, the agreement has what amounts to a two-tier structure: an official one and an unofficial one. The official tier includes the four signatories to the 1969 agreement, while the unofficial one is composed of the TBV territories which have signed bilateral economic agreements with South Africa for a portion of the common pool *but* which is taken out of South Africa's own share. The arrangement between Transkei and South Africa 'provides for the continued free movement of goods and services between South Africa and Transkei after the latter attains independence, and for the continued application by Transkei after that date of the common customs, excise and sales duties applicable in the customs union area'.[20] Similarly-worded bilateral agreements were also signed between South Africa and the other 'independent' homelands. Yet such political/economic agreements can hardly be considered as a change in the legal status of South Africa itself (i.e. whether it can divest itself of portions of the territory under its sovereignty). If the TVB homelands are 'sovereign states' as South Africa repeatedly declares them to be, then the Republic is breaching the SACU customs agreement by continuing to receive goods duty-free from them and providing them with a share of the common pool, even if from its own share. The BLS countries could claim this change of status as the grounds for re-negotiating the SACU agreement. But such an attempt to utilise this issue as a political pressure point is more likely to result in the collapse of SACU in its present form.[21] South Africa, for its part, has continued to push its proposed 'economic constellation of states in Southern Africa' concept as an expanded alternative, though only the TBV homelands have shown any interest in it.[22]

Another pressure point upon the BLS countries is Article 4, under which all customs tariffs and sales duties into the common customs area shall be those 'in force in South Africa from time to time' (para. 1). With the exception of a full rebate on such duties from goods imported under disaster relief, technical assistance agreements and obligations under any multilateral international agreements, or alternatively with the prior approval of all the SACU members, South Africa possesses fiscal decision-making powers for the entire common customs area. Similarly, any rebates, refunds or drawbacks for goods imported for the BLS local industries must be identical to those for corresponding South African industries (para. 2). A recent example of South Africa's powers is its imposition of a 10 per cent surcharge in

March 1982 on almost all imports entering the common customs area. While this is thought to produce an additional R500 million in the common revenue pool and thus a larger revenue return to each SACU member state, it was done by South Africa in view of its own worsening balance of payments crisis as a result of the enormous fall in the world price of gold. In an official response, the Lesotho Finance Minister, Mr K.T.J. Rakhatla, in his 6 April budget speech for the 1982–3 financial year, pointed out that South Africa's imposed import surcharge would immediately affect Lesotho's imported inflation but, possible higher receipts under the SACU formula would only be available in 1984–5.[23] 'Botswana and Swaziland experienced the same effects. The South African decisions have produced considerable fluctuations in the BLS customs revenue. As a result of South Africa's abolition of previous import surcharges in 1980 as well as the large price increase in petrol imports, the BLS countries (as well as the TBV homelands) experienced 'directly lower increases in customs revenue allocated than the relevant increases in their calculated imports suggested'.[24] In view of its powers under the SACU agreement, South Africa would seem quite capable of affecting or even pressuring its smaller BLS neighbours.

A recent South African analysis considered the use of economic techniques in the country's regional foreign policy.[25] After listing the various economic levers available to the Republic to pressure its regional neighbours and comparing them to the practical economic, political and legal constraints, the study made two general conclusions: that it is not possible to precisely determine (1) the consequences of using any particular economic lever, or (2) whether a specific economic lever would achieve a non-economic objective. Lesotho waited for over eighteen months for a delivery of refined oil from Maputo (Mozambique). Originally donated by Algeria to Lesotho to lessen its dependence upon South Africa, the Lesotho government publicly complained about the delay in obtaining South African government permits which are required to allow the oil to be shipped through South Africa.[26] While this could just be an example of bureaucratic delay or rail transport holdup, the end-result of disrupting a neighbouring country's imports is to put pressure on that country's economy. In different circumstances such pressure could result in achieving foreign economic or perhaps, even non-economic objectives; in this case, it has only resulted in a public complaint from the Lesotho government against South Africa's 'continuing attempt to destabilise its neighbouring countries'.

While South Africa appears to be quite prepared to use SACU as an instrument of national foreign policy for its objective of maintaining a complaisant (or at least non-belligerent) buffer of neighbouring countries, the BLS countries have three less effective options. First, they can (and do) project the view that South Africa's economic domination of the region continues to exploit their populations and economies. This view provides public encouragement to South Africa to reduce the more exploitative aspects of their economic relationship and further acts as an inducement for foreign assistance to help the BLS countries lessen their dependence on South Africa. The dependency relationship between black Southern Africa and the Republic is made known in regional forums like the Organisation of African Unity (OAU) and the Southern African Development Coordination Conference (SADCC), as well as in international forums such as the United Nations (UN), the Commonwealth and the Nonaligned Movement. Another option is to threaten to withdraw from SACU unless a number of BLS proposed changes to the agreement are made. While any member can withdraw under the current agreement after one year's notice, this 'play our way or we quit' policy could just as likely result in a possible South African withdrawal. The third option available is for the BLS to remain within SACU while seeking further renegotiation of those sections of the agreement which are most disruptive to their economic planning and foreign economic relations. These include: the level of revenue-sharing, time-lag for revenue repayment, and restrictions on economic agreements outside the common customs area.

It should be noted that a possible fourth option (a derivative of the third one) might also exist. In this case, the BLS countries would remain within the agreement while seeking to lessen their economic dependence upon South Africa by means of widening their foreign economic links both within and outside Africa. But this option is currently restricted by the SACU agreement. Under Article 19, no member state can enter separately into, or amend a trade agreement with a country outside the common customs area without the prior concurrence of the other members; thus necessitating South Africa's prior agreement. This is the likely reason why the 1978 Lesotho-Mozambique trade agreement has remained unratified. It also explains why the BLS countries initially withheld their signatures from the Eastern and Southern African Preferential Trade Area (ESAPTA) agreement at the December 1981 meeting in Lusaka. (Lesotho and Swaziland subsequently signed the agreement.) In the case of the Lome Convention, the BLS countries' obligations to the convention were initially seen as conflicting with their SACU membership, in so far as the European Economic Community's condition of entry that the BLS countries' agreed to charge no more duty for EEC imports than for their 'most favoured nations' (MFN) imports was concerned. Yet this would conflict with the higher non-MFN customs duties set by South Africa for the common customs area. With the approval of both South Africa and the signatories to the convention (i.e. the EEC countries and the ACP developing countries), the BLS countries divided their total duty paid on imports into two components: a fiscal duty applied to imports from all countries and a customs duty (which could be higher) applied to countries without MFN status. When both duties were charged on any particular import, the BLS countries' total duty would equal that which South Africa would have charged; thus upholding the condition in the SACU agreement that all members have to charge the same duty on goods imported into the common customs area.[27]

To what degree have these options worked in practice? The BLS countries have made considerable use of regional and international forums (and through them, to influence world opinion) to denounce South Africa's *apartheid* system and its regional economic dominance and to press for renegotiation of the more exploitative sections of the agreement. As for the threat to withdraw, this can only be used once since if the threat is challenged and is not carried out, it will be shown to be a bluff giving less credibility to similar threats in the future. Further, both South Africa and the BLS countries have the right to withdraw, making this option a very sharp double-edged sword. Who then is more vulnerable to the collapse of the customs union? South Africa would lose some economic leverage though making some financial savings (i.e. the 42% compensation in the revenue formula), while the BLS countries at present lack a replacement customs infrastructure although they are likely to benefit from regaining fiscal decision-making autonomy. At present, there appears to be no clear-cut answer to this question. As for staying within the agreement and pushing for further renegotiation, this is the currently accepted policy amongst the BLS members of SACU, the South African pressure for the inclusion of the TBV homelands notwithstanding.

Why, then, do the BLS countries remain within the customs union? First, they receive a major portion of their government revenue from their SACU revenue share and the revenue-sharing formula does provide a 1.42 enhancement factor as compensation for the loss of fiscal decision-making powers. Second, if the BLS countries did decide to withdraw, they would all need to considerably enlarge their governmental infrastructure for collection of customs and excise duties and for regulating the resultant financial affairs. And finally, South Africa has taken the position that member states must either remain within the present agreement, renegotiate a completely new agreement (i.e. inclusion of the TBV homelands), or withdraw from the agreement completely: an 'all or nothing' position. Thus the decision to remain within the customs union can be seen as the best of three poor choices.

Institutional Modifier of Member States' Behaviour

The second role which international organisations can play is that of an institutional modifier upon its member states' behaviour, according to Pentland. He argues that international organisations become 'an institutional manifestation of the general set of restraints placed on states by the international system' and this results from them being 'institutional channels, obstacles, and aids collectively created by states which modify the traditionally *laissez-faire* character of their relationships'.[28] He went on to list four key aspects of the structural pattern of the international system in determining the extent of the modifying process: (1) the degree of polarisation, (2) the power and status hierarchies, (3) the linkage of central system and regional subsystem, and (4) the degree of transnational interdependence. In the case of SACU, this chapter will consider these aspects as relating to the Southern African regional system and the African continental system, though reference will also be made to the international system as a whole. This approach should permit a closer consideration of the effectiveness of SACU as an institutional modifier.

In relation to the degree of polarisation, SACU is superimposed upon two major polarising factors. The first is the type of sociopolitical system operated within each of the member states. Because South Africa maintains a system of white-minority government and racial separation, this places it in a position of conflict or at least confrontation with the BLS member states, as well as with the rest of Africa and most of the world. As a result, no diplomatic relations are maintained by the BLS countries with South Africa nor is there an institutional structure for SACU (i.e. a permanent secretariat). There is, rather, a functional Customs Union Commission which meets once a year in ordinary session to consider any issue, including revenue shares, arising from the operation of the customs union. These annual meetings are held in the capital of each of the four member states in turn. In the absence of diplomatic relations in the form of diplomatic recognition and established embassies, government-to-government interactions of a political or social nature are conducted *via* correspondence, telephone and even 'open statements' carried in the mass media. This division is further emphasised by the repeated denouncements of the *apartheid* system by the BLS countries in various international forums, while also pointing out at the same time, that geographical contiguity and economic integration prevents them from breaking off economic relations.

The second polarising factor is the disparity in the size and development of the economies of the SACU member states. In terms of GNP per capita figures for 1980 (preliminary), the World Bank lists US $2290 for South Africa in comparison to US $910 for Botswana, US $680 for Swaziland and US $390 for Lesotho; see Table 13.3. Similarly the combined populations of the BLS countries is less than 10 per cent of that of South Africa. These two facts clearly show the small size of the BLS national markets and their total foreign and domestic output. Furthermore, Botswana and Lesotho have been included in the United Nations' designated 31 'Least Developed Countries' (i.e. the poorest of the developing countries).[29] This disparity between South Africa and the BLS countries in economic terms has further maintained the asymmetrical nature of their relationship.

Dependent upon South Africa for a large portion of their government revenue in the form of shares from the common customs pool, for their manufactured goods and food, and for wage employment, the BLS countries are open to South African economic pressure. But in what way can this fact be seen in terms of power and status hierarchies? South Africa does possess economic power over the BLS countries, though this power is constrained, to a degree, by South Africa's isolated 'pariah state' position[30] (due to its *apartheid* system) and by its attempts to project an overseas image of 'good neighbourliness' with the surrounding African countries to offset

Table 13.3 Population, GNP, and GNP per Capita of SACU Members (1980)

	Population mid-1980	GNP at market prices (US $/millions)	GNP per capita (US $)
South Africa	29 285 000	66 960	2290
Lesotho	1 341 000	520	390
Botswana	800 000	730	910
Swaziland	557 000	380	680

Source: *1981 World Bank Atlas: Gross National Product Population and Growth Rates* (Washington, DC: World Bank, 1982), p. 12.

hostile world opinion. It is this hostile world opinion which denies South Africa the *de jure* status of regional power despite the *de facto* recognition of its 'newly developed' economy. South Africa is definitely the dominant member of SACU if only through its agreed-upon right to make common fiscal decisions for all member states and the size of its national economy.

SACU has been unable to act as an institutional linkage between either the Southern African regional system or the African continental system and the central system due to South Africa'a membership. South Africa itself is denied membership in such Third World organisations as the OAU and the Non-aligned Movement, to which the BLS countries belong. Its 'pariah state' status has diminished its international affiliations, through such measures as its forced withdrawal from the Commonwealth in 1961, its suspension from the regular sessions of the UN General Assembly in 1974 (though still a UN member), the loss of its seat on the International Atomic Energy Agency governing board in 1977 (though still an IAEA member), etc. Instead it is the BLS countries which have the established economic-institutional linkage to the central system *via* Third World institutions, such as the Economic Commission for Africa (ECA) to the United Nations (in addition to their membership in SADCC and ESAPTA) and the 'Group of 77' to UNCTAD. Despite the economic pressure which South Africa can bring to bear upon the BLS countries, it seems unlikely that the Republic can transform this pressure into favourable statements and actions by the BLS countries in those international organisations where it is denied membership. The BLS countries have followed a pattern of louder verbal opposition to the *apartheid* policies of South Africa (especially since the independence of Angola and Mozambique in 1975) rather than a more moderate stance.[31] But their continued membership in SACU has required them to justify this position in various international forums.[32]

In relation to the degree of transnational interdependence, SACU is a direct reflection of the high level of dependence of the BLS countries upon South Africa, rather than a situation of interdependence. The geographical factors (such as landlocked territory and common boundaries) and economic factors (such as interlinked transportation, migrant employment and capital investment patterns) show this asymmetrical relationship of the BLS countries with South Africa rather than a symmetrical (or near-symmetrical) one of interdependence. SACU is an institutional recognition of the economic integration of the four countries, without affecting their asymmetrical relationship. To consider this point, it would be useful to discuss three aspects of this relationship: free movement of goods within the common customs area; energy and natural resources transfers between SACU members; and the effects of possible economic sanctions upon the BLS members of SACU.

There are no quantitative restrictions or imposed duties on goods grown, produced or manufactured within the common customs area and imported into another of the member states (Article 2 of the 1969 Customs Union Agreement). This means that any governmental agency, private company, commercial operation or even an individaul citizen is free to conduct business transactions in any of the member states, though subject to national licensing laws, health restrictions (e.g. movement of livestock), etc. Similarly there is no restriction upon the movement of money within the Rand Monetary Area (i.e. South Africa, Lesotho and Swaziland; Botswana withdrew in 1976). While South African goods dominate the markets of the BLS countries owing to their larger economies of scale and short transport distances (than non-SACU produced goods), the BLS countries can freely ship their own locally manufactured goods into South Africa to try to increase their potential marketing area. Under the SACU agreement, the BLS countries are permitted to levy additional duties on goods manufactured within the common customs area if these are in competition with new 'pioneer' industries established in any one of the BLS countries (Article 6). But prior consultation with the other member states is required before imposing such duties, and this protection for pioneer industries extends for only the first eight years without the further consent of the other members. Owing to the very small manufacturing sectors in the BLS countries and the large South African manufacturing sector, this free movement of goods primarily benefits South African business by making client-markets out of the BLS economies.

In addition, the BLS countries have been held up to the charge of importing cheap 'foreign' goods (i.e. originating from countries outside the common customs area) into South Africa. Reportedly goods manufactured in whole or in part in such countries as Zimbabwe, Mozambique and even in Taiwan are shipped to a BLS country for duty-free import into South Africa. Both Botswana and Swaziland share a common border with a non-SACU country, in addition to which Botswanan has a free-trade pact with Zimbabwe. The goods cited include plastic buckets, cement, furniture, knitted clothing and textiles. South African businessmen have claimed that this practice 'is not far removed from smuggling' and have pressed for South African government action to halt these cheap imports from the BLS countries for several years.[33]

In the area of energy and natural resources transfers, there is a high degree of dependence by the BLS countries upon South Africa. The Electricity Supply Commission (ESCOM) of South Africa supplies electricity to the BLS countries *via* transmission lines off the national grid.[34] Similarly coal is shipped by rail to the BLS countries for use in small thermal power stations and for consumer heating and cooking. This dependent aspect of SACU economic integration may be offset somewhat in the future by a number of proposed BLS projects. These include the Lesotho Highlands water project to sell water to South Africa (plus some electricity generation for use within Lesotho itself), a rail link from the Eastern Transvaal to Richards Bay (Natal) *via* Swaziland which would provide the latter with rail transit revenue, and a rail link through northern Transvaal for future Botswana coal exports overseas (though this also would result in additional South African rail transit revenue).[35] Each of these projects would result in increasing future BLS revenue sources, though further integrating their economies into South Africa's. But as long as each of the four SACU member states believes that it is in their individual interests (i.e. primarily that it brings in government revenue) to maintain their current level of economic integration and possibly to even increase it, none is likely to withdraw from the common customs union or even to take extreme positions on SACU policy decisions which could force one or more other members to withdraw.

The third aspect is the future possibility of externally-imposed economic sanctions against South Africa. Originally proposed in the early 1960s, economic sanctions have repeatedly been called for in various international forums (i.e. UN, OAU, the Commonwealth, the Non-aligned Movement, etc.) to attempt to force South Africa to abandon its *apartheid* system and to adopt a system of non-racial majority rule. But any attempt to impose economic sanctions against South Africa would certainly result in serious economic disruption within the BLS countries and certain neighbouring ones as well. This point, as well as the general refusal of the Western countries to support such a policy, has resulted in its non-implementation. At the recent International Conference on Sanctions against South Africa, the international community was again urged to provide assistance to the neighbouring countries which would be adversely affected by a programme of sanctions against South Africa. Such an assistance programme 'should include the provision of supplies of food, oil and other essential commodities, and the establishment of facilities for their stockpiling, as well as necessary financial assistance.'[36] In assessing the effect of trade sanctions against South Africa in relation to the other SACU countries, one researcher observed that the problems for SACU members (i.e. the BLS countries) were 'very different from those of other countries in the region' in terms of South Africa's high degree of control over their trade, the degree of BLS trade which takes place through South African commercial channels, and the penetration of South African capital into the economies of the BLS countries. He went on to point out that there is a quantitative difference between South Africa's domination of the SACU member states and the other countries in the region resulting in a qualitative difference, and that it is important that any consideration of the regional implications of a sanctions strategy should treat these two groups of countries separately.[37]

SACU cannot act as an institutional modifier over the behaviour of its member states, for two reasons. South Africa's *apartheid* policy results in a clear polarisation within the membership of SACU and within both the Southern African region and Africa as a whole. Similarly South Africa has been denied or pressured to withdraw its membership from a number of international organisations. Its domination of SACU can be seen as the primary reason for the rejection of SACU from institutional links with Third World economic organisations. The second reason is that South Africa economically dominates SACU and, to a large degree, most of the economic interactions in the region. This has led to increasing efforts among the other regional countries to establish institutional links to coordinate their development programmes and to decrease their dependence upon South Africa. Thus there is little likelihood that SACU will in the future develop a permanent institutional structure; rather, alternative structures (e.g. SADCC or ESAPTA) are more likely to provide any future institutional modifying role for the Southern African region.

Autonomous Regional Actor

Pentland's third proposed role for international organisations is as an autonomous actor in the global system. In the case of SACU, this would be as an autonomous actor with a regional rather than international scope. He argues that 'organisations are created and sustained by the states in a collective act of self-limitation or self-enhancement, and there is certainly no expectation that they will come to coexist with, or even supersede, their creators as the dominant actors in the international system'. Rather than, as member-states of an organisation, relinquish part of their national sovereignty to the organisation, they become increasingly integrated into a new international actor, in order 'to achieve some degree of autonomy [of action] and some capacity to influence [or resist the influences of] other actors'.[38] He makes the further point that the organisation's development can best be seen in terms of its administrative arm or secretariat.[39] The fact that SACU has no permanent administrative institution is not due to a nominal level of organisational development, but rather to the polarised views of the member states over how political power in their relative systems should be distributed; this polarisation also prevented the establishment of formal diplomatic links. By way of comparison, the more recently-established SADCC has already created a small permanent secretariat (located in Gaberone, Botswana) with an executive secretary (Arthur Blumeris of Zimbabwe) to coordinate the interactions of the member states (each of which is responsible for one or more sectors of regional economic policy coordination).[40]

At present, SACU is unlikely to develop to a higher level of economic integration, whether by establishing a strong organisational secretariat or by further formal economic integration resulting in a common market or economic union among its member states, for a number of reasons; this is not withstanding the fact that the BLS countries are entering into joint economic projects with South Africa in order to increase their sources of revenue. The first of these reasons, as mentioned above, is that the BLS countries are strongly opposed to the South African apartheid system and the dominant role that South Africa already plays in their national economies. Botswana's President Quett Masire recently pointed out that 'diversifying its options [for regional economic development, i.e. SADCC] did not mean that Botswana had any immediate plans to interfere with the Southern African Customs Union'.[41] Similarly, the Lesotho Planning Minister, Mr Evaristus Sekhonyana, has declared that 'Lesotho seeks to change her economic relationship with South Africa from "heavy dependence" to "mutual interdependence"'.[42] And Swaziland, currently lobbying for acceptance of its 'border adjustment land and population-nationality transfer deal' with South Africa by the rest of Africa including the ANC, would seem to have also decided to maintain its SACU economic links with South Africa.

A second reason is that the BLS countries, while not opting out of SACU, have repeatedly sought to lessen their economic dependence on South Africa or to convert these relations into ones of interdependence. This objective of what might be referred to as 'gradual disengagement' from the possibility of total integration into South Africa's economy, has taken a number of forms. One was the creation of their own national currencies. After being a *de facto* part of the monetary area using South African currency (the *rand*) for many years, each of the BLS countries has attempted to distance itself from South African monetary control, though in different ways and to different degrees.[43] During the last stages of the negotiations for a proposed rand monetary area agreement (RMA), Botswana decided not to join the agreement in September 1974. But it continued to use the rand until its own central bank was established and it had introduced its own currency, the *pula*, in August 1976. Swaziland and Lesotho, on the other hand, signed the RMA agreement with South Africa in December 1974. This was despite the fact that Swaziland had three months earlier issued its own currency, the *lilangeni*, for circulation within its own borders and regulated by a newly-established monetary authority. Lesotho followed Swaziland's example in January 1980 when it also introduced its own currency, the *loti*. Both the *lilangeni* and the *loti* were placed on a par with the rand and backed by interest-bearing rand deposits with the South African Reserve Bank, but both countries continued to treat the rand as a legal, though foreign, currency within their borders.

Another form that this gradual disengagement has taken is where the BLS countries have joined additional economic affiliations besides SACU. These include both trading agreements (i.e. the Lome Convention and ESAPTA) and economic cooperation groupings (i.e. UNCTAD Group of 77 and SADCC). In the case of the trading agreements, the BLS countries have had to obtain prior consent from South Africa as stipulated in the SACU agreement. In both of the above mentioned agreements, this consent was ultimately given. Botswana, though, has not yet signed the ESAPTA agreement. With regard to the economic cooperation groupings, SACU regulations do not restrict BLS membership in them as they are not organisations which regulate or interfere with trade regionally or inter-regionally. Rather they are attempts to coordinate the economic development of the less-developed ones. As President Masire has stated, SADCC was not intended to compete with SACU but was to be complementary to it, with one of its main purposes being to make its member states economically independent.[44]

While actively participating in a number of economic affiliations to advance their national economic growth, the BLS countries have strictly refused to join or in any way participate in the South African proposed 'Constellation of Southern African States'. These proposals were based on the South African assumption that increased regional cooperation in the economic field could lead to cooperation in the political and even security fields.[45] But to date the only interest shown in these proposals has come from South Africa's own 'independent homelands'. At a one-day conference at Pretoria, then South African Prime Minister P.W. Botha and the TBV homeland leaders issued a joint statement calling for a multilateral programme for regional and development cooperation entailing coordinated action on the four broad fronts of interstate relations, economic and social affairs, and security, within the framework of the proposed constellation of states. They also agreed to establish a multilateral development bank and to consider the eventual creation of a single customs union for all states in the region.[46] Both the proposal for such a constellation and for the inclusion of the TBV homelands (which now includes Ciskei, despite Transkei's vehement opposition to its 'independence') in an enlarged customs union have been rejected by the BLS countries. In fact, if South Africa were to continue to press for these proposals, they can be seen as the dividing issue upon which SACU could collapse.

A third reason why SACU is unlikely to become an autonomous actor is the possibility that South Africa might also decide to disengage from the BLS countries. Informed sources in Johannesburg suggest two possible reasons for South Africa taking such an apparently drastic, about-face decision. First is that the customs union has been seen as being too expensive to South Africa in terms of its administrative costs. Besides, there have been suggestions that the SACU revenue shares made to the BLS countries (bearing in mind the 1.42 multiplier in the revenue-sharing formula) are substantially more than their collected customs duties and that this extra revenue, taken out of South Africa's share, could be going to help develop its underdeveloped homelands. (The other possible reason is in the event that South Africa actually gave the BLS countries an ultimatum: either the TBV homelands were to be included in a renegotiated SACU agreement or South Africa would itself withdraw.) It is, however, unlikely that South Africa would at the moment withdraw from SACU in that the customs union currently provides the Republic with several very strong levers of economic pressure to bring to bear on the BLS countries, some of which would be lost if the SACU agreement collapsed. Further, the removal of a 'free movement of goods' policy along its borders with the BLS countries would increase South Africa's administrative costs in relation to import-export trade, customs and excise collection, and even anti-smuggling operations. In addition, South Africa has been currently giving a portion of its own customs revenue-share to the TBV homelands to bolster their meagre sources of revenue, and it is difficult to see a collapse of SACU as the result of the current revenue-sharing formula to the BLS countries while this 'second tier' sharing continues.

A final point on this issue of an autonomous actor needs to be made. This is that if the political tensions inside South Africa or even just within the region increase, SACU may not survive the resulting pressures of competing political forces, in the view of at least one informed observer.[47] Because of the increasing ANC sabotage campaign within South Africa and the increased South African military and other destabilising actions against the Frontline States, there is a strong possibility that SACU could collapse due to a violent upheaval within or along the borders of South Africa.

SACU's Future Prospects

At the beginning of this chapter, I posed two questions in relation to the Southern African Customs Union. First, did SACU have a role to play in building Third World solidarity and economic development, as well as helping to bring about the sought-after NIEO? And second, can SACU be better seen in terms of these possible roles (i.e. an instrument of national foreign policy, an institutional modifier of member-states' behaviour, and an autonomous regional actor) which it could and does play in international relations? Taking this second question first, I will outline SACU's capacity to play each of these three roles and its future prospects as a regional organisation in the short- (1–5 years), medium- (5–15 years), and long-term (15 years plus).

SACU has been and will continue to be one of the major economic instruments of South Africa's foreign policy within the region in both the short- and medium-term, despite hints of possible South African disengagement from the common customs union. It provides the Republic with several institutionalised levers of economic pressure upon the BLS countries while concentrating fiscal decision-making for SACU within the responsibility of the South African government. But even if South Africa were to withdraw, the size and development of its economy would still determine to a large degree the inter-regional pattern of commercial transactions and customs tariffs. Such economic levers of influence and pressure as tariff rates, re-export duties, monetary regulations on movements of capital (into and out of South Africa) over neighbouring countries will still remain under South African government control; other levers (e.g. capital investment funds and commodity marketing) would continue to be dominated by South African corporations and private commercial interests.

By comparison, the BLS countries have few, if any means of utilising SACU as an economic instrument of their respective foreign policies. To threaten to withdraw from SACU is unlikely to result in positive gains for the BLS countries even if they ultimately agreed to remain members or from their resultant independent customs and financial status if they actually did withdraw. Their national markets and commercial transactions would still be strongly affected, if not actually dominated, by South Africa's economy in either case. So in the short- and medium-term, the BLS countries are unable to utilise SACU as a foreign policy instrument except to press for the revision of those sections of the agreement which result in hindering or disrupting the development of their national economies, yet maintaining their high level of dependence upon South Africa. It would appear that BLS membership in SACU will continue, as 'it seems highly probable that the advantages [of membership] outweigh the disadvantages' if there is no basic change in the current economic policies of th BLS countries and no radical change within South Africa itself.[48] In the long-term, it is unlikely that SACU will continue in its present form due to projected population and economic conditions in South Africa and to increasing domestic violence as a result of its *apartheid* policies. In view of the evidence, the BLS countries have little choice in what has been referred to as their 'politics of dependence': attempting to improve their benefits from SACU membership while having few alternatives to their continued dependence upon South Africa. Pentland's argument that 'international organisations' can be utilised as an instrument of national foreign policy would appear to be proven by South Africa's behaviour, even if not by that of the BLS countries (which can be accounted for by their lack of levers of economic pressure).

It is unlikely that SACU can or will in the future act in the role of an institutional modifier upon its member states' behaviour. There are several reasons for this conclusion. First is that there is a wide disparity between the size and development of the South African economy and those of the BLS countries. Next is that there is an asymmetrical relationship between South Africa and the BLS countries as a result of the high level of dependence by the latter upon South Africa for government revenue (i.e. customs shares), manufactured goods and food, and even employment. And third, there is no actual institutional structure, such as a permanent secretariat, to act as a conduit for modifying each of the member states' behaviour. Neither is a future institutional structure likely as the customs union commission meets only once a year and there are no diplomatic relations maintained between the BLS countries and South Africa. South Africa's dominant economic position in the region precludes SACU acting in this role. To test Pentland's argument for this role for SACU, a situation of interdependent influence (even if unequal) would have to be achieved among the member states. Such a situation would be contingent upon two factors. First that the member states continued to view SACU membership as being in their best interests (i.e. maintaining their economies while permitting increased economic development, especially the BLS countries). And second, that a radical change in the socio-political structure within South Africa would have to be accompanied by a substantial regional growth programme funded by South Africa (possibly with extra-regional foreign assistance) to reduce the asymmetrical relationship with the less-developed members of SACU. Such a situation of improved interdependence (i.e. reduced dependence) could lead to a higher level of economic integration based upon SACU with a perhaps enlarged membership, though it is equally possible that a strengthened ESAPTA-type organisation could provide the necessary institutional structure in the short- and medium-term.

Similarly, SACU is unable to become an autonomous regional actor partly due to its current level of economic integration and partly due to the polarised divisions along racial lines within the region. A radical change within South Africa as considered above could alter this situation. But the currently proposed internal political reforms by the white minority government under Prime Minister P.W. Botha (i.e. an executive president and a three-chamber legislature [a 'parliament' each for the whites, the Asians, and the coloureds], with no political power for the majority black population)[49] would not reduce the racial confrontation inherent in South Africa. Without radical internal change in the Republic and increased economic interdependence for the BLS countries, SACU could collapse in response to increasing violent tensions in the region. What appears certain is that the future socio-political system of South Africa will ultimately dictate what form economic interactions will take within the Southern African region: whether at a higher level of economic integration, increased economic interdependence, or continued economic dependence. Finally, the possibility exists that ESAPTA (or a similar regional organisation) may well provide the institutional structure for those economic interactions, rather than SACU.

To return to the first question of whether SACU has a role to play in bringing about a future NEIO, a recent UNCTAD report excluded SACU from its listing of Third World economic cooperation and integration groupings, though listing SADCC and ESAPTA.[50] This is basically due to South Africa's domestic *apartheid* policies and to its more-developed status compared to its neighbouring African countries. These two factors account for South Africa's economic dominance over the BLS member states of SACU in particular and over the other African countries of the region in general. By refusing to end or even reduce this position of dominance, minority-ruled South Africa has been ostracised both politically and economically by the majority of Third World countries (i.e. the Non-aligned Movement and the UNCTAD Group of 77 respectively). But it should be noted that the white minority government's view of South Africa is not as a developing Third World country, but as a newly-industrialised country with economic and cultural attachments to the West ('the First World').[51]

If SACU is prevented, due to South Africa's membership, from providing an institutional structure for Third World economic cooperation, is there a viable alternative institution open to the BLS countries? A strengthened ESAPTA (or perhaps a re-structured SADCC) could provide the BLS countries with an institutional link into Third World economic cooperation as well as contributing a Southern African point of view to the North-South dialogue. The Executive Secretary for the UN Economic Commission for Africa, Dr Adebayo Adedeji, recently stated that the creation of ESAPTA was a major breakthrough in the development of larger African markets through multinational regional cooperation, as opposed to the fragmentation of Africa into small national markets which aggravated its already deteriorating economic conditions.[52] If Third World unity is to have any meaning in terms of global economic, social and financial cooperation, African regional organisations must establish new systems of economic relations to contribute to this cooperation. African member states must reduce their asymmetrical dependence on more-developed countries and increase their individual and collective self-reliance. SACU is unable to fill this institutional role for the BLS countries, though this chapter argues that a strengthened ESAPTA could perhaps play such a role in the short- and medium-term. But it must also be noted that continued BLS membership in SACU is more a case of geographical fact and economic necessity than a question of free choice.

Notes

1 'UNITAR Conference holds that Regionalism is an integral part of New Economic Order', *UN Chronicle* (New York), Vol. 17 (No. 6), July 1980, p. 49.
2 *Ibid*.
3 Prior to their independence, they were known as Bechuanaland (1966),

Basutoland (1966), and Swaziland (1968) respectively.

4   Charles Pentland, 'International Organisations and their Roles', in M. Smith, R. Little and M. Shackleton (eds) *Perspectives on World Politics* (London: Croom Helm, 1981), pp. 226–32.

5   For the definitional purposes of this chapter, SACU is seen by the author as a multi-state, intergovernmental organisation operating within the Southern African region of the African continent, as opposed to an alternative view of Southern Africa as a subregion of an African region of the world. Similarly, Pentland's use of the concept of 'international organisation' has been interpreted to include any multi-state, intergovernmental organisation which is seen as an actor in international relations regardless of whether its primary focus is regional or subregional, rather than global. See William D. Coplin, *Introduction to International Politics* (Englewood Cliffs, N.J.: Prentice-Hall, 1980, 3rd Edition), pp. 119–122.

6   Most of the information for this section was derived from the following sources: Peter Robson, 'Economic Integration in Southern Africa', *Journal of Modern African Studies* (Cambridge), Vol. 5 (No. 4), December 1967, pp. 469–90; Biff Turner, 'A Fresh Start for the Southern African Customs Union', *African Affairs* (London), Vol. 70 (No. 280), July 1971, pp. 269–76; P.M. Landell-Mills, 'The 1969 Southern African Customs Union Agreement', *Journal of Modern African Studies*, Vol. 9 (No. 2), August 1971, pp. 263–81; and Donald K. Kowet, *Land, Labour Migration and Politics in Southern Africa: Botswana, Lesotho and Swaziland* (Uppsala: Scandinavian Institute of African Studies, 1978), chapter 5.

7   D.V. Cowon, 'Towards a common market in Southern Africa', *Optima* (Johannesburg), Vol. 17 (No. 2), June 1967, p. 44.

8   Robson, *op. cit.*, pp. 476–80 (see note 6 above).

9   'Joint Communiqué by the Minister of Finance of Botswana, the Minister of Finance of Lesotho, the Minister of Economic Affairs of South Africa and the Minister of Finance of Swaziland', issued by the Department of Information at the request of the Department of Foreign Affairs (Pretoria), 11 December 1969, ref. 380/69, mimeo.

10   Republic of South Africa, 'Customs Union Agreement between the Governments of South Africa, Botswana, Lesotho and Swaziland', *Government Gazette* (Pretoria), Vol. 54 (No. 2584), No. R. 3914, 12 December 1969, (hereafter "Customs Union Agreement").

11   Turner, *op. cit.*, p. 273 (see note 6 above).

12   The share of the common revenue pool which each of the BLS countries would receive under the 1969 customs union agreement's revenue-sharing formula is calculated as follows:

$$\frac{A + B + C}{D + E + F + G} \times H \times 1.42 = \text{revenue share}$$

A = value of imports (figure of two years previously) of the country;
B = value of the country's production (and consumption) of excisable goods;
C = value of the country's production (and consumption) of sales tax goods;
D = c.i.f. value of the total customs area imports (1968: R1992 million);

E = customs duties paid on D (1968: R312m);
F = value of excisable sales duty goods produced and consumed in customs area (1968: R700m);
G = excise and sales duties paid on F (1968: R312m); and
H = common revenue pool (1968: R463m; this figure did not include sales tax, as it did for 1966).

The available import figures for this period were: Botswana R19.9m (1967), Lesotho R23.9m (1968). After the BLS countries had received their respective revenue shares, South Africa would receive the remainder of the common revenue pool. Source: *Financial Mail* (Johannesburg), 19 December 1960, pp. 1295–96.

13   'Treble gain for SA neighbours', *The Star* (Johannesburg), 18 February 1970.

14   James H. Cobbe, 'Integration among Unequals: the Southern African Customs Union and Development' *World Development* (London), Vol. 8 (No. 4), April 1980, p. 330.

15   Pentland, *op. cit.*, p. 226 (see note 4 above).

16   K.J. Holsti, *International Politics: A Framework for Analysis* (London: Prentice-Hall International, 1972, 2nd edition), p. 240.

17   Briefing at the Department of Customs and Excise, Maseru (Lesotho), 16 March 1982.

18   'Customs union partnership plan', *Rand Daily Mail* (Johannesburg), 26 October 1976.

19   'Kei not at customs talks', *Rand Daily Mail*, 25 March 1977.

20   *Rand Daily Mail*, 26 October 1977.

21   James H. Cobbe kindly brought this point, and several others, to my attention.

22   See 'Constellation: Economic Accord', *Informa* (Department of Foreign Affairs and Information, Pretoria), Vol. 27 (No. 9), October 1980, pp. 1–5.

23   'Lesotho', *Standard Chartered Review* (London), June 1982, p. 39.

24   Wolfgang H. Thomas, 'Financing Socio-Economic Development in the Black Homelands of South Africa', *Journal of Contemporary African Studies* (Pretoria), Vol. 1 (No. 1), October 1981, p. 163.

25   D.J. Geldenhuys, 'Some Strategic Implications of Regional Economic Relationships for the Republic of South Africa', *ISSUP Strategic Review* (Pretoria), January 1981, pp. 14–30.

26   *Rand Daily Mail*, 3 August 1982.

27   Derek J. Hudson, 'Botswana's Membership of the Southern African Customs Union', in Charles Harvey (ed.), *Papers on the Economy of Botswana* (London: Heinemann, 1981), pp. 156–7. Also see Ralph I. Onwuka, 'The Lome Convention: a Machinery for Economic Dependence or Interdependence?', *Quarterly Journal of Administration* (Ile-Ife), Vol. XIII (Nos 3 and 4), April/July 1979, pp. 277–92.

28   Pentland, *op. cit.*, p. 228 (see note 4 above).

29   Compiled from *1981 World Bank Atlas: Gross National Product, Population and Growth Rates* (Washington, D.C.: World Bank, 1982), p. 12

and United Nations Conference on the Least Developed Countries (Paris, 1–14 September 1981), *Fact Sheets LDC 1, 2, 7 & 20*, 1981.

30 See P.C.J. Vala, 'South Africa as a pariah international state', *International Affairs Bulletin* (Johannesburg), Vol. 1 (No. 3), 1977, pp. 121–41.

31 In the case of Lesotho, see David Hirschmann, 'Changes in Lesotho's Policy towards South Africa', *African Affairs* (London), Vol. 78 (No. 311), April 1979, pp. 177–96.

32 *Measures for Strengthening Economic Integration and Cooperation among Developing Countries at the Sub-regional, Regional and Interregional Levels* (Geneva: UNCTAD Secretariat, UNCTAD/ST/ECDC/17, 27 April 1982).

33 "Customs Union: Stop the smugglers", *Financial Mail* (Johanesburg), 31 August 1979, p. 846.

34 Until recently Botswana was self-sufficient in electricity from its own coal-fired thermal generating plant. But the huge energy requirements of the new DeBeer's Jwaneng diamond mine has necessitated that Botswana now purchase the additional electrical power from the ESCOM national grid.

35 See 'Lesotho is to sell two rivers', *New African* (London), May 1982, p. 42; Bernard Simon; 'Swaziland to build rail link', *Financial Times* (London), 5 January 1982; and 'New Botswana coal mine pact signed', *The Star Weekly* (Johannesburg), 17 July 1982.

36 *Paris Declaration on Sanctions against South Africa* (New York: United Nations Centre against *Apartheid*, 17 July 1982.

37 R.J.Davies, *Trade Sanctions and Regional Impact in Southern Africa* (London: Africa Bureau, 1981), p. 34 (also see pp. 26–30).

38 Pentland, *op. cit.*, p. 230 (see note 4 above).

39 *Ibid.*, p. 231.

40 'Arthur Blumeris of SADCC', *The Star*, 25 August 1982.

41 Wilf Nussey, 'Masire fears SA gearing for attack', *The Star*, 2 December 1981.

42 'Lesotho seeks to shake off SA dependence', *The Star*, 9 June 1982.

43 For a detailed analysis of these monetary arrangements, see Francis d'A Collings, *et. al.*, 'The Rand and the Monetary Systems of Botswana, Lesotho and Swaziland', *Journal of Modern African Studies* (Cambridge), Vol. 16 (No. 1), March 1978, pp. 97–121.

44 *The Star*, 2 December 1981.

45 This point is made in more detail in D.J. Geldenhuya and T.D. Venter, 'Regional co-operation in Southern Africa: a constellations of states?', *International Affairs Bulletin*, Vol. 3 (No. 3), December 1979, pp. 50–60.

46 'Constellation: Economic Accord', *Informa* (Pretoria: Department of Foreign Affairs and Information), Vol. 27 (No. 9), October 1980, pp. 1–5. For a current outline of South African government plans, see 'The Promotion of Industrial Development: An Element of a co-ordinated Regional Development Strategy for Southern Africa', a supplement to *South Africa Digest* (Pretoria: DFAI), 2 April 1982. These plans include only South Africa and its homeland areas.

47 'Customs union may fail', *The Star Weekly*, 24 October 1981.

48 Cobbe, *op. cit.*, p. 334 (see note 14 above). An earlier, unpublished survey on Lesotho's SACU membership reached the opposite conclusion, i.e. that SACU membership on the whole was bad for Lesotho. John Gray concluded that:

> the benefits are immediate, obvious and short-term – revenue bonus for the government, the availability of goods for the consumer and the lure of the South African market for the producer. The disadvantages are insidious and long-term – the creation of revenue dependence of the Lesotho government on Pretoria, the high cost structure facing consumer and producer because of the trade diversion costs of the tariff, and above all the failure to develop industrially.

John Gray, 'Lesotho and the Southern African Customs Union', National University of Lesotho, Faculty of Social Sciences Staff Seminar Paper No. 20, September 1979, p. 14.

49 For a liberal South African critique of these and other proposals, see Lawrence Schlemmer and David Welsh, 'South Africa's constitutional and political prospects', *Optima*, Vol. 30 (No. 4), June 1982, pp. 210–32.

50 See footnote 32.

51 for example, see *Republic of South Africa: 20 Years of Progress* (Pretoria: DFAI, May 1981).

52 Adebayo Adedeji, *A Preliminary Assessment of the Economic Performance in 1981 and Prospects for 1982: End-of-Year Statement* (Addis Ababa: Economic Commission for Africa, 30 December 1981, mimeo), pp. 5–6.

Conclusion

Evaluating the future of integration in Africa is of course, not an easy task. This is because we are dealing with a dynamic political environment making any predictions about its future a risky adventure. This is mainly because the African environment whose future we want to predict is largely beyond our control. Nonetheless, we have attempted an evaluation of the future prospects of regionalism in Africa. We did this in several ways. First, we approached the issue historically, that is, drawing conclusions from, and making suggestions based on the past experiences of regionalism in the continent. Finally, we prognosticated into the future by answering some of the questions raised by the contributors in their various chapters: (i) What conclusions can we draw from/or what lessons can we learn from the success or failure of previous integration schemes on the continent? The answers to this question inevitably led us to the second question, (ii) under what circumstances can regional economic arrangements succeed in Africa?; (iii) is the presence of small subregional groupings within bigger ones harmful to the success of the bigger ones?; finally, (iv) are loose integration schemes more resilient than their highly institutionalised counterparts? To be more specific, is SADCC more viable than ECOWAS as Ravenhill seems to suggest?

Some of these questions we have already discussed in the introduction. However, one of the important issues that remains to be answered concerns the impact of small subregional groups such as Mano River Union and CEAO, on bigger arrangements such as ECOWAS in West Africa. The general conclusion which many contributors reached is that the focus and objectives of small subregional schemes may conflict with or even overlap with those of the much bigger ones. Some contributors have pointed out, for instance, that there is an overlap of objectives and focus between ECOWAS and the intended African Common Market.

We believe, however, that there is no categorical 'yes' or 'no'

Contributors

Layi Abegunrin is a Lecturer in the Department of International Relations, University of Ife, Nigeria.

S.K.B. Asante is a Professor in the Department of Political Science, University of Ghana.

I. Diaku is an Associate Professor of Economics, Imo State University, Nigeria.

Isebill Gruhn is a Professor of Politics and former Acting Dean of the School of Social Studies, University of California, Santa Cruz.

A. Hazlewood is a Professor of Economics, Oxford University.

Robert D.A. Henderson is Sessional Professor at the University of Western Ontario, Canada. He has previously worked in Nigeria, Kenya and Lesotho.

W. Tom Imobighe is a Senior Fellow, Nigerian Institute For Policy and Strategic Studies, Kuru-Jos, Nigeria.

W.A. Ndongko is a Professor of Economics, University of Yaounde, Cameroon.

Ralph I. Onwuka is a Senior Lecturer and former Acting Head of the Department of International Relations, University of Ife, Nigeria. He is currently the Editor-in-Chief of the *Nigerian Journal of International Studies*.

John Ravenhill is an Associate Professor of Government, University of Sydney, Australia.

Amadu Sesay is a Lecturer in the Department of International Relations, University of Ife, Nigeria.

Timothy Shaw is a Professor in the Department of Political Science, Dalhousie University, Halifax, Canada.

answer to the question. Much would, first of all, depend on the motives behind the formation of the subregional integration schemes. For instance, if they are seen merely as half-way houses to a better future in the region concerned, then their presence would not pose a threat to the survival or success of the bigger association. On the other hand, their existence within the regional scheme would pose a serious obstacle to the latter's success if they compete with rather than complement each other. This is the case with the experience of ECOWAS and CEAO as Asante has pointed out in chapter 5. CEAO is dysfunctional in ECOWAS because of its French connection as well as strong French influence in the member states. Secondly, the leaders of some of the key states in CEAO – Ivory Coast and Senegal – have perceptions of Nigeria, the most important member in ECOWAS, which portray that country as hegemonial and sub-imperial in the subregion. Thus, CEAO was set up, among other things, as a counterpoise to perceived Nigerian dominance of, and influence in West Africa. It would take some time to divest the Francophone states of this impression. And while it lasts, it could only make the task of integration more difficult within ECOWAS. This is especially so, if the community does not yield immediate practical benefits to its entire membership. In short, unless a bigger regional integration scheme is seen as beneficial to their particular interests, smaller arrangements within it would want to hold on to their sub-groupings until they are convinced that the bigger grouping serves their interest better and more efficiently.

Another question which was raised in various chapters is that of the loose versus the highly institutional regional arrangements. For instance, Ravenhill came out clearly in favour of the informal SADCC arrangements as opposed to what he considers to be a very bureaucratised and grandiose ECOWAS scheme. But does SADCC really have a much better chance of success than ECOWAS simply because it is more down-to-earth in terms of its objectives and institutions? The answer seems to be, 'not really'. We believe that one has to go beyond the institutional set-up of SADCC and take into consideration the peculiar environment within which it has to operate. One also has to consider the resources available to the Community. As for the first point, the environment within which SADCC operates is definitely more fluid and 'hostile' than that of ECOWAS. The constant attacks and threats from South Africa against SADCC members and the 'hostage' relationship between some of the Community's members and racist Pretoria, would tend to give the organisation low survival marks in spite of its loose structure. Besides that, default by any of its members – e.g. failure to implement projects – could put the whole scheme into jeopardy. More important, SADCC's reliance on external sources for finance has also made it vulnerable to both internal and external pressures. As Abegunrin has argued in chapter 11, a lot of SADCC's programmes have not been implemented, simply because the expected funds from external sources have not arrived.

However, given the importance of the politics of the region to the very Western sources from whom assistance is being sought, as well as SADCC's own objectives, it is doubtful whether the West would want to see a situation which would make the independent black states in Southern Africa strong enough to pose an economic and military threat to South Africa, which is still considered to be a vital link in the West's strategic and economic thinking. Thus the problems of funding of cooperation programmes and the dependence on the West for international capital remain interconnected and interchangeable.

We believe, then, that the fact that ECOWAS has embarked on more grandiose projects does not make it less likely to succeed than SADCC *per se*. In fact, we could say that a solid base is what is needed in any large grouping like ECOWAS. This is because, although the West African environment is less delicate than that in Southern Africa, it nevertheless has its own peculiar circumstances; for instance, the language barrier, and the leadership conflict between some of the key Francophone states (e.g. Senegal, Ivory Coast) and Nigeria. Thus, without a solid foundation from which to operate, the Community could disintegrate under the slightest pressure from any of the above states.

What ECOWAS has to guard against, and which Ravenhill rightly pointed out in his chapter, is the temptation for grandiose or even doubtful projects whose benefits are not immediately perceived. The most clear case in point here is the Protocol on the Free Movement of Peoples of ECOWAS which encouraged a large influx of community members to the most prosperous Partner State, Nigeria, thereby creating a lot of social, economic and even security problems for that country. When the pressure became unbearable, Nigeria decided to expell those ECOWAS citizens who did not have valid travel documents or, who had overstayed the statutory ninety-day period as provided for in the Protocol of the Free Movement of Peoples. The action provoked a lot of criticism not only from non-ECOWAS members but also from Ghana, Liberia, Sierra Leone and Guinea. Thus, directly or indirectly, the Protocol has dented the ECOWAS spirit.

Clearly, then, there can be no categorical affirmatives to all the questions raised in the previous paragraphs, or indeed the book, because a variety of factors account for the success or failure of

regional integration ventures in Africa. There are a lot of [u]
factors which make outright prognostications about the presen[t]
future state of regionalism in the continent a risky exercise. This [is not]
to say, however, that there is no future for regionalism in Afric[a.] [On]
the contrary, in spite of the obstacles highlighted above and i[n]
other chapters, we still believe that regionalism has a precarious f[uture]
in the continent.

The success of regional integration schemes either at present [or in]
the future, would require a lot of planning, political will and sacr[ifice]
on the part of African leaders if they are to be successful. We bel[ieve]
that a strong political will and careful planning coupled with wha[t we]
may call the 'favourable external response', would augur well [for]
regionalism both at the sub-regional and continental levels. [The]
impact of the adverse external environment which has resulted [in]
declining and/or stagnant economic growth in most African stat[es]
and lower prices for Africa's export commodities in the face of m[uch]
higher prices for imports, cannot be overstressed. Unless Afric[an]
leaders join their boot strings and weave ladders that would take the[m]
to higher economic performance, their mutual future remains ve[ry]
bleak. Fortunately, most African leaders seem to appreciate t[he]
importance of this point. Thus, regionalism is today much mo[re]
solidly based than in previous years. Moreover, the idea of sel[f-]
sufficiency and integration among African countries has mor[e]
followers today than at any other time since the dawn o[f]
independence. We believe, then, that a start has been made in the righ[t]
direction. Given the necessary political will and sacrifices on the par[t]
of Africa's leaders, the continent's future should be promising. In
short, we believe that there is a future for regionalism in Africa.

Select Bibliography

Books

1. Ali Mazrui, A. & Hasu Patel, H. (eds), *Africa in World Affairs: The Next Thirty Years* (New York: Third Press 1973).
2. André Anguile & Jacques David, *L'Afrique Sans Frontières* (Monaco: Paul Bory, 1965).
3. Arthur Hazlewood (ed.), *African Integration and Disintegration – Case Studies in Economic and Political Union* (London: Oxford University Press, 1967).
4. Arthur Hazlewood, *Economic Integration: The East African Experience* (London: Heinemann, 1975).
5. Anthony G. Hopkins, *An Economic History of West Africa* (London: Longman, 1975).
6. Bela Balassa, *The Theory of Economic Integration* (London: George Allen & Unwin, 1965).
7. Berhanykun Ademicael, *The OAU and the UN* (New York: Africana, 1976).
8. B.N.T. Mutharika, *Towards Multinational Economic Cooperation of Africa* (New York: Praeger, 1972).
9. Charles Harvey (ed.), *Papers on the Economy of Botswana* (London: Heinemann, 1981).
10. Chimelu Chime, *Integration and Politics Among African States: Limitations and Horizons of Mid-Term Theorising* (Uppsala: Scandinavian Institute of African Studies, 1977).
11. Christian P. Potholm & Fredland A. Richard (eds), *Integration and Disintegration in East Africa* (Lanham, Maryland: University Press of America, 1980).
12. Clarence Zuvekas, *Economic Development* (London: Macmillan, 1979).
13. Colin Legum et. al., *Africa in the 1980s: A Continent in Crisis* (New York: McGraw Hill, 1979).
14. David Mitrany, *The Functional Theory of Politics* (London: Martin Roberts, 1975).
15. Donald K. Kowet, *Land, Labour, Migration and Politics in Southern Africa: Botswana, Lesotho and Swaziland* (Uppsala: Scandinavian Institute of African Studies, 1978).

16 Douglas Anglin, Timothy Shaw and Carl Windstrand (eds), *Canada, Scandinavia and Southern Africa* (Stockholm: Almqvist and Wiksell, 1978).
17 Ebong Ime, *Development Financing Under Constraints* (Research Institute of the Friedrick-Ebert-Foundation, 1974).
18 Ernest B. Hass, *The Obsolescence of Regional Integration Theory* (Berkeley: Institute of International Studies, University of California, 1975).
19 G. Lanning & M. Mueller, *Africa Undermined* (Harmondsworth: Penguin, 1979).
20 G.M. Carter, & P. O'Meara (eds), *Southern Africa: The Continuing Crisis* (Bloomington: Indiana University Press, 1979).
21 Reginald H. Green & A. Seidman, *Unity or Poverty? The Economics of Pan-Africanism* (Harmondsworth: Penguin, 1968).
22 Gunnar Myrdal, *Economic Theory and Underdeveloped Nations* (London: Duckworth, 1957).
23 Guy Arnold & Ruth Weiss, *Strategic Highways of Africa* (London: Friedmann, 1977).
24 H. Brunschwig, *Mythes et Réalités de l'Impérialisme Colonial Français*, 1871–1914 (Paris: Armand Colin, 1960).
25 I. Diaku, *Industrial Finance in Nigeria: A Study of Sources, Methods and Impact of Industrial Development Financing in a Developing Economy* (Longman Nigeria).
26 Immanuel Wallerstein, *Africa: The Politics of Unity* (New York: Vintage Books, 1967).
27 Isebill V. Gruhn, *Regionalism Reconsidered: The Economic Commission For Africa* (Boulder, Colorado: Westview Press, 1979).
28 Jacob Viner, *The Customs Union Issue* (New York: Carnegie Endowment For International Peace, 1950).
29 James N. Rosenau, Kenneth W. Thompson and Garvin Boyd (eds), *World Politics: An Introduction* (New York: Free Press, 1976).
30 John P. Renninger, *Multinational Cooperation for Development in West Africa* (New York: Pergamon Press, 1979).
31 John White, *Regional Development Banks* (London: Overseas Development Institute, 1970).
32 Jonathan H. Chleshe *The Challenge of Developing Intra-African Trade* (Nairobi: East African Literature Bureau, 1977).
33 Joseph Nye, *Pan-Africanism and East African Integration* (Cambridge: Harvard University Press, 1966).
34 J. De Dreux-Breeze, *Le Problème du regroupement en Afrique Equatoriale Du Régime Colonial à'l Union Douanière et Econ-omique de l'Afrique Centrale* (Paris: R. Pichon et R. Durand-Auzias, 1968).
35 J.G. Liebenow, *Liberia: The Evolution of Privilege* (Ithaca: Cornell University Press, 1969).
36 J.K. Holsti, *International Politics: A Framework For Analysis* (London: Prentice-Hall International, 1972).

37 J.R. Davis, *Trade Sanctions And Regional Impact in Southern Africa* (London: Africa Bureau, 1981).
38 Junta del Acuerdo de Cartegena, *Technology, Policy and Economic Development* (Ottawa: International Development Centre, 1976).
39 Kwame Nkrumah, *Neocolonialism: The Last Stage of Imperialism* (New York: International, 1966).
40 Louis J. Cantori, & Steven L. Spiegel, *The International Politics of Regions: A Comparative Approach* (Englewood Cliffs: Prentice-Hall, 1970).
41 Louis Shon (ed.) *Basic Documents on African Organisations* (New York: Oceanic Publications Inc. 1971).
42 Lynn K. Mytelka, *Africa in the 1980s* (New York: McGraw Hill, 1979).
43 Lynn K. Mytelka, *Bargaining In A Third World Integrative System* (unpublished manuscript), 1972.
44 May Palmberg, *Problems of Socialist Orientation in Africa*, (New York: Africana, 1978).
45 Melvyn B. Krauss (ed.), *The Economics of Integration* (London: Allen & Unwin, 1973).
46 Michael Clough (ed.), *Political Change in Southern Africa* (Berkeley, Institute of International Affairs, University of California, 1982).
47 Michael Wolfers, *Politics in The Organisation of African Unity* (London: Methuen, 1976).
48 M. Smith, R. Little, & M. Shackleton, *Perspective on World Politics*, (London: Croom Helm, 1981).
49 Norman Hillmer & Garth Stevenson (eds) *Foremost Nation: Canadian Foreign Policy And a Changing World* (Toronto: McClelland & Steward, 1977).
50 Peter C.W. Gutkink & Immanuel Wallerstein (eds) *The Political Economy of Contemporary Africa* (Beverley Hills: Sage, 1976).
51 Peter Robson, *The Economics of International Integration:* (London: George Allen & Unwin, 1980).
52 Philips Ndegwa, *The Common Market And Development in East Africa* (Kampala: East African Publishing House, 1968).
53 Ralph I. Onwuka, *Development and Integration in West Africa: The Case of the Economic Community of West African States (ECOWAS)* (Ife: University Press, 1982).
54 Richard A. Falk & Saul Mendlovitz (eds), *Regional Politics & World Order* (San Francisco: W.H. Freeman, 1974).
55 Robert Keohane & Joseph S. Nye (eds), *Transnational Relations And World Politics* (Cambridge: Harvard University Press, 1973).
56 Roland Oliver & Antony Atmore, *Africa Since 1800* (Cambridge: Cambridge University Press, 1969).
57 Roland St John MacDonald et al. (eds), *The International Law And Policy of Human Welfare* (The Netherlands: Sijthoff & Noordhoff, 1978).
58 R.W. Clower et al, *Growth Without Development* (Evanston: North Western Press, 1966).

59 Sidney Dell, *A Latin American Common Market*? (London: Oxford University Press, 1966).
60 *The World Economic Crisis: A Commonwealth Perspective* (London: Commonwealth Secretariat, 1980).
61 William A. Hance, *Population Migration And Urbanization In Africa* (New York: Columbia University Press, 1970).
62 Timothy M. Shaw (ed.), *Alternative Futures for Africa* (Boulder, Colorado: Westview Press, 1982).
63 Timothy M. Shaw (ed.) *Futures of Africa* (Boulder, Colorado: Westview Press, 1979).
64 Timothy M. Shaw & Kenneth A. Heard (eds) *The Politics of Africa: Dependence And Development* (New York: Africana, 1979).
65 Victor T. Levine, *The Cameroons from Mandate to Independence* (Berkeley: University of California Press, 1964).
66 Willy Brandt, *North-South: A Programme for Survival* (Cambridge: Massachusetts, 1980).
67 William A. Hance, *Population, Migration and Urbanisation In Africa* (New York: Columbia University Press, 1970).
68 William W. Coplain, *Introduction to International Politics* (Englewood Cliffs, NJ: Prentice-Hall, 1980).
69 Zdenek Cervenka, *The Unfinished Quest for Unity: Africa And The OAU* (New York: Africana, 1977).

Articles

1 Aaron Segal, 'The Integration of Developing Countries: Some Thoughts On East Africa and Central America.' *Journal of Common Market Studies*, 5(4) 1967.
2 Aguibou Yansane, 'The State of Economic Integration in North West Africa, South of the Sahara: The Emergence of the Economic Community of West African States (ECOWAS)' *African Studies Review* XX(2) September 1977.
3 Amadu Sesay, 'The Liberian Revolution: Forward March, Stop, About-face Turn' *Conflict Quarterly* (forthcoming).
4 Amadu Sesay, 'Societal Inequality, Ethnic Heterogeneity and Political Instability: The Case of Liberia' *Plural Societies*, vol. II, No. 3, (Autumn 1980).
5 Andrew Liddell, 'Financial Cooperation in Africa – French Style,' *The Banker*, 129 (No. 643) September, 1979.
6 Biff Turner, 'A Fresh Start for Southern African Customs Union,' *African Affairs*, (London) vol. 70 (No. 280) July 1971.
7 C.A. Cooper and B.F. Massell, 'Towards A General Theory of Custom Union: A General Survey,' *Economic Journal*, 70, No. 279, (September 1960).
8 Constantine V. Vaitsos, 'Crisis in Regional Economic Cooperation (Integration) Among Developing Countries: A Survey' *World Development* 6 (June 1978).

9   D.J. Goldenhuys and J.D. Venter, 'Regional Cooperation in Southern Africa: A Constellation of States?' *International Affairs Bulletin*, vol. 3, No. 3 (December 1979).
10 D.V. Cowen, 'Towards a Common Market in Southern Africa,' *Optima* (Johannesburg), vol. 17, No. 2 (June 1967).
11 Felipe Pazos, 'Regional Integration of Trade Among Less Developed Countries,' *World Development*, 1, No. 7 (July 1973).
12 Francis d'A Collings, et. al., 'The Rand and the Monetary Systems of Botswana, Lesotho and Swaziland,' *Journal of Modern African Studies* (Cambridge) vol. 16 (No. 1), March 1978.
13 James H. Cobbe, 'Integration Among Unequals: The Southern African Customs Union and Development,' *World Development* (London), vol. 8 (No. 4), April 1980.
14 James A. Goldsborough, 'Dateline Paris: Africa's Policeman,' *Foreign Policy*, 33 (Winter 1978–1979).
15 John Ravenhill, 'Regional Integration and Development in Africa: Lessons from the East African Community', *Journal of Commonwealth and Comparative Politics*, November, 1979.
16 Lawrence Schlemmer and David Welsh, 'South Africa's Constitutional and Political Prospects,' *Optima,* vol. 30, (No. 4), June 1982.
17 L. Rood, 'Nationalisation and Indigenisation in Africa,' *Journal of African Studies*, 14(3), 1976.
18 Mamadon Bathily, 'The West African Economic Community,' *The Courier*, 34 (Nov.–Dec. 1975).
19 M.B. Akpan, 'Black Imperialism: Americo-Liberian Rule Over the African Peoples of Liberia, 1841–1964,' *Canadian Journal of African Studies*, vol. 7, No. 2, 1973.
20 Micah S. Tsomondo, 'From Pan Africanism To Socialism: The Modernisation of an African Liberation Ideology,' *Issue* 5:4 (Winter 1975).
21 N. Leff, 'Technology Transfer and US Foreign Policy: The Developing Countries,' *Orbis* 23(1), Spring 1979.
22 Olatunde J. B. Ojo, 'Nigeria and ECOWAS' *International Organisation*, 34(4) Autumn 1980.
23 Olayiwola Abegunrin, 'The Southern Nine,' *Current Bibliography on African Affairs*, vol. 14, No. 4 (Summer 1982).
24 P.C.J. Vala, 'South Africa As A Pariah International State,' *International Affairs Bulletin* (Johannesburg) vol. 1 (No. 3), 1977.
25 Peter Robson, 'Economic Integration In Southern Africa,' *Journal of Modern African Studies* (Cambridge) vol. 5, (No. 4), December 1967.
26 P.M. Landell-Mills, 'The 1969 Southern African Customs Union Agreement,' *Journal of Modern African Studies*, vol. 9 (No. 2), August 1971.
27 Rafael Vargas-Hidalgo, 'The Crisis of Andean Pact: Lessons for Integration Among Developing Countries,' *Journal of Common Market Studies*, 8(3) March 1979.
28 Rainer Kuehn and Frank Seelow, 'ECOWAS and CEAO: Regional

Cooperation in West Africa,' *Development and Cooperation* 3, May–June 1980.
29. Raymond W. Copson, 'African Integrational Politics: Under-development and Conflicts in the Seventies,' *Orbis* 22:1 (Spring 1978).
30. R.G. Lipsey, 'The Theory of Customs Union: A General Survey', *Economic Journal* 70, No. 279 (September 1960).
31. R.I. Onwuka, 'The ECOWAS Treaty: Inching Towards Implementation,' *World Today* (London), 36(2), 1980.
32. R.I. Onwuka, 'The Lome Convention: A Machinery for Economic Dependence or Interdependence,' *Quartery Journal of Administration*, (Ile-Ife), April 1979.
33. R.I. Onwuka, 'Independence Within ECOWAS: I', *West Africa*, 10 October 1977.
34. Robert K. Merton, 'The Matthew Effect in Science', *Science* 159 (January 1968).
35. Robert W. Jackman, 'Dependence or Foreign Investment and Economic Growth In the Third World', *World Politics* XXXIV, 2 (January 1982).
36. Timothy M. Shaw, 'Inequalities And Interdependence in Africa And Latin America: Subimperialism And Semi-Industrialism In The Semi-Periphery,' *Cultures et Developpement*, 10:(2) 1978.
37. Timothy M. Shaw, 'Kenya and South Africa: Subimperialist States,' *Orbis*, 21(2) Summer 1977.
38. Timothy M. Shaw, 'Inequalities And Conflict in Contemporary Africa,' *International Perspectives* (May/June 1978).
39. Timothy M. Shaw, 'Regional Cooperation and Conflict in Africa,' *International Journal* 30:4 (Autumn 1975).
40. William P. Avery & James D. Cochrane, 'Innovation in Latin American Regionalism: The Andean Common Market,' *International Organisation*, 27(2) Spring 1973.

Appendix

African Regional and Subregional Economic Institutions

1. **ADB** (African Development Bank)
   Founded/established   4 August 1963.
   Membership   All independent African states. There are, however, non-African members. These are: Argentina, Austria, Belgium, Brazil, Canada, Denmark, England, France, West Germany, Italy, Japan, South Korea, Kuwait, Netherlands, Norway, Saudi Arabia, Spain, Sweden, Switzerland, United Kingdom, United States and Yugoslavia.

2. **ADF** (African Development Fund)
   Founded/established   30 June 1973.
   Membership   All independent African states (plus non-African members: Argentina, Austria, Belgium, Brazil, Canada, Denmark, Finland, France, West Germany, Italy, Japan, South Korea, Kuwait, Netherlands, Norway, Saudi Arabia, Spain, Sweden, Switzerland, United Kingdom, United States and Yugoslavia).

3. **ECA** (This is a shorthand for the United Nations Economic Commission for Africa, UNECA.)
   Founded   1945
   Membership   All independent African states.

4. **ECOWAS** (Economic Community of West African States)
   Founded/established   28 May 1975
   Membership   (16) Benin, Gabon, Gambia, Ghana, Guinea, Guinea Bissau, Ivory Coast, Liberia, Mali, Mauritania, Niger, Nigeria, Senegal, Sierra Leone, Togo and Burkina Faso.

5 **CEAO** (Communauté Economique de l'Afrique de l'Ouest)
   Founded/established May 1970
   Membership (6) Ivory Coast, Mali, Mauritania, Niger, Senegal, and Burkina Faso.

6 **EAC** (East African Community)
   Founded/established 1967
   Disbanded 1977
   Membership (3) Kenya, Tanzania and Uganda.

7 **MRU** (Mano River Union)
   Founded/established 3 October 1973.
   Membership (3) (originally 2: Liberia and Sierra Leone, Guinea's accession to the Union in October 1980 brought the membership to 3).

8 **OAU** (Organisation of African Unity)
   Founded/established 25 May 1963
   Membership All independent African states.

9 **SADCC** (Southern African Development and Coordination Conference)
   Founded/established 1 April 1980
   Membership (9) Angola, Botswana, Lesotho, Malawi, Mozambique, Swaziland, Tanzania, Zambia and Zimbabwe.

10 **UDEAC** (L'Union Douanière et Economique de l'Afrique Centrale) (Central African Customs and Economic Union).
   Founded/established 8 December 1964
   Membership (4) Cameroon, Central African Republic, Congo and Gabon.

Index

ACM, 59-65; draft protocol on, 60; feasibility of, 61-5; and UDEAC, 101
ADB, 62; and AFTA, 68; capital subscriptions to, 42-3; future of, 54-6; loans of, 52-3; location of, 44-5; major functionaries of, 39-40; management of, 38-9; non-African participation in, 41-2, 42-3; origin of, 36-9; performance of, 47, 51-3; and SADCC, 198-9; subscriptions, defaulters of, 48
ADF, 50-1; and the ADB, 53-4
AFTA, integration into, 66-7
Abidjan (location of ADB), 44, 45
Abidjan, treaty of, 75
Adedeji, Adebayo (head of ECA), 31-2
administration: of EAC, 177-8; of ECOWAS defence pact, 119-21
Africa Group, 29
Africa Hall, 22
'African Character' of ADB, 38, 42
African Economic Community, 59
agriculture, 198; in the MRU, 128-9; in SADCC, 194
aid, 62; bilateral, in MRU, 136-7; management of, 37; multilateral, in MRU, 137-41; technological, dependence on, 141-2; and UDEAC, 104
Amin, General (Ugandan Head), 183
Andean Pact, 165-6
Anglophone countries, and CEAO, 77, 84
Angola, *see* SADCC

apartheid, 230
arms trade, 18
Arusha Conference, 219
Arusha Ministerial Meeting, 58, 59
Authority, the, (EAC), 177
Authority of Heads of State and Government (ECOWAS), 80, 119
autonomy: constraints on, 16-8; and integration, 209

BCDI (CEAO), 80
BCEAO, 62
BLS countries: disengagement of, 243-4; other communities for, 249; revenue for, 231-2; *see also* SACU
BLS economies, control of by SACU, 231-5
BLS, and justification of SACU membership, 238, 239-40
balance of payments, 181-3
bank, *see* ADB, EADB
banks, and AFTA, 68
Blumeris, Arthur (head of SADCC), 192
Botswana, *see* SADCC, SACU
boundaries, colonial, 96
boundary disputes, 17
Brazzaville Treaty, 98

CCCE, 160
CEAO: and ECOWAS, 215; institutional pattern of, 79-80; internal disagreements in, 84; origins of, 75-82; success of, 87; treaty, principle objectives of,

267

79–80; as West African-wide group, 77; *see also* ECOWAS
CET, of the MRU, 129–30
Cameroon, *see* UDEAC
capital: and SADCC projects, 198–9; and TNCs, 155–6
capital subscriptions, to ADB, 42–3
capitalist intervention, 17, 18
Central African Republic, *see* UDEAC
centre/periphery model of production, 10
colonial armies, 114–5
colonialism, and regional groupings, 83
colonies, and TNCs, 152–3
command structure, of ECOWAS defence pact, 120, 121
Commander, of AAFC, 120–1
commissions, of the OAU, 25–6
common market, *see* ACM, AFTA, economic communities, PTA
communications: and dependence on Pretoria, 199–200; of front line states, 196–7; integrated, 67; programme (ECOWAS), 88; undeveloped state of, 12; and viability of UDEAC, 99–100
communities, factors favouring success of, 187–9; *see also* economic communities
community membership, cost/benefit of, 184–5
concessions, to TNCs, 161–2
Conference of Heads of State and Government (CEAO), 79
Congo, *see* UDEAC
consensus, in defence pacts, 111–3
consolidated revenue fund, 231–2; of SACU, 229
constellations, 190
cooperation: distribution of benefits of in EAC, 173–4, 175–82 *passim*; nationally based, 219
Copson, Raymond, *quoted*, 17
cost/benefit of community membership, 184–5
Council of Heads of State (UDEAC), 98
Council of Ministers: of CEAO, 80; of ECOWAS, 80

currencies: in MRU, 131; in BLS countries, 244
customs union, 64, 90; EAC as, 173; MRU as, 131; SACU as, 226; *see also* free trade area
customs union commission (SACU), 237

DELCO, 162
Defence Commission (ECOWAS), 120
Defence Council (ECOWAS), 119–20
defence pact (ECOWAS), analysis of, 118–22
defence pacts, consensus in, 111–3
defence protocol, and ECOWAS, 215–6
defence, regional, 110–13
developed countries: and ADB, 43–4; and ADF, 50–1
development plans, of SADCC, 193–5
development: radical, 13–14; and TNCs, 158–60
development strategy, 13
development-orientated integration, 150–1
Diori, President of Niger, 77
diplomacy, and regional integration, 14–15
distribution, equable, in regional communities, 208–9
Doe, Commander (Liberian Head), 132
duplication of industries, and transfer tax, 175–6

EAC, 2, 64; problems underlying, 173–4
EADB, 176–7
EADE, 174
ECA, 15, 24–34; and African Development Bank, 36, 37; and the formation of UDEAC, 103; future of, 32–4; ECA, problems of (1963), 26; role of, 24
ECA/OAU, 28–30
ECOSOC, 24

ECOWAS, 64, 151-2: and Andean Pact compared, 165-6; and CEAO, 215; and control of TNCs, 165-7; critique of, 213-7; and defence commitments, 116-7; defence pact, 122-3, (analysis of, 118-22; command structure of, 120, 121; viability of, 113-8); forces (financial provision for, 121-2; integration of, 114-5); fund, 62, 216; institutional pattern of, 80; and MRU, 130; origins of, 76-82; problems of, 3, 87-8; and South Africa, 5
ECOWAS/CEAO: areas of conflict 90-2; cooperation of, 89-90; dissimilarities between, 82-4; similarities between, 78-82
ECOWAS treaty, principle objectives of, 78-9
EEC: and CEAO, 76; and MRU, 137, 139, 140, 141; and SACU, 235-6; and SADCC, 199; and UDEAC, 104-5
EFTA, 65-6
Economic Commission, of the OAU, 61
economic communities: defence implications of, 116-7; as modifiers of states' behaviour, 237; sub-regional, 64-5; *see also* communities
economic dominance, of South Africa, 229-32, 233-7 *passim*
economic growth, and TNCs, 158-60
economic system, world, dependence on, 15-16
economics, and the ECA, 24
employment, and TNCs, 163-4
energy transfers, within SACU, 241
equality, myth of, 9
Equatorial Customs Union, *see* UDE
Executive Secretariat of the Community (ECOWAS), 80
export manufacturing, 10
extractive enterprises, 153-5, 163

FCD, 81

farming, in Zimbabwe and Zambia, 198
financial provision of ECOWAS forces, 121-2
flexibility: and regionalism, 212-3; of SADCC, 218
foreign exchange: in EAC, 182; and migrant workers, 196
foreign policy, 12; of South Africa, 234-5
foreign sources, dependence on, 106
franc zone, and ECOWAS, 215
France, 93; and aid to UDEAC, 104; and CEAO, 83; and ECOWAS, 76; and franc zone, 215; and UDEAC, 100
Francophone countries, and the ADB, 43, 45, *see also* CEAO
free trade, and the ACM, 60-1
free trade area, 85, 90, 91, *see also* AFTA
Frontline States, 191, 192-5, 217-8
fund: of CEAO, 81, 86; of ECOWAS, 81, 86, 87, 216
fund, consolidated revenue, 229, 231-2
fund, solidarity (UDEAC), 98-9
funding, of ADB, 37-8

GNP of SACU members, 238
Gaberone, 192
Gabon, *see* UDEAC
Gambia, *see* ECOWAS
Gardiner, Robert (executive secretary of ECA), 27-9
General Secretariat: of CEAO, 80; of UDEAC, 98
Germany, West, and MRU, 136-7, 139
Ghana, *see* ECOWAS
government of EAC, 177-8
Guinea, *see* MRU
Guinea-Bissau, *see* ECOWAS

harmonisation: in ECOWAS, 214-5; in MRU, 129
homelands, 232-3, 244-5

ideology: and harmonisation, 179,

183–4, 185; orthodox, 9; radical, 10
import surcharges, 233–4
income, redistribution of, 165
incrementalism, 210–13
independence, and community cooperation, 178
industrial products, and preferential trade, 85, 85–6
industrialisation: dependent, 18; difficulties of, 126, 127; and MRU, 128; and perceived military threats, 117–8
industries, duplication of, 175–6; integration of, 67
inequalities, and interaction, 11
integration, 11: of colonial armies, 114–5; development-orientated, 150–1; of ECOWAS forces, 114–5; in East Africa, colonial, 173; economic, and the OAU, 58, 59; levels of, 151–2; reasons for, 96–7; regional, and self-sufficiency, 149–50; see also regionalism
integrative forces, within UDEAC, 99–105
interactions, economic, 151–2
interdependence, as goal of BLS countries, 243–4
intervention, extracontinental, 16–18
intra-African trade, 11–12
investment, foreign, 69–70; by TNCs in West Africa, 156; see also TNC
Ivory Coast, and the ADB, 45; see also CEAO

Jeanneney report, 104

Kaunda, Kenneth (President of Zambia), 191–2, *quoted*, 193
Kenya, as privileged partner in EAC, 173–4, see also EAC
Khama, Seretse, 192–3 *quoted*, 217

labour, migrant, 195–6

Lagos Plan of Action, 5–6, 30, 33–4, 58–9, 61–2
Lesotho, *see* SADCC, SACU
Liberia, *see* MRU
liquidation, 162
loans, of ADB, 52–3
Lusaka constellation, 190, 191–2
Lusaka economic declaration, 192

MNC, and investment code of MRU, 143; in Liberia, 135; and market integration, 208; *see also* TNC
MNR, 197, 198
MRU, 2–3, 64–5, 144–5; budgets of, 139, 140, 141; and ECOWAS, 90, 130; failure of, 133; and foreign aid, 134–41; formation of, 125–8; internal dissension in, 128–30, 132; investment code of, 142–4
Malawi, *see* SADCC
Mali, *see* CEAO
Management Committee (UDEAC), 98
market integration, 209, 207–8, 221
Mauritania, and the CEAO, 84
Mazuri, Ali, 61
migrant labour, 195–6, 215
mining, 153–5, 163
modification, institutional, of states' behaviour, 237–42, 247–8
monetary harmonisation, 215
monetary system, common, 100
mono-economies, 126, 127
Monrovia symposium, 58–9
Mozambique, and SADCC, 202; *see also* SADCC
multinationals, *see* TNC

NIEO, 12
Namibia, *see* SADCC
nationalisation, 155, 160, 162
nationalism, 12
Netherlands, and MRU, 136, 139, 140, 141
Niger, *see* CEAO
Nigeria: direct tax revenue of (1979–80), 159, 159–60; and ECOWAS, 82–3; and TNCs, 161;

see also ECOWAS
Nkrumah, President of Ghana, 157–8
non-Africans, and the ADB, 53
nonalignment, 12

OAU, 14–15, 16; aims of, 25; charter of, 25; and colonialism, 28; founding of, 26–7; future of, 33–4; and the Lusaka summit, 193; and the Monrovia symposium, 58
OAU/ECA cooperation, 28–30
OCPE, 80
oil supplies, 194, 195
origin, rules of, 70
orthodox/radical approach to regional integration, 14–16

PTA, 66
pan-Africanism, 14, 12
planning: for development of industry in EAC, 180–1; and regionalism, 210–13
politics: and ECOWAS/CEAO, 81–2; of integration, 208; and UDEAC, 102, 106
preference system, 70
preferential tax status, within CEAO, 85
preferential trade area, 202
production, internationalisation of, 10
projects, of ADB, 47, 52

radical/traditional approach to foreign policy, 13
raw materials, 117–8
reciprocity, and free trade areas, 67
recruitment problems, of ADB, 40–1
regional integration, 10, 14–16; difficulty of, 207–10
regionalism, 205–6; and flexibility, 212–3; incremental approach to, 210–13
resource development, joint, 211
resource, 9, 62; of ADB, 47–8

road transport, in EAC, 179–80

SACU, 220; present agreement of, 228–9; and EEC, 235–6; energy transfer within, 241; future of, 246–9; and homelands issue, 232–3; origins of, 226–9; trade within, 240
SADCC, 4–5; flexibility of, 218, 219; independence of, 192–5; objectives of, 192–5; organisation of, 218–20, 220–1; origins of, 190, 191–2, 217–8; and SACU, 244; trade in, 200–1
sanctions, effects of, 241–2
Senegal, *see* CEAO
share capital, of ADB, 38
Sierra Leone, *see* MRU, *see* ECOWAS
smuggling, 129
socialist states, intervention of, 17
solidarity fund: of CEAO, 86; UDEAC, 98–9
South Africa: dependence on by frontline states, 218; foreign policy techniques, 234–5; and the formation of SADCC, 190–2; influence of over SACU, 229–37; as 'pariah' state, 238–9; and revenue-sharing, 227–8; *see also* SACU, SADCC
Southern Africa; independence of, 192–5; trade of 200–2
Southern Nine, 191
state trading, 180
statistics, 51
Stevens, Siaka (Sierra Leone president), 132, 133
stock, capital, of the ADB, 48–50
Stockholm Convention (EFTA), 65–6
sub-imperialism, 9, 10
subscription, to ADB, 45–6, 48, 49
Swaziland, *see* SACU, *see* SADCC

TBV homelands, 232–3, 244–5
TNC: and AFTA integration, 69–70; colonial, 152–3; control of by ECOWAS, 165–7; social

271

effects of, 164; in West Africa, 153–4; *see also* MNC
Tanzania, 179; *see also* EAC, SADCC
tariffs, 126, 151
tax, 208; TCR, 85, 86, 91; and TNCs, 159–60, 161; transfer, 175–6, 180
technical assistance, to ADB, 41, 41–2
technical staff, lack of, 167
technology: dependence on in MRU, 141–2; and the ECA, 24; and TNCs, 156–7
technology policy, for ECOWAS, 166–7
telecommunications and transport programme (ECOWAS), 88
Telli, Diallo (head of OAU), 28–9
territorial disputes, 17
Togo, *see* ECOWAS
Tolbert, William, (Liberian president), 132, 133
tourism, in EAC, 178–9
trade, 11–12, 63–4, 207–8, 211; in CEAO, 84–5; in ECOWAS, 85–6, 214; in MRU, 130–1; in SACU, 240; in Southern Africa, 200–1
trade barriers, 66
trade liberalisations, incompatibility of (ECOWAS/CEAO), 90–2
trading, by state, 180

traditional/radical approach, to foreign policy, 13
transfer tax, 175–6, 180
transport, 67, 178–80

UDEAC, 98–9, 103
UEAC, 100
UN: and ECA, 24; and EAC, 172–3; and MRU, 138
UNCTAD, and the formation of UDEAC, 103
UNDP, and the formation of MRU, 134
UNITA, 198
Uganda, *see* EAC
underdevelopment, agents of, 155
union industries, 134
Union Investment Code, 142–4
Upper Volta, *see* CEAO

vice-presidents, of ADB, 39–40
voting, and ADB, 46–7, 49

western involvement, in MRU, 134–45

Zambia, *see* SADCC
Zartman, *quoted*, 9, 16
Zimbabwe, 200; *see also* SADCC

DATE DUE